ASVAB
CORE REVIEW

Fifth Edition

LEARNINGEXPRESS®

NEW YORK

Cataloging-in-Publication Data is on file with the Library of Congress.

ISBN: 978-1-61103-053-2

Printed in the United States of America

9 8 7 6 5 4 3 2 1

Fifth Edition

Regarding the Information in This Book
We attempt to verify the information presented in our books prior to publication. It is always a good idea, however, to double-check such important information as minimum requirements, application and testing procedures, and deadlines with your local recruitment agency, as such information can change from time to time.

For information on LearningExpress, other LearningExpress products, or bulk sales,
please write to us at:
    224 W. 29th Street
    3rd Floor
    New York, NY 10001

CONTENTS

CHAPTER 1   What Is the ASVAB Core?   1

CHAPTER 2   Getting into the Military   7

CHAPTER 3   The Score You Need to Enlist   15

CHAPTER 4   The LearningExpress Test Preparation System   21

CHAPTER 5   Practice ASVAB Core Test 1   37

CHAPTER 6   Math Review   71

CHAPTER 7   Math Practice   101

CHAPTER 8   Word Knowledge Review   115

CHAPTER 9   Word Knowledge Practice   125

CHAPTER 10   Paragraph Comprehension Review   135

CHAPTER 11   Reading Practice   145

CHAPTER 12   Practice ASVAB Core Test 2   157

CHAPTER 13   Practice ASVAB Core Test 3   189

ADDITIONAL ONLINE PRACTICE   220

1 ▶ WHAT IS THE ASVAB CORE?

CHAPTER SUMMARY

In order to enlist in the military, you have to take the Armed Services Vocational Aptitude Battery (ASVAB). But you have to pass only *four* of the subtests on the ASVAB to qualify for enlistment. This chapter explains those four subtests and shows you how to use this book to score your best.

The Armed Services Vocational Aptitude Battery (ASVAB) is comprised of individual subtests that assess an enlistee's different skills and aptitudes. The majority of the subtests—General Science, Auto and Shop, Mechanical Comprehension, Assembling Objects, and Electronics Information—are designed to determine what your aptitudes are for different jobs in the military. However, four of the ASVAB subtests—Arithmetic Reasoning, Word Knowledge, Paragraph Comprehension, and Mathematics Knowledge—count toward your Armed Forces Qualifying Test (AFQT) score, which determines whether you can enlist in the military. This book covers *only* those four subtests that count toward your AFQT score. Those four tests are referred to in this book as the ASVAB *core*.

ASVAB:
Paper and Pencil versus CAT

Depending on where an enlistee takes the ASVAB, he or she will take either the computer version of the ASVAB, called the CAT-ASVAB, or the paper-and-pencil version. Candidates taking the ASVAB at a Military Entrance Processing Station (MEPS) will take the computer version, while candidates taking the ASVAB at a Military Entrance Test (MET) site will most likely take the paper-and-pencil version. The paper-and-pencil version of the ASVAB consists of either eight subtests (if you're a student) or nine subtests (if you're a candidate for enlistment).

The majority of military applicants—about 70%—take the CAT-ASVAB. The CAT-ASVAB is a computer-adaptive test, which means that the test adapts to your ability level. The computer will give you the first question, and, if you answer correctly, it gives you another question on the same subject—but one that is a bit harder than the first. The questions get harder as you progress, and after you answer a certain number of questions correctly the computer skips to the next subtest.

The following is additional information about the CAT-ASVAB:

- It consists of ten subtests—the Auto Information and Shop Information subtests are administered separately. However, the results are combined into one score (labeled AS).
- The test takes half an hour to complete.
- Each subtest must be completed within a certain time frame. Most individuals complete the subtests within the time allotted.

- Once you have completed a subtest, you do not have to wait for everyone else to finish—you can move on to the next subtest.
- As you complete each subtest, the computer displays the number of items and amount of time remaining for that subtest in the lower right-hand corner of the screen.
- Once an answer has been submitted, you cannot review or change it.
- Test scores are available as soon as you complete the test.
- If you choose to take the CAT-ASVAB, you will be trained on answering test questions, using the computer keyboard and mouse, and getting help before starting the exam.

Please Note: If you are a recruit, chances are you're going to take the CAT-ASVAB. However, because this book is geared toward strengthening your skills through practice, the practice AFQTs found here follow the paper-and-pencil specifications, which include a higher number of questions.

The number of subtests, number of questions, and time limits for the CAT-ASVAB differ from the paper-and-pencil version in the following ways. Note that the bolded items count toward the Armed Forces Qualifying Test (AFQT) score.

NUMBERS OF ITEMS AND TESTING TIME FOR THE PAPER-AND-PENCIL ASVAB

SUBTEST	NUMBER OF QUESTIONS	TIME (MINUTES)
General Science (GS)	25	11
Arithmetic Reasoning (AR)	30	36
Word Knowledge (WK)	35	11
Paragraph Comprehension (PC)	15	13
Mathematics Knowledge (MK)	25	24
Electronics Information (EI)	20	9
Auto and Shop Information (AS)	25	11
Mechanical Comprehension (MC)	25	19
Assembling Objects* (AO)	25	15
Institutional Version Totals	**200 Items**	**134 Minutes**
Production Version Totals	**225 Items**	**149 Minutes**

*The Assembling Objects (AO) subtest is not included in the institutional version of the ASVAB taken by high school students as part of the ASVAB Career Exploration Program.

NUMBERS OF ITEMS AND TESTING TIME FOR THE CAT-ASVAB

SUBTEST	NUMBER OF QUESTIONS	TIME (MINUTES)
General Science (GS)	16	8
Arithmetic Reasoning (AR)	16	39
Word Knowledge (WK)	16	8
Paragraph Comprehension (PC)	11	22
Mathematics Knowledge (MK)	16	20
Electronics Information (EI)	16	8
Auto Information (AI)	11	7
Shop Information (SI)	11	6
Mechanical Comprehension (MC)	16	20
Assembling Objects (AO)	16	16
Totals	**145 Items**	**154 Minutes**

The Four ASVAB Core Subtests

The following is a more detailed description of each of the four subtests that count toward the AFQT score.

Part 1: Arithmetic Reasoning

The Arithmetic Reasoning subtest consists of word problems describing everyday life situations, which are designed to measure your reasoning skills and understanding of:

- operations with whole numbers
- operations with fractions and decimals or money
- ratio and proportion
- interest and percentage
- measurement of perimeters, areas, volumes, and time and temperature

Chapter 6 reviews math and Chapter 7 gives you extra practice in math.

Part 2: Word Knowledge

The Word Knowledge subtest consists of questions that ask you to choose the correct definitions of verbs, nouns, adjectives, and adverbs. These questions come in two forms:

- definitions presented alone, with no context
- words in the context of a short sentence

The vocabulary skills you need for the Word Knowledge subtest are presented in Chapter 8. Chapter 9 gives you more practice using these skills.

Part 3: Paragraph Comprehension

The Paragraph Comprehension subtest consists of questions based on several short passages written on a variety of topics. No prior knowledge of the subject will be required—all the information you will need to answer the questions will be found in the passage. The questions test two different skills:

- **Literal comprehension:** your ability to identify stated facts, identify reworded facts, and determine the sequence of events
- **Implicit, inferential, or critical comprehension:** your ability to draw conclusions; identify the main idea of a paragraph; determine the author's purpose, mood, or tone; and identify style and technique

Chapter 10 gives you the skills you need to do well on this subtest. Chapter 11 gives you more instruction on how to read well, and also gives you more practice reading questions.

Part 4: Mathematics Knowledge

The Mathematics Knowledge subtest consists of questions designed to measure your understanding of mathematical concepts, principles, and procedures. The emphasis is on your ability to recognize and apply basic mathematical principles. The questions cover:

- **Number theory:** factors, multiples, reciprocals, number properties, primes, integers
- **Numeration:** fractional parts, decimals, percentages, and conversions; order of operations; exponents; rounding; reducing fractions; roots and radicals; signed numbers
- **Algebraic operations and equations:** solving or determining equations, factoring, simplifying algebraic expressions, converting a sentence to an equation
- **Geometry and measurement:** coordinates and slope, Pythagorean theorem, angle measurement, properties of polygons and circles, perimeter, area, volume, unit conversion
- **Probability:** determining the likelihood of an event occurring or not occurring

These mathematical concepts are covered in Chapter 6 of this book, and Chapter 7 presents more problems for extra practice.

Arranging to Take the ASVAB

Approximately 12,000 high schools across the United States offer the ASVAB. If you are in high school, ask your guidance counselor about taking the ASVAB. Many high schools offer it at a specific time during the school year. If you missed your school's offering of the ASVAB, chances are a neighboring school will be offering it at another time during the school year.

If you're out of high school, go to the nearest recruiter of the branch of the armed services that you're interested in. There is no charge to take the ASVAB. Taking the exam doesn't obligate you to join the military, although you can probably expect a persuasive sales pitch about the opportunities available in the Army, Air Force, Navy, Marine Corps, and U.S. Coast Guard. The military service in charge of maintaining the administrative elements of the ASVAB is the Army, but all armed services use the information provided by the test results. For more details about the ASVAB, visit the ASVAB website at http://official-asvab.com.

What the ASVAB Means for You

If you want to enter the military, everything is riding on your ASVAB score. Your scores on the four subtests of the ASVAB covered in this book—the AFQT—determine whether you can get in at all. Once you are in, scores on the other subtests determine for which jobs, or Military Occupational Specialties, you will be allowed to train. For instance, if you want to learn to be a computer operator, you need good scores in Paragraph Comprehension, Word Knowledge, Mathematics Knowledge, General Science, and Mechanical Comprehension. But if you don't meet a certain minimum score in Paragraph Comprehension, Word Knowledge, Arithmetic Reasoning, and Mathematics Knowledge, you won't even be able to enlist.

If you are looking toward a career in the armed forces, you need to score well on the ASVAB. Fortunately, this book is here to help.

How to Use This Book to Increase Your Score

The key to success in almost any field is to prepare intensively. One of the very best ways to prepare for the ASVAB is to read and study this book, take the practice tests, and measure how you are progressing.

To ensure you are clear on the basic information, start by reading Chapter 2, which explains the recruitment and enlistment process and how the ASVAB fits into that process. To learn more about the score you need to enlist, read Chapter 3.

Next, Chapter 4 takes you through the Learning-Express Test Preparation System. The nine steps in this chapter will ensure you are in top physical and mental shape to do your best on test day.

Armed with the knowledge you have gained in the first four chapters, take the first of three practice tests in Chapter 5. By taking this test, you will be able to see how you would perform if it were test day. Evaluating your score will enable you to identify your strengths and weaknesses in order to tailor the rest of your preparation before the actual test. Chapters 6 through 11 include targeted review and practice for each of the four subtests that count toward the all-important AFQT score.

Finally, Chapters 12 and 13 include two additional practice tests. Use these two tests to track your progress from the time of the first test. You can return to the review and practice chapters as needed to ensure that you are focusing on the material you find most difficult.

Practice and preparation are the keys to doing well on this exam. This book will give you everything you need to score your best. Good luck!

2 ▶ GETTING INTO THE MILITARY

CHAPTER SUMMARY

You may find joining the military an appealing career choice. Once you have made the decision that the military is where you are headed, you will need to be armed with information about the enlistment process. That information is what this chapter has to offer.

Your introduction to the military enlistment process usually starts with a visit to your local recruiting office. A search on the Internet for *military recruiter*, along with your geographical location, should provide you with the information you are looking for. Remember, all military service branches have a robust online presence through their various web pages, and you can find a great deal of information there:

- **Navy:** www.navy.com
- **Army:** www.goarmy.com
- **Air Force:** www.airforce.com
- **Marine Corps:** www.marines.com
- **United States Coast Guard:** www.gocoastguard.com

Don't narrow your options too soon, though. If you are thinking of a career in the military, visit a recruiter from each of the five branches—Army, Navy, Air Force, Marines, and Coast Guard. There are lots of similarities, but the subtle differences in what each branch of service has to offer could make a difference in your career.

Basic Requirements

There are certain requirements you will have to meet in order to enlist in any branch of the military. Some of these requirements vary with each branch, so make sure you ask your recruiter any questions you may have. You must:

- be between 17 and 39 years of age, and have a parent or guardian's permission if you are under 18
- be a U.S. citizen or permanent resident with a green card
- have a high school diploma or GED
- be drug-free
- have a clean arrest record

It is important to be truthful with your recruiter about any trouble you have had in the past with drugs or with the law. Criminal history checks are conducted on applicants. However, some kinds of problems can be overcome if they are really *in the past*, not current difficulties. Check with your recruiter.

Working With Your Recruiter

The recruiter is there to help you. In speaking with him or her, you will have the opportunity to ask as many questions as you want and to get a detailed picture of what each branch has to offer if you shop around. All recruiters will have brochures, videotapes, pamphlets, and years of personal experience to offer as resources. Don't be afraid to bring along a parent, guardian, or trusted friend to help you ask questions. In fact, it is highly encouraged—they might ask helpful questions that you had not thought of.

You can ask about the service and its benefits—salaries and fringe benefits, postings, and educational opportunities, including financial aid for college once you get out. (See the table on pages 10–11 for the basic salary for various grades of enlisted personnel

in all the services.) The recruiter will also ask about you: your education, your physical and mental health, and all sorts of in-depth questions about your goals, interests, hobbies, and life experience.

Before you take the Armed Services Vocational Aptitude Battery (ASVAB), you will be given a brief test designed to give the recruiter an idea of how well you will perform on the real test. This pretest covers math and vocabulary. Although the ASVAB has other subtests, it's the math and verbal portions that determine whether you pass the test. The other sections are designed to discover what your aptitudes are for different jobs. There is no limit to how many times you can take this brief test in the recruiter's office.

The recruiter will talk to you about the benefits of enlisting: the pay, the travel, the experience, the training. You and the recruiter can also start to discuss the kinds of jobs available to you in the military. But before that discussion can go very far, you will have to be tested to see if you can enlist, and if so, what specialties you qualify for. That's where your trip to the Military Entrance Processing Station comes in.

Military Entrance Processing Station (MEPS)

The recruiter will schedule you for a trip to a MEPS facility in your area (there are 65 facilities located throughout the United States) for required testing and evaluation. Depending on the service and location, your MEPS visit will take one or two days. You will travel as a guest by plane, train, bus, or car, depending on how far you live from the nearest facility. MEPS schedules vary from area to area, but they all operate five days a week and are open a few Saturdays during the year.

The MEPS is where all applicants for every branch of the military begin the enlistment process. So, even if the Marine Corps is your future employer, you can expect to see staff wearing Navy blue, Army green, or Air Force blue. When you walk through the

IMPORTANT DOCUMENTS

Throughout the enlistment process, you will have to present certain documents. Have the following available to ensure you are prepared:

- birth certificate, proof of permanent residency, or other proof of citizenship and date of birth
- valid Social Security card or two other pieces of Social Security identification
- high school diploma or GED certificate
- letter or transcript documenting your midterm graduation from high school, if applicable
- college transcript, if applicable, showing credits earned
- parental or guardian consent form if you are under 18 years old
- doctor's letter if you have, or have a history of, special medical condition(s)
- marriage certificate, if applicable
- divorce papers, if applicable

door, you will check in at the control desk and be sent to the liaison office for your branch of the service.

Your MEPS Day at a Glance

During your day at MEPS you will go through three phases:

- mental (aptitude) testing
- medical exam
- administrative procedures

Your schedule may vary from the one outlined here, depending on how much of the process you have completed in advance. Some applicants, for example, may have already taken the ASVAB at a Mobile Examining Team (MET) site near their hometown recruiting station.

Mental (Aptitude) Testing

Your day at MEPS will most likely begin with the ASVAB, if you haven't already taken it. (See Chapter 1, "What Is the ASVAB Core?") Don't underestimate the impact the ASVAB will have on your entry into the military. Results of the ASVAB test and the physical and mental exam you receive during the

entrance process are used to determine whether you can join the branch of the military you prefer and which training programs you are qualified to enter.

Some MEPS conduct ASVAB testing on computers. The computer version of the test takes one hour and forty minutes to complete, as opposed to over two hours for the paper-and-pencil version. The computer ASVAB works a little differently than the paper versions. The computer will give you the first question, and, if you get this question right, it gives you another question on the same subject—but this question is a bit harder than the first one. The questions get harder as you progress, and, after you answer a certain number correctly, the computer skips to the next subtest. So, you could get eight questions right, for example, and then the computer might go to the next subtest instead of requiring you to answer every question in that one subtest.

Some MEPS do not have enough computers to test everyone. If you notice that some applicants are taken to a room with the computer testing and the others are required to take the ASVAB with pencil and paper, don't worry. Either way, the information and skills you need remain the same.

MONTHLY BASIC PAY TABLE
THE 2015 MILITARY PAY CHART
COMMISSIONED OFFICERS

Pay Grade	≤2	Over 2	Over 3	Over 4	Over 6	Over 8	Over 10	Over 12	Over 14	Over 16	Over 18	Over 20	Over 22	Over 24	Over 26
O-10 See Note 1												16072	16151	16487	17072
O-9												14057	14620	14552	15062
O-8	96946	10272	10488	10549	10819	11269	11374	11802	11925	12293	12827	13319	13647	13647	13647
O-7	8264	8649	8826	8967	9223	9476	9768	10059	10451	10269	12044	12044	12044	12044	12044
O-6 See Note 2	6187	6797	7243	7243	7270	7582	7623	7623	8057	8823	9272	9721	9977	10236	10738
O-5	5157	5810	6212	6288	6539	6689	7019	7261	7574	8054	8281	8506	8762	8762	8762
O-4	4450	5152	5495	5572	5891	6233	6659	6991	7221	7353	7430	7430	7430	7430	7430
O-3	3913	4435	4787	5219	5469	5744	5922	6213	6365	6365	6365	6365	6365	6365	6365
O-2	3381	3850	4434	4584	4678	4678	4678	4678	4678	4678	4678	4678	4678	4678	4678
O-1	2934	3054	3692	3692	3692	3692	3692	3692	3692	3692	3692	3692	3692	3692	3692

COMMISSIONED OFFICERS WITH OVER 4 YEARS OF ACTIVE SERVICE AS AN ENLISTED MEMBER OR WARRANT OFFICER

See Note 3	≤2	Over 2	Over 3	Over 4	Over 6	Over 8	Over 10	Over 12	Over 14	Over 16	Over 18	Over 20	Over 22	Over 24	Over 26
O-3E				5219	5469	5744	5922	6213	6459	6601	6793	6793	6793	6793	6793
O-2E				4584	4678	4828	5079	5273	5418	5418	5418	5418	5418	5418	5418
O-1E				3692	3942	4088	4237	4384	4584	4584	4584	4584	4584	4584	4584

WARRANT OFFICERS

	≤2	Over 2	Over 3	Over 4	Over 6	Over 8	Over 10	Over 12	Over 14	Over 16	Over 18	Over 20	Over 22	Over 24	Over 26
W-5												7190	7554	7826	8127
W-4	4043	4350	4474	4497	4809	5018	5230	5549	5828	6094	6312	6524	6836	7092	7384
W-3	3692	3846	4004	4056	4221	4547	4886	5045	5230	5420	5762	5993	6132	6278	6477
W-2	3267	3576	3672	3737	3949	4278	4442	4602	4799	4952	5091	5258	5367	5454	5454
W-1	2868	3177	3260	3435	3643	3948	4091	4290	4487	4641	4783	4956	4956	4956	4956

ENLISTED MEMBERS

	Years of Service														
	≤2	Over 2	Over 3	Over 4	Over 6	Over 8	Over 10	Over 12	Over 14	Over 16	Over 18	Over 20	Over 22	Over 24	Over 26
E-9							4885	4997	5135	5299	5465	5730	5955	6191	6552
E-8						3999	4176	4285	4417	4559	4815	4945	5167	5289	5591
E-7	2780	3034	3150	3304	3425	3631	3747	3953	4215	4242	4367	4415	4578	4665	4996
E-6	2318	2550	2663	2772	2885	3143	3244	3437	3496	3540	3590	3590	3590	3590	3590
E-5	2203	2351	2465	2581	2762	2951	3107	3126	3126	3126	3126	3126	3126	3126	3126
E-4	2020	2123	2238	2351	2452	2452	2452	2452	2452	2452	2452	2452	2452	2452	2452
E-3	1823	1938	2055	2055	2055	2055	2055	2055	2055	2055	2055	2055	2055	2055	2055
E-2	1734	1734	1734	1734	1734	1734	1734	1734	1734	1734	1734	1734	1734	1734	1734
E-1	1547	1547	1547	1547	1547	1547	1547	1547	1547	1547	1547	1547	1547	1547	1547

NOTE 1. Basic pay for an O-7 to O-10 is limited by Level II of the Executive Schedule. Basic pay for O-6 and below is limited by Level V of the Executive Schedule.
NOTE 2. O-6 and below is limited by Level V of the Executive Schedule.
NOTE 3. Applicable to O-1 to O-3 with at least 4 years and 1 day of active duty or more than 1460 points as a warrant and/or enlisted member.

Medical Exam

Next is the medical exam. All of the doctors you will see at this point are civilians. You will see them at least three times during the day. During the first visit, you and the medical staff will thoroughly review your medical prescreening form, your medical history form, and all the medical records you have been told by your recruiter to bring along. This meeting will be one on one.

After this meeting, you will move on to the examining room. You'll strip down to your underwear and perform a series of about 20 exercises that will let the medical staff see how your limbs and joints work. You may be with a group of other applicants of the same sex during this examination or you may be alone with the doctor.

Your third meeting with the doctor will be where you receive a routine physical. Among the procedures you can expect are:

- blood pressure evaluation
- pulse rate evaluation
- heart and lung check
- evaluation of blood and urine samples
- eye exam
- hearing and vision exams
- height-proportional-to-weight check
- HIV test
- drug and alcohol tests
- specialized test if required

Female applicants will be given a drape or gown during the physical. This exam will be conducted in private, and a female attendant will accompany you. Women will also receive a pregnancy test.

After these checks, you will find out whether your physical condition is adequate. If the medical staff uncovers a problem that will keep you from joining the service, they will discuss the matter with you. In some cases the doctor may tell you that you are being disqualified at the moment, but that you can come back at a later date to try again. For example, if you are overweight, you could lose weight and then come back to the MEPS for another try.

If the doctor wants to have a medical specialist examine you for some reason, you may have to stay overnight, or the doctor may schedule an appointment for a later date—at the military's expense, of course. Unless you do need to see a specialist, the medical exam should take no more than three hours.

Paperwork

The rest of your day will be taken up with administrative concerns. First you will meet with the guidance counselor for your branch of the service. He or she will take the results of your physical test, your ASVAB scores, and all the other information you have provided and enter this information into a computer system. The computer will show which military jobs are best suited to you. Then you can begin asking questions about your career options. Before you leave the room, you will know:

- for which jobs you are qualified
- which jobs suit your personality, abilities, and interests
- which jobs are available
- when that training is available

You will also be able to decide whether you prefer to enter the military on this very day or to go in under the Delayed Entry Program. Some applicants raise their right hand during swearing-in ceremonies at the end of the processing day, while others prefer to go home and decide what they want to do.

Either way, it's critical that you ask as many questions as possible during this visit with the counselor. Take your time, and be sure you know what you want before you go any further in the process. Be aware, though, that the seats in the popular training programs go fast. The earlier you make your decision, the more likely you will have a chance to get what you really want.

Delayed Entry Programs

Delayed entry programs allow you to enlist with your chosen branch of the military and report for duty up to 365 days later. This is a popular program for students who are still in high school or for those who have other obligations that prevent them from leaving for basic training right away.

Officer

If your desire is to become an officer in the military, all service branches have enlisted-to-officer ascension programs where you can achieve your goal. The manner in which you perform your assignments during your enlisted commitment is one of the major criteria in being accepted to an enlisted-to-officer program, so scoring well on the ASVAB and getting assigned in a field where you have the chance to excel are extremely important.

Basic Training

Everything you have done has been leading up to this moment—the day you leave for Basic Training. You will report back to the MEPS to prepare to leave for Basic Training. If you have been in the Delayed Entry Program, you will get a last-minute mini-physical to make sure your condition is still up to par. You will also be asked about any changes that might affect your eligibility since the last time you were at MEPS. If you have been arrested or had any medical problems, now is the time to speak up.

Your orders and records will be completed at MEPS, and then you are on your way to Basic Training, by plane, bus, or car, at military expense. Where you train will depend on the branch of service. The Air Force, Navy, and Coast Guard each have one training facility. The Marines have two, and the Army has four because where the Army sends you will depend on the specialized training you signed up for at MEPS.

The First Few Days

No matter which branch of service you join, the first few days of Basic Training are similar. You will spend time at an intake facility, where you will be assigned to a Basic Training unit and undergo a quick-paced introduction to your branch of the service. Your days will include:

- orientation briefings
- uniform distribution
- records processing
- I.D. card preparation
- barracks upkeep training
- drill and ceremony instruction
- physical training (PT)

You will be assigned to a group of recruits ranging from 35 to 80 people. The Navy calls this training group a "company," the Army and Marine Corps call it a "platoon," and the Air Force calls it a "flight." And let's not forget your "supervisor" for these early days of your military career—the drill instructor. This is your primary instructor throughout your entire stay at Basic Training.

BRANCH	LOCATION OF TRAINING FACILITY	LENGTH OF TRAINING
Army	Fort Jackson, Columbia, SC; Fort Leonard Wood, Waynesville, MO; Fort Sill, Lawton, OK; Fort Benning, Columbus, GA	10 weeks
Navy	Great Lakes Recruit Training Depot, Great Lakes, IL	7 to 9 weeks
Air Force	Lackland Air Force Base, San Antonio, TX	$8\frac{1}{2}$ weeks
Marine Corps	Parris Island, SC*, or San Diego, CA	12 weeks
Coast Guard	Cape May, NJ	8 weeks

*All women, plus men from the East Coast, attend Basic Training at Parris Island. All men from the West Coast attend at San Diego.

The Following Weeks

You can expect your training day to start around 5 a.m. and officially end around 9 p.m. Most Saturdays and Sundays are light training days. You won't have much free time, and your ability to travel away from your unit on weekends will be very limited, if you get this privilege at all. In most cases you will not be eligible to take leave (vacation time) until after Basic Training, although exceptions can sometimes be made in case of family emergency.

The subjects you learn in Basic Training include:

- military courtesy
- military regulations
- military rules of conduct
- hygiene and sanitation
- organization and mission
- handling and care of weapons
- tactics and training related specifically to your service

While you are in Basic Training, you can expect plenty of physical training. Physical fitness is critical for trainees, and your drill instructor will keep tabs on your progress throughout Basic Training by giving you tests periodically. Your best bet is to start a running and weight-lifting program *the instant* you make your decision to join the military. Recruits in all branches of the service run mile after mile, perform hundreds of sit-ups and push-ups, and become closely acquainted with obstacle courses. These courses differ in appearance from facility to facility, but they all require the same things: plenty of upper body strength and overall endurance, as well as the will to succeed.

ACTIVE DUTY ENLISTMENT DURATIONS BY BRANCH	
BRANCH OF SERVICE	**TERMS OF ENLISTMENT**
Army	2–6 years
Navy	3–5 years
Air Force	4 or 6 years
Marine Corps	4–6 years
Coast Guard	4 or 6 years

Lifetime Opportunities

Basic training, no matter which branch of the service you choose, is a time in your life that you will never forget. No one is promising you it will be pleasant, but during this time you will forge friendships you will keep for the rest of your life. And the opportunities you will have during and after your military service will be unparalleled. You may choose a lifetime career in the military, or you may use it as a springboard to a rewarding career in the private sector. Either way, your future starts now and this book is designed to prepare you for it.

3 ▶ THE SCORE YOU NEED TO ENLIST

CHAPTER SUMMARY

To get the most out of this book, you must know the score you need to get into the service branch of your choice. This chapter walks you step by step through the process of converting your scores on the practice tests in this book into the scores the military uses, so you can tell whether you make the grade.

hen you take the three practice tests in this book, you will want to know whether your scores measure up. You will need some patience here. There are several different kinds of composite scores you will need to compute from your raw scores on the individual parts of the ASVAB.

Calculating Your Score

Your first step is to convert the raw scores you get on your first practice exam (Chapter 5) to the scores the military uses to compute the composite score that says whether you can enlist. This is the Armed Forces Qualifying Test score, or AFQT.

In the table on page 16, write your scores on the Practice ASVAB Core Test 1 in the column that says "Raw Score" under Practice Test 1. Your raw score is simply the number you got right on that subtest. For the raw score in the last blank, Verbal Expression (VE), add together your raw scores on both the Word Knowledge (WK) and Paragraph Comprehension (PC) subtests.

Note that blanks are also provided for Practice ASVAB Core Test 2 and Practice ASVAB Core Test 3; you can fill in those blanks when you take those tests. This table will help you keep track of your improvement as you work through the practice tests in this book.

All the score conversions throughout this chapter are approximate. Different versions of the ASVAB vary in their score conversions, and your scores on the practice tests in this book will not be exactly the same as your score on the real ASVAB. Use the exams in this book to get an *approximate* idea of where you stand and how much you are improving.

YOUR SCORES						
	PRACTICE TEST 1		PRACTICE TEST 2		PRACTICE TEST 3	
SUBTEST	RAW SCORE	SCALED SCORE	RAW SCORE	SCALED SCORE	RAW SCORE	SCALED SCORE
Arithmetic Reasoning (AR)						
Word Knowledge (WK)						
Paragraph Comprehension (PC)						
Mathematics Knowledge (MK)						
Verbal Expression (VE = WK + PC)						

Now you need to fill in the column on the "Your Scores" table labeled "Scaled Score." The following table shows you approximate correlations between raw scores and scaled scores for each subtest. On the left are raw scores. The other columns show the equivalent scaled score for each test. Make sure you're using the column for the proper subtest. The subtests are labeled with the abbreviations shown in the left-hand column of the preceding table.

RAW TO SCALED SCORE CONVERSION					
RAW	AR	WK	PC	MK	VE
0	26	20	20	27	20
1	26	20	20	27	20
2	28	20	20	28	20
3	29	22	23	30	20
4	31	23	26	32	20
5	32	24	30	33	20
6	33	25	33	35	20
7	35	27	36	37	21
8	36	28	39	38	22
9	37	29	42	40	23
10	39	30	45	42	24
11	40	32	48	43	25
12	42	33	51	45	26
13	43	34	54	47	27
14	44	35	58	48	27
15	46	36	61	50	28
16	47	38		52	29
17	48	39		53	30
18	50	40		55	31
19	51	41		56	32
20	53	43		58	33
21	54	44		60	34
22	55	45		61	35
23	57	46		63	36
24	58	47		65	37
25	59	49		66	37
26	61	50			38
27	62	51			39
28	63	52			40
29	65	54			41
30	66	55			42
31		56			43
32		57			44
33		58			45
34		60			46
35		61			47
36					48
37					48
38					49
39					50
40					51
41					52
42					53
43					54
44					55
45					56
46					57
47					58
48					58
49					59
50					60

Find the subtest you want to score in the boxes on the top. Then, on the left column, find your raw score for that subtest. Follow the raw-score row to the right until you get to the proper subtest. That number is your scaled score for this subtest.

Do You Qualify?

Now that you have your scaled score for each subtest filled in on the table on page 16, you are ready for the next step: finding out whether your score will get you into the military. Remember to use only your *scaled scores,* not your raw scores, for these conversions.

The Armed Forces Qualifying Test (AFQT) Score

All branches of the military compute your AFQT score—the one that determines whether you can enlist—in the same way. Only the Verbal Expression (which you determined by adding Word Knowledge and Paragraph Comprehension scores and then converting to a scaled score), Arithmetic Reasoning, and Mathematics Knowledge scaled scores count toward your AFQT. The military just wants to know whether you have basic reading and arithmetic skills. The score conversion goes like this:

$$2(VE) + AR + MK = AFQT$$

In other words, your AFQT (scaled score) is your Verbal Expression scaled score, doubled, added to your Arithmetic Reasoning and Mathematics Knowledge scaled scores. Fill in the blanks here to find your AFQT on Practice Test 1.

VE score _____   × 2 =   _____

AR score   _____

MK score   +   _____

AFQT Scaled Score   _____

There's one last step. Take the AFQT scaled score and find it in the column labeled "Scaled Score" on the next page. Look up the corresponding "Percentile" score. This is approximately equivalent to the score the military will use.

The Army and National Guard require a minimum AFQT score of 31 to qualify for enlistment. Navy recruits must score at least 35 on the AFQT; the Marine Corps requires a minimum of 32, the Coast Guard requires a minimum of 40, and the Air Force requires a minimum of 36. Check with your recruiter for any changes to this requirement.

If your AFQT on the first practice test isn't up to 31, don't despair. You are using this book to help you improve your score, after all, and you have just gotten started. Remember, too, that your score on these practice exams may not be exactly the same as your score on the actual test.

A higher score, however, makes you more attractive to recruiters, and depending on your score on individual subtests, it may qualify you for more of the occupational specialties you want.

Use the following table to convert your AFQT scaled score to the AFQT percentile score. After you have figured out your scaled score using the formula on this page, find it on the following table to see what your AFQT percentile score is. This will tell you whether you have received the minimum score to enlist in the branch of the military you've chosen.

AFQT SCALED SCORE TO PERCENTILE CONVERSION

SCALED SCORE	PERCENTILE	SCALED SCORE	PERCENTILE	SCALED SCORE	PERCENTILE
≤109	1	185	33	218	68
110–118	2	186	34	219	69
119–124	3	187–188	35	220–221	70
125–133	4	189	36	222	71
134–137	5	190	38	223	72
138–141	6	191	39	224	73
142–145	7	192	40	225	74
146–147	8	193	41	226	75
148–151	9	194	42	227	76
152–153	10	195	43	228	77
154–156	11	196	44	229	78
157	12	197	45	230	79
158–159	13	198	46	231	80
160	14	199	47	232	81
161–162	15	200	48	233–234	82
163–164	16	201	49	235	83
165–166	17	202	50	236	84
167	18	203	51	237–238	85
168–169	19	204	52	239	86
170	20	205	53	240	87
171	21	206	54	241–242	88
172–173	22	207	55	243	89
174	23	208	56	244–245	90
175	24	209	57	246	91
176–177	25	210	59	247–248	92
178	26	211	60	249–251	93
179	27	212	61	252–253	94
180	28	213	62	254–256	95
181	29	214	63	257–259	96
182	30	215	64	260–263	97
183	31	216	66	264–268	98
184	32	217	67	≥269	99

THE LEARNINGEXPRESS TEST PREPARATION SYSTEM

CHAPTER SUMMARY

Taking the ASVAB can be tough. It demands a lot of preparation if you want to achieve a top score. Whether you get into the military depends on how well you do on the AFQT portion of the exam. The LearningExpress Test Preparation System, developed exclusively for LearningExpress by leading test experts, gives you the discipline and attitude you need to be a winner.

Getting Ready for the ASVAB

Fact: Taking the ASVAB isn't easy, and neither is getting ready for it. Your future military career depends on your passing the core section of the ASVAB—Arithmetic Reasoning, Word Knowledge, Paragraph Comprehension, and Mathematics Knowledge. By focusing on these four subtests, you have taken your first step to getting into the military. However, there are all sorts of pitfalls that can prevent you from doing your best on this all-important portion of the exam. Here are some of the obstacles that can stand in the way of your success:

- being unfamiliar with the format of the exam
- being paralyzed by test anxiety
- leaving your preparation until the last minute
- not preparing at all!
- not knowing vital test-taking skills: how to pace yourself through the exam, how to use the process of elimination, and when to guess
- not being in tip-top mental and physical shape
- planning poorly by arriving late at the test site, working on an empty stomach, or forgetting to dress in layers and shivering through the exam because the room is cold

What is the common denominator in all these test-taking pitfalls? One word: *control*. Who is in control, you or the exam?

Here is some good news: The LearningExpress Test Preparation System puts you in control. In just nine easy-to-follow steps, you will learn everything you need to know to make sure that you are in charge of your preparation and your performance on the exam. Other test takers may let the test get the better of them; other test takers may be unprepared or out of shape, but not you. You will have taken all the necessary steps to get a passing AFQT score.

Here's how the LearningExpress Test Preparation System works: Nine easy steps lead you through everything you need to know and do to get ready to master your exam. Each of the steps listed here includes reading about the step and one or more activities. It's important that you do the activities along with the reading, or you won't be getting the full benefit of the system. Each step tells you approximately how much time to allow for completion.

Step 1: Get Information	30 minutes
Step 2: Conquer Test Anxiety	20 minutes
Step 3: Make a Plan	50 minutes
Step 4: Learn to Manage Your Time	10 minutes
Step 5: Learn to Use the Process of Elimination	20 minutes
Step 6: Know When to Guess	20 minutes
Step 7: Reach Your Peak Performance Zone	10 minutes
Step 8: Get Your Act Together	10 minutes
Step 9: Do It!	10 minutes
Total	**3 hours**

We estimate that working through the entire system will take you approximately three hours, though it's perfectly okay if you work faster or slower than the time estimates assume. If you can take a whole afternoon or evening, you can work through the whole LearningExpress Test Preparation System in one sitting. Otherwise, you can break it up and do just one or two steps a day for the next several days. It's up to you—remember, you are in control.

Step 1: Get Information

Time to complete: 30 minutes
Activity: Read Chapter 1, "What Is the ASVAB Core?"

Knowledge is power. The first step in the Learning-Express Test Preparation System is finding out everything you can about the ASVAB core. Once you have your information, the next steps will show you what to do with it.

Part A: Straight Talk About the ASVAB

Basically, the U.S. military invented the idea of standardized testing, starting around the time of World War I. The Department of Defense wanted to make sure that its recruits were trainable—not that they already knew the skills they needed to serve in the armed forces, but that they could learn those skills.

The ASVAB started as an intelligence test, but now it is a test of specific aptitudes and abilities. While some of these aptitudes, such as reading and math problem-solving skills, are important in almost any job, others, such as electronics and automotive principles, are quite specialized. These more specialized subtests don't count toward your AFQT score. Only the four subtests covered in this book count toward the AFQT score.

It's important for you to realize that your score on the AFQT does not determine what kind of person you are. There are all kinds of things a written exam like this can't test: whether you can follow orders, whether you can become part of a unit that works together to accomplish a task, and so on. Those kinds of things are hard to evaluate, while a test is easy to evaluate.

This is not to say that the exam is not important! Your chances of getting into the military still depend on your getting a good score on the subtests of the ASVAB core. And that's why you're here—using the LearningExpress Test Preparation System to achieve success on the exam.

Part B: What Is on the Test

If you haven't already done so, stop here and read Chapter 1 of this book, which gives you an overview of the ASVAB core.

Step 2: Conquer Test Anxiety

Time to complete: 20 minutes
Activity: Take the Test Stress Quiz

Having complete information about the exam is the first step in getting control of the exam. Next, you have to overcome one of the biggest obstacles to test success: test anxiety. Test anxiety not only impairs your performance on the exam itself, but also keeps you from preparing. In Step 2, you will learn stress management techniques that will help you succeed on your exam. Learn these strategies now and practice them as you work through the exams in this book so they will be second nature to you by exam day.

Combating Test Anxiety

The first thing you need to know is that a little test anxiety is a good thing. Everyone gets nervous before a big exam—and if that nervousness motivates you to prepare thoroughly, so much the better. It's said that Sir Laurence Olivier, one of the foremost British actors of the twentieth century, felt ill before every performance. His stage fright didn't impair his

performance; in fact, it probably gave him a little extra edge—just the kind of edge needed to do well, whether on a stage or in a testing room.

On page 25 is the Test Stress Quiz. Stop and answer the questions to find out whether your level of test anxiety is something you should be concerned about.

Stress Management Before the Test

If you feel your level of anxiety getting the best of you in the weeks before the test, here is what you need to do to bring the level down again.

- **Be prepared.** There is nothing like knowing what to expect and being prepared for it to put you in control of test anxiety. That's why you're reading this book. Use it faithfully, and remind yourself that you are better prepared than most of the people taking the test.
- **Practice self-confidence.** A positive attitude is a great way to combat test anxiety. This is no time to be humble or shy. Stand in front of the mirror and say to your reflection, "I'm prepared. I'm full of self-confidence. I'm going to ace this test. I know I can do it." Say it into a tape recorder and play it back once a day. If you hear it often enough, you will believe it.
- **Fight negative messages.** Every time someone starts telling you how hard the exam is or how difficult it is to get a high score, start repeating your self-confidence messages. Don't listen to the negative messages. Turn on your tape recorder and listen to your affirmations.
- **Visualize.** Imagine yourself reporting for duty on your first day as a military trainee. Think of yourself wearing your uniform and learning skills you will use for the rest of your life. Visualizing success can help make it happen—and it reminds you of why you are working so hard preparing for the exam.

- **Exercise.** Physical activity helps calm your body and focus your mind. Besides, being in good physical shape can actually help you do well on the exam. Go for a run, lift weights, go swimming—and do it regularly.

Stress Management on Test Day

There are several ways you can reduce your level of anxiety on test day. They will work best if you practice them in the weeks before the test so you know which ones work best for you.

- **Deep breathing.** Take a deep breath while you count to five. Hold it for a count of one, then let it out for a count of five. Repeat several times.
- **Move your body.** Try rolling your head in a circle. Rotate your shoulders. Shake your hands from the wrist. Many people find these movements relaxing.
- **Visualize again.** Think of the place where you are most relaxed: lying on a beach in the sun, walking through the park, or whatever you enjoy. Now close your eyes and imagine you are actually there. If you practice in advance, you will find that you only need a few seconds of this exercise to experience a significant increase in your sense of well-being.

When anxiety threatens to overwhelm you during the exam, there are still things you can do to manage the stress level.

- **Repeat your self-confidence messages.** You should have them memorized by now. Say them silently to yourself, and believe them!
- **Visualize one more time.** This time, visualize yourself moving smoothly and quickly through the test, answering every question correctly and finishing just before the time is up. Like most visualization techniques, this one works best if you have practiced it ahead of time.
- **Find an easy question.** Skim over the test until you find an easy question, and answer it. Getting even one question finished gets you into the test-taking groove.
- **Take a mental break.** Everyone loses concentration once in a while during a long test. It's normal, so you shouldn't worry about it. Instead, accept what has happened. Say to yourself, "Hey, I lost it there for a minute. My brain is taking a break." Put down your pencil, close your eyes, and do some deep breathing for a few seconds. Then you're ready to go back to work.

Try these techniques ahead of time, and see if they work for you!

You only need to worry about test anxiety if it is extreme enough to impair your performance. The following questionnaire will provide a diagnosis of your level of test anxiety. In the blank before each statement, write the number that most accurately describes your experience.

0 = Never   1 = Once or twice   2 = Sometimes   3 = Often

_____ I have gotten so nervous before an exam that I simply put down the books and didn't study for it.

_____ I have experienced disabling physical symptoms such as vomiting and severe headaches because I was nervous about an exam.

_____ I have simply not showed up for an exam because I was scared to take it.

_____ I have experienced dizziness and disorientation while taking an exam.

_____ I have had trouble filling in the little circles because my hands were shaking too hard.

_____ I have failed an exam because I was too nervous to complete it.

_____ **Total: Add up the numbers in the blanks.**

Your Test Stress Score

Here are the steps you should take, depending on your score. If you scored:

- **Below 3,** your level of test anxiety is nothing to worry about; it's probably just enough to give you that little extra edge.
- **Between 3 and 6,** your test anxiety may be enough to impair your performance, and you should practice the stress management techniques listed in this section to try to bring your test anxiety down to manageable levels.
- **Above 6,** your level of test anxiety is a serious concern. In addition to practicing the stress management techniques listed in this section, you may want to seek additional, personal help. Call your community college and ask for the academic counselor. Tell the counselor that you have a level of test anxiety that sometimes keeps you from being able to take an exam. The counselor may be able to help you or may suggest someone else you can talk to.

Step 3: Make a Plan

Time to complete: 50 minutes
Activity: Construct a study plan

Maybe the most important thing you can do to get control of yourself and your exam is to make a study plan. Too many people fail to prepare simply because they fail to plan. Spending hours on the day before the exam poring over sample test questions not only raises your level of test anxiety, it is simply no substitute for careful preparation.

On the following pages are two sample schedules, based on the amount of time you have to prepare for the ASVAB. If you are the kind of person who needs deadlines and assignments to motivate you for a project, use them as is. If you are the kind of person who doesn't like to follow other people's plans, you can use the suggested schedules here to construct your own.

Even more important than making a plan is making a commitment. You can't improve your skills in the four areas tested on the ASVAB core overnight. You have to set aside some time every day for study and practice. Try for at least 30 minutes a day. Thirty minutes daily will do you much more good than two hours on Saturday.

Don't put off your study until the day before the exam. Start now. A few minutes a day, with half an hour or more on weekends, can make a big difference in your score.

Step 4:
Learn to Manage Your Time

Time to complete: 10 minutes to read, many hours of practice!
Activities: Practice these strategies as you take the sample tests in this book

Steps 4, 5, and 6 of the LearningExpress Test Preparation System put you in charge of your exam by showing you test-taking strategies that work. Practice these strategies as you take the sample tests in this book, and then you will be ready to use them on test day.

First, you will take control of your time on the exam. Each of the four subtests of the ASVAB core is timed separately. Most allow you enough time to complete the section, though none allows a lot of extra time. You should use your time wisely to avoid

making errors. Here are some general tips for the whole exam:

- **Listen carefully to directions.** By the time you get to the exam, you should know how all the subtests work, but listen just in case something has changed.
- **Pace yourself.** Glance at your watch every few minutes, and compare the time to your progress on the subtest. When one-quarter of the time has elapsed, you should be one-quarter of the way through the subtest, and so on. If you're falling behind, pick up the pace a bit.
- **Keep moving.** Don't waste time on one question. If you don't know the answer, skip the question and move on. Circle the number of the question in your test booklet in case you have time to come back to it later.
- **Keep track of your place on the answer sheet.** If you skip a question, make sure you skip on the answer sheet too. Check yourself every 5–10 questions to make sure the question number and the answer sheet number match up.
- **Don't rush.** Though you should keep moving, rushing won't help. Try to keep calm and work methodically and quickly.

Schedule A: The Two-Week Plan

If you have at least two weeks before you take the ASVAB, you have plenty of time to prepare—as long as you don't waste it! If you have less than two weeks, turn to Schedule B.

TIME	PREPARATION
Day 1	Take the first practice exam in Chapter 5. Score the exam and identify two areas that you will concentrate on before you take the second practice exam.
Days 2–5	Study the areas you identified as your weaknesses. Don't forget, there are review lessons and practice questions for Math, Reading, and Vocabulary in Chapters 6–11. Review these chapters in detail to improve your score on the next practice test.
Day 6	Take the second practice exam in Chapter 12 and calculate your score. Identify one area to concentrate on before you take the third practice exam.
Days 7–9	Study the one area you identified for further review. Again, use the Math, Reading, and Vocabulary chapters for help.
Day 10	Take the last practice exam in Chapter 13. Score the test. Note how much you have improved!
Days 11–13	Take an overview of all your study materials, focusing on your strengths and improving on your weaknesses.
Day before the exam	Relax. Do something unrelated to the exam and go to bed at a reasonable hour.

Schedule B: The One-Week Plan

If you have a week or less before you take the exam, use this seven-day schedule to help you make the most of your time.

TIME	PREPARATION
Day 1	Take the first practice exam in Chapter 5 and review the answers and explanations. Note which topics you need to review most.
Day 2	Review one area that gave you trouble on the first practice exam. Use the review lessons and practice questions in Chapters 6–11 to hone your skills.
Day 3	Take the second practice exam in Chapter 12 and score it.
Day 4	If your score on the second practice exam doesn't show improvement on the two areas you studied, continue to use the review chapters to improve some skills and reinforce others. If you did improve in those areas, choose a new weak area to study today.
Day 5	Take the third practice exam in Chapter 13 and score it. See how much you have improved since the first practice test!
Day 6	Use your last study day to brush up on any areas that are still giving you trouble. Use the review and practice chapters.
Day before the exam	Relax. Do something unrelated to the exam and go to bed at a reasonable hour.

Step 5: Learn to Use the Process of Elimination

Time to complete: 20 minutes
Activity: Complete Using the Process of Elimination worksheet

After time management, your next most important tool for taking control of your exam is using the process of elimination wisely. It's standard test-taking wisdom that you should always read all the answer choices before choosing your answer. This helps you find the right answer by eliminating wrong answer choices.

You should always use the process of elimination on tough questions, even if the right answer jumps out at you. Sometimes the answer that jumps out isn't right after all. You should always proceed through the answer choices in order. You can start with answer choice **a** and eliminate any choices that are clearly incorrect.

Let's say you're facing a vocabulary question that goes like this:

"Biology uses a <u>binomial</u> system of classification." In this sentence, the word <u>binomial</u> most nearly means

a. understanding the law.
b. having two names.
c. scientifically sound.
d. having a double meaning.

If you happen to know what *binomial* means, of course, you don't need to use the process of elimination, but let's assume you don't. So, you look at the answer choices. "understanding the law" sure doesn't sound like something having to do with biology. So you eliminate choice **a**—and now you only have three answer choices to deal with. Mark an **X** next to choice **a** so you never have to read it again.

Now, move on to the other answer choices. If you know that the prefix *bi-* means *two,* as in *bicycle,* you will flag choice **b** as a possible answer. Mark a check mark beside it, meaning "good answer, I might use this one."

Choice **c**, "scientifically sound," is a possibility. At least it's about science, not law. It could work here, although when you think about it, having a "scientifically sound" classification system in a scientific field is kind of redundant. You remember the *bi-* in *binomial,* and probably continue to like choice **b** better. But you're not sure, so you put a question mark next to **c**, meaning "well, maybe."

Now, choice **d**, "having a double meaning." You're still keeping in mind that *bi-* means *two,* so this one looks possible at first. But then you look again at the sentence the word belongs in, and you think, "Why would biology want a system of classification that has two meanings? That wouldn't work very well!" If you're really taken with the idea that *bi-* means *two,* you might put a question mark here. But if you're feeling a little more confident, you'll put an **X**. You already have a better answer picked out.

Now your question looks like this:

"Biology uses a <u>binomial</u> system of classification." In this sentence, the word <u>binomial</u> most nearly means

 X a. understanding the law.
 ✓ b. having two names.
 ? c. scientifically sound.
 ? d. having a double meaning.

You've got just one checkmark for a good answer. If you're pressed for time, you should simply mark choice **b** on your answer sheet. If you have the time to be extra careful, you could compare your check-mark answer to your question-mark answers to make sure that it's better. (It is: The *binomial* system in biology is the one that gives a two-part genus and species name like *homo sapiens.*)

It's good to have a system for marking good, bad, and maybe answers. Here's one recommendation:

X = bad
✓ = good
? = maybe

If you don't like these marks, devise your own system. Just make sure you do it long before test day—

while you're working through the practice exams in this book—so you won't have to worry about it during the test.

Even when you think you are absolutely clueless about a question, you can often use the process of elimination to get rid of one answer choice. If so, you are better prepared to make an educated guess, as you will see in Step 6. More often, the process of elimination allows you to get down to only *two* possibly right answers. Then, you're in a strong position to guess. And sometimes, even though you don't know the right answer, you can make a fairly certain guess by elimintating those that don't fit, as you did in the previous example.

Try using your powers of elimination on the questions in the worksheet "Using the Process of Elimination" that follows. The answer explanations there show one possible way you might use the process to arrive at the right answer.

The process of elimination is a tool for the next step, which is knowing when to guess.

USING THE PROCESS OF ELIMINATION

Use the process of elimination to answer the following questions.

1. Isa is as old as Meghan will be in five years. The difference between Ed's age and Meghan's age is twice the difference between Ilsa's age and Meghan's age. Ed is 29. How old is Ilsa?
   a. 4
   b. 10
   c. 19
   d. 24

2. "All drivers of commercial vehicles must carry a valid commercial driver's license whenever operating a commercial vehicle." According to this sentence, which of the following people does NOT need to carry a commercial driver's license?
   a. a truck driver idling his engine while waiting to be directed to a loading dock
   b. a bus operator backing her bus out of the way of another bus in the bus lot
   c. a taxi driver driving his personal car to the grocery store
   d. a limousine driver taking the limousine to her home after dropping off her last passenger of the evening

3. Smoking tobacco has been linked to
   a. increased risk of stroke and heart attack.
   b. all forms of respiratory disease.
   c. increasing mortality rates over the past ten years.
   d. juvenile delinquency.

4. Which of the following words is spelled correctly?
   a. incorrigible
   b. outragous
   c. domestickated
   d. understandible

Answers

Here are the answers, as well as some suggestions as to how you might have used the process of elimination to find them.

1. d. You should have eliminated choice **a** off the bat. Ilsa can't be four years old if Meghan is going to be Ilsa's age in five years. The best way to eliminate other answer choices is to try plugging them in to the information given in the problem. For instance, for choice **b**, if Ilsa is 10, then Meghan must be 5. The difference in their ages is 5. The difference between Ed's age, 29, and Meghan's age, 5, is 24. Is 24 two times 5? No. Then choice **b** is wrong. You could eliminate choice **c** in the same way and be left with choice **d**.

2. c. Note the word *not* in the question, and go through the answers one by one. Is the truck driver in choice **a** "operating a commercial vehicle"? Yes, idling counts as "operating," so he needs to have a commercial driver's license. Likewise, the bus operator in choice **b** is operating a commercial vehicle; the question doesn't say the operator has to be on the street. The limo driver in choice **d** is operating a commercial vehicle, even if it doesn't have passenger in it. However, the cabbie in choice **c** is *not* operating a commercial vehicle, but his own private car.

3. a. You could eliminate choice **b** simply because of the presence of the word *all*. Such absolutes hardly ever appear in correct answer choices. Choice **c** looks attractive until you think a little about what you know—aren't fewer people smoking these days, rather than more? So how could smoking be responsible for a higher mortality rate? (If you didn't know that *mortality rate* means the rate at which people die, you might keep this choice as a possibility, but you'd still be able to eliminate two choices and have only two to choose from.) Choice **d** is plain silly, so you could eliminate that one, too. You're left with the correct choice, **a**.

4. a. How you used the process of elimination here depends on which words you recognized as being spelled incorrectly. If you knew that the correct spellings were *outrageous, domesticated*, and *understandable*, then you were home free. You probably knew that at least one of those words was wrong!

Step 6: Know When to Guess

Time to complete: 20 minutes
Activity: Complete worksheet on Your Guessing Ability

Armed with the process of elimination, you are ready to take control of one of the big questions in test taking: Should I guess? The answer is "Yes." Some exams have what is called a "guessing penalty," in which a fraction of your wrong answers is subtracted from your right answers, but the ASVAB isn't one of them. The number of questions you answer correctly yields your raw score. So you have nothing to lose and everything to gain by guessing.

To find out whether you're a good guesser, complete the "Your Guessing Ability" worksheet. Even if you're a play-it-safe person with lousy intuition, you are still safe in guessing every time. The best thing would be if you could overcome your anxieties and go ahead and mark an answer. But you may want to have a sense of how good your intuition is before you go into the exam.

YOUR GUESSING ABILITY

The following are ten really hard questions. You are not supposed to know the answers. Rather, this is an assessment of your ability to guess when you don't have a clue. Read each question carefully, just as if you did expect to answer it. If you have any knowledge at all about the subject of the question, use that knowledge to help you eliminate wrong answer choices.

ANSWER GRID

1.	ⓐ	ⓑ	ⓒ	ⓓ	**5.**	ⓐ	ⓑ	ⓒ	ⓓ	**9.**	ⓐ	ⓑ	ⓒ	ⓓ
2.	ⓐ	ⓑ	ⓒ	ⓓ	**6.**	ⓐ	ⓑ	ⓒ	ⓓ	**10.**	ⓐ	ⓑ	ⓒ	ⓓ
3.	ⓐ	ⓑ	ⓒ	ⓓ	**7.**	ⓐ	ⓑ	ⓒ	ⓓ				
4.	ⓐ	ⓑ	ⓒ	ⓓ	**8.**	ⓐ	ⓑ	ⓒ	ⓓ				

1. September 7 is Independence Day in
   a. India.
   b. Costa Rica.
   c. Brazil.
   d. Australia.

2. Which of the following is the formula for determining the momentum of an object?
   a. $p = mv$
   b. $F = ma$
   c. $P = IV$
   d. $E = mc^2$

3. Because of the expansion of the universe, the stars and other celestial bodies are all moving away from each other. This phenomenon is known as
   a. Newton's first law.
   b. the big bang.
   c. gravitational collapse.
   d. Hubble flow.

4. American author Gertrude Stein was born in
   a. 1713.
   b. 1830.
   c. 1874.
   d. 1901.

5. Which of the following is NOT one of the Five Classics attributed to Confucius?
   a. the *I Ching*
   b. the *Book of Holiness*
   c. the *Spring and Autumn Annals*
   d. the *Book of History*

6. The religious and philosophical doctrine that holds that the universe is constantly in a struggle between good and evil is known as
   a. Pelagianism.
   b. Manichaeanism.
   c. neo-Hegelianism.
   d. Epicureanism.

7. The third chief justice of the U.S. Supreme Court was
  a. John Blair.
  b. William Cushing.
  c. James Wilson.
  d. John Jay.

8. Which of the following is the poisonous portion of a daffodil?
  a. the bulb
  b. the leaves
  c. the stem
  d. the flowers

9. The winner of the Masters golf tournament in 1953 was
  a. Sam Snead.
  b. Cary Middlecoff.
  c. Arnold Palmer.
  d. Ben Hogan.

10. The state with the highest per capita personal income in 1980 was
  a. Alaska.
  b. Connecticut.
  c. New York.
  d. Texas.

Answers

Check your answers against the following correct answers.

1. c.
2. a.
3. d.
4. c.
5. b.
6. b.
7. b.
8. a.
9. d.
10. a.

How Did You Do?

You may have simply gotten lucky and actually known the answer to one or two questions. In addition, your guessing was more successful if you were able to use the process of elimination on any of the questions. Maybe you didn't know who the third chief justice was (question 7), but you knew that John Jay was the first. In that case, you would have eliminated choice **d** and therefore improved your odds of guessing correctly from one in four to one in three.

According to probability, you should get $2\frac{1}{2}$ answers correct, so getting either two or three right would be average. If you got four or more right, you may be a really terrific guesser. If you got one or none right, you may be a really bad guesser.

Keep in mind, though, that this is only a small sample. You should continue to keep track of your guessing ability as you work through the sample questions in this book. Circle the numbers of questions you are unsure of as you make your guess; or, if you don't have time while you take the practice exams, go back afterward and try to remember which questions you guessed at. Remember, on an exam with four answer choices, your chances of getting a correct answer is one in four. So keep a separate "guessing" score for each exam. How many questions did you guess on? How many did you get right? If the number you got right is at least one-fourth of the number of questions you guessed on, you are at least an average guesser, maybe better.

Step 7: Reach Your Peak Performance Zone

Time to complete: 10 minutes to read, weeks to complete!
Activity: Complete the Physical Preparation Checklist

To get ready for a challenge like a big exam, you have to take control of your physical, as well as your mental, state. Exercise, proper diet, and rest will ensure that your body works with, rather than against, your mind on test day, as well as during your preparation.

Exercise

If you don't already have a regular exercise program, the time during which you are preparing for an exam is actually an excellent time to start one. You will have to be fit to make it through the first weeks of basic training. If you're already keeping fit, don't let the pressure of preparing for an exam fool you into quitting now. Exercise helps reduce stress by pumping good-feeling hormones called endorphins into your system. It also increases the oxygen supply throughout your body, including your brain, so you will be at peak performance on test day.

A half hour of vigorous activity every day—enough to raise a sweat—should be your aim. If you are really pressed for time, every other day is okay. Choose an activity you like and get out there and do it. Jogging with a friend always makes the time go faster.

But don't overdo it; you don't want to exhaust yourself. Moderation is the key.

Diet

First of all, cut out the junk. Go easy on caffeine and nicotine, and eliminate alcohol from your system at least two weeks before the exam. Promise yourself a treat the night after the exam, if need be.

What your body needs for peak performance is simply a balanced diet. Eat plenty of fruits and vegetables, along with protein and complex carbohydrates.

Rest

You probably know how much sleep you need every night to be at your best, even if you don't always get it. Make sure you do get that much sleep, though, for at least a week before the exam. Moderation is important here, too. Extra sleep will just make you groggy.

If you are not a morning person and your exam will be given in the morning, you should reset your internal clock so that your body doesn't think you're taking an exam at 3:00 a.m. You have to start this process well before the exam. Get up half an hour earlier each morning, and then go to bed half an hour earlier that night. Don't try it the other way around. You will just toss and turn if you go to bed early without having gotten up early. The next morning, get up another half an hour earlier, and so on. How long you will have to do this depends on how late you're used to getting up.

Use the Physical Preparation Checklist on page 35 to make sure you are in tip-top form.

Step 8: Get Your Act Together

Time to complete: 10 minutes to read,
time to complete will vary
Activity: Complete Final Preparations Checklist

You are in control of your mind and body; you are in charge of test anxiety, your preparation, and your test-taking strategies. Now it's time to take charge of external factors, like the testing site and the materials you need to take the exam.

Getting to the MEPS

You will be the guest of the Department of Defense on your trip to the Military Entrance Processing Station (MEPS). You will probably be scheduled to spend a full day at the MEPS, though if it's far from your hometown, you may have to go the night before. Your recruiter will tell you when and where you will be picked up for your trip to the MEPS. Make sure you know how to get to that location, if it's not your recruiting station, and how long it will take to get there. Figure out how early you will have to wake up that morning, and get up at that time every day for the week before your MEPS day.

Gather Your Materials

The night before the exam, lay out the clothes you will wear and the materials you have to bring with you to the MEPS. Plan on dressing in layers; you won't have any control over the temperature of the examination room. Have a sweater or jacket you can take off if it's warm. Use the checklist on the Final Preparations worksheet on page 36 to help you pull together what you will need.

Don't Skip Breakfast

Even if you don't usually eat breakfast, do so on exam morning. A cup of coffee doesn't count. Don't choose doughnuts or other sweet foods, either. A sugar high will leave you with a sugar low in the middle of the exam. A mix of protein and carbohydrates is best: cereal with milk, or eggs with toast, will do your body a world of good.

Step 9: Do It!

Time to complete: 10 minutes, plus test-taking time
Activity: Ace the ASVAB core!

Fast forward to exam day. You are ready. You made a study plan and followed through. You practiced your test-taking strategies while working through this book. You are in control of your physical, mental, and emotional state. You know when and where to show up and what to bring with you. In other words, you are better prepared than most of the other people taking the ASVAB with you. You are psyched.

Just one more thing. When you've finished your day at the MEPS, you will have earned a reward. Plan a celebration. Call up your friends and plan a party, or have a nice dinner for two—whatever your heart desires. Give yourself something to look forward to.

Then, do it. Take the ASVAB, full of confidence, armed with the test-taking strategies you have mastered. You are in control of yourself, your environment, and your performance on the exam. You are ready to succeed. Go in there, ace the exam, and look forward to your future military career!

For the week before the test, write down: 1) what physical exercise you engaged in and for how long, and 2) what you ate for each meal. Remember, you're aiming for at least half an hour of exercise every other day (preferably every day), and a balanced diet that's light on junk food.

Exam minus 7 days

Exercise: _____ for _____ minutes

Breakfast: _____

Lunch: _____

Dinner: _____

Snacks: _____

Exam minus 6 days

Exercise: _____ for _____ minutes

Breakfast: _____

Lunch: _____

Dinner: _____

Snacks: _____

Exam minus 5 days

Exercise: _____ for _____ minutes

Breakfast: _____

Lunch: _____

Dinner: _____

Snacks: _____

Exam minus 4 days

Exercise: _____ for _____ minutes

Breakfast: _____

Lunch: _____

Dinner: _____

Snacks: _____

Exam minus 3 days

Exercise: _____ for _____ minutes

Breakfast: _____

Lunch: _____

Dinner: _____

Snacks: _____

Exam minus 2 days

Exercise: _____ for _____ minutes

Breakfast: _____

Lunch: _____

Dinner: _____

Snacks: _____

Exam minus 1 day

Exercise: _____ for _____ minutes

Breakfast: _____

Lunch: _____

Dinner: _____

Snacks: _____

FINAL PREPARATIONS

Getting to the MEPS Pickup Site

Location of pickup site: _____

Date: _____

Departure time: _____

Do I know how to get to the pickup site?   Yes ___   No ___   *If no, make a trial run.*

Time it will take to get to the pickup site: _____

Things to Lay Out the Night Before

Clothes I will wear   _____

Sweater/jacket   _____

Watch   _____

Photo ID   _____

Other   _____

5 ▶ PRACTICE ASVAB CORE TEST 1

CHAPTER SUMMARY

This is the first of three practice tests based on the subtests of the ASVAB that count toward your AFQT score. Use this test to see how you would do if you were to take the exam today.

The four subtests of the ASVAB that count toward your Armed Forces Qualifying Test (AFQT) score—Arithmetic Reasoning, Word Knowledge, Paragraph Comprehension, and Mathematics Knowledge—are included in the practice test that follows.

The amount of time allowed for each subtest will be found at the beginning of that subtest. For now, don't worry too much about timing. Just take the tests, focusing on being as relaxed as you can. The answer sheet you should use for answering the questions is on page 39. Complete answer explanations follow the test.

Part 1: Arithmetic Reasoning

1.	ⓐ	ⓑ	ⓒ	ⓓ
2.	ⓐ	ⓑ	ⓒ	ⓓ
3.	ⓐ	ⓑ	ⓒ	ⓓ
4.	ⓐ	ⓑ	ⓒ	ⓓ
5.	ⓐ	ⓑ	ⓒ	ⓓ
6.	ⓐ	ⓑ	ⓒ	ⓓ
7.	ⓐ	ⓑ	ⓒ	ⓓ
8.	ⓐ	ⓑ	ⓒ	ⓓ
9.	ⓐ	ⓑ	ⓒ	ⓓ
10.	ⓐ	ⓑ	ⓒ	ⓓ

11.	ⓐ	ⓑ	ⓒ	ⓓ
12.	ⓐ	ⓑ	ⓒ	ⓓ
13.	ⓐ	ⓑ	ⓒ	ⓓ
14.	ⓐ	ⓑ	ⓒ	ⓓ
15.	ⓐ	ⓑ	ⓒ	ⓓ
16.	ⓐ	ⓑ	ⓒ	ⓓ
17.	ⓐ	ⓑ	ⓒ	ⓓ
18.	ⓐ	ⓑ	ⓒ	ⓓ
19.	ⓐ	ⓑ	ⓒ	ⓓ
20.	ⓐ	ⓑ	ⓒ	ⓓ

21.	ⓐ	ⓑ	ⓒ	ⓓ
22.	ⓐ	ⓑ	ⓒ	ⓓ
23.	ⓐ	ⓑ	ⓒ	ⓓ
24.	ⓐ	ⓑ	ⓒ	ⓓ
25.	ⓐ	ⓑ	ⓒ	ⓓ
26.	ⓐ	ⓑ	ⓒ	ⓓ
27.	ⓐ	ⓑ	ⓒ	ⓓ
28.	ⓐ	ⓑ	ⓒ	ⓓ
29.	ⓐ	ⓑ	ⓒ	ⓓ
30.	ⓐ	ⓑ	ⓒ	ⓓ

Part 2: Word Knowledge

1.	ⓐ	ⓑ	ⓒ	ⓓ
2.	ⓐ	ⓑ	ⓒ	ⓓ
3.	ⓐ	ⓑ	ⓒ	ⓓ
4.	ⓐ	ⓑ	ⓒ	ⓓ
5.	ⓐ	ⓑ	ⓒ	ⓓ
6.	ⓐ	ⓑ	ⓒ	ⓓ
7.	ⓐ	ⓑ	ⓒ	ⓓ
8.	ⓐ	ⓑ	ⓒ	ⓓ
9.	ⓐ	ⓑ	ⓒ	ⓓ
10.	ⓐ	ⓑ	ⓒ	ⓓ
11.	ⓐ	ⓑ	ⓒ	ⓓ
12.	ⓐ	ⓑ	ⓒ	ⓓ

13.	ⓐ	ⓑ	ⓒ	ⓓ
14.	ⓐ	ⓑ	ⓒ	ⓓ
15.	ⓐ	ⓑ	ⓒ	ⓓ
16.	ⓐ	ⓑ	ⓒ	ⓓ
17.	ⓐ	ⓑ	ⓒ	ⓓ
18.	ⓐ	ⓑ	ⓒ	ⓓ
19.	ⓐ	ⓑ	ⓒ	ⓓ
20.	ⓐ	ⓑ	ⓒ	ⓓ
21.	ⓐ	ⓑ	ⓒ	ⓓ
22.	ⓐ	ⓑ	ⓒ	ⓓ
23.	ⓐ	ⓑ	ⓒ	ⓓ
24.	ⓐ	ⓑ	ⓒ	ⓓ

25.	ⓐ	ⓑ	ⓒ	ⓓ
26.	ⓐ	ⓑ	ⓒ	ⓓ
27.	ⓐ	ⓑ	ⓒ	ⓓ
28.	ⓐ	ⓑ	ⓒ	ⓓ
29.	ⓐ	ⓑ	ⓒ	ⓓ
30.	ⓐ	ⓑ	ⓒ	ⓓ
31.	ⓐ	ⓑ	ⓒ	ⓓ
32.	ⓐ	ⓑ	ⓒ	ⓓ
33.	ⓐ	ⓑ	ⓒ	ⓓ
34.	ⓐ	ⓑ	ⓒ	ⓓ
35.	ⓐ	ⓑ	ⓒ	ⓓ

Part 3: Paragraph Comprehension

1.	ⓐ	ⓑ	ⓒ	ⓓ
2.	ⓐ	ⓑ	ⓒ	ⓓ
3.	ⓐ	ⓑ	ⓒ	ⓓ
4.	ⓐ	ⓑ	ⓒ	ⓓ
5.	ⓐ	ⓑ	ⓒ	ⓓ

6.	ⓐ	ⓑ	ⓒ	ⓓ
7.	ⓐ	ⓑ	ⓒ	ⓓ
8.	ⓐ	ⓑ	ⓒ	ⓓ
9.	ⓐ	ⓑ	ⓒ	ⓓ
10.	ⓐ	ⓑ	ⓒ	ⓓ

11.	ⓐ	ⓑ	ⓒ	ⓓ
12.	ⓐ	ⓑ	ⓒ	ⓓ
13.	ⓐ	ⓑ	ⓒ	ⓓ
14.	ⓐ	ⓑ	ⓒ	ⓓ
15.	ⓐ	ⓑ	ⓒ	ⓓ

Part 4: Mathematics Knowledge

1.	ⓐ	ⓑ	ⓒ	ⓓ
2.	ⓐ	ⓑ	ⓒ	ⓓ
3.	ⓐ	ⓑ	ⓒ	ⓓ
4.	ⓐ	ⓑ	ⓒ	ⓓ
5.	ⓐ	ⓑ	ⓒ	ⓓ
6.	ⓐ	ⓑ	ⓒ	ⓓ
7.	ⓐ	ⓑ	ⓒ	ⓓ
8.	ⓐ	ⓑ	ⓒ	ⓓ
9.	ⓐ	ⓑ	ⓒ	ⓓ

10.	ⓐ	ⓑ	ⓒ	ⓓ
11.	ⓐ	ⓑ	ⓒ	ⓓ
12.	ⓐ	ⓑ	ⓒ	ⓓ
13.	ⓐ	ⓑ	ⓒ	ⓓ
14.	ⓐ	ⓑ	ⓒ	ⓓ
15.	ⓐ	ⓑ	ⓒ	ⓓ
16.	ⓐ	ⓑ	ⓒ	ⓓ
17.	ⓐ	ⓑ	ⓒ	ⓓ
18.	ⓐ	ⓑ	ⓒ	ⓓ

19.	ⓐ	ⓑ	ⓒ	ⓓ
20.	ⓐ	ⓑ	ⓒ	ⓓ
21.	ⓐ	ⓑ	ⓒ	ⓓ
22.	ⓐ	ⓑ	ⓒ	ⓓ
23.	ⓐ	ⓑ	ⓒ	ⓓ
24.	ⓐ	ⓑ	ⓒ	ⓓ
25.	ⓐ	ⓑ	ⓒ	ⓓ

Part 1: Arithmetic Reasoning

Time: 36 minutes

1. If Ellen has $36.00 to spend at the flower market, and lilies cost $1.80 each, how many lilies can she purchase?
   a. 18
   b. 20
   c. 24
   d. 36

2. An aquarium has a base length of 12 inches and a width of 5 inches. If the aquarium is 10 inches tall, what is the total volume?
   a. 460 cubic inches
   b. 340 cubic inches
   c. 600 cubic inches
   d. 720 cubic inches

3. A man turns in a woman's handbag to the Lost and Found Department of a large downtown store. The man informs the clerk in charge that he found the handbag on the floor beside an entranceway. The clerk estimates that the handbag is worth approximately $150. Inside, the clerk finds the following items:

1 leather makeup case valued at	$65
1 vial of perfume, unopened, valued at	$75
1 pair of earrings valued at	$150
cash	$178

   The clerk is writing a report to be submitted along with the found property. What should he write as the total value of the found cash and property?
   a. $468
   b. $608
   c. $618
   d. $718

Use the following information to answer questions 4–6.

The cost of movie theater tickets is $7.50 for adults and $5 for children ages 12 and under. On Saturday and Sunday afternoons until 4:00 p.m., there is a matinee price: $5.50 for adults and $3 for children ages 12 and under. Special group discounts are available for groups of 30 or more people.

4. Which of these can be determined from the information given in the passage?
   a. how much it will cost a family of four to buy movie theater tickets on Saturday afternoon
   b. the difference between the cost of two movie theater tickets on Tuesday night and the cost of one ticket on Sunday at 3:00 p.m.
   c. how much movie theater tickets will cost each person if he or she is part of a group of 40 people
   d. the difference between the cost of a movie theater ticket for an adult on Friday night and a movie theater ticket for a 13-year-old on Saturday at 1:00 p.m.

5. The Reaves family includes one adult, one 15-year-old, one 12-year-old, and one 11-year-old. How much would the Reaves family save by going to a Saturday matinee at 3:30 p.m. instead of a regularly priced movie at 7 p.m.?
   a. $25.00
   b. $22.50
   c. $17.00
   d. $8.00

6. Using the passage, how can you find the difference in price between a movie theater ticket for an adult and a movie theater ticket for a child under the age of 12, if the tickets are for a show at 3:00 p.m. on a Saturday?
   a. subtract $3.00 from $5.50
   b. subtract $5.00 from $7.50
   c. subtract $7.50 from $5.50
   d. add $5.50 and $3.00 and divide by 2

7. It takes a typist 0.75 seconds to type one word. At this rate, how many words can he type in 60 seconds?
   a. 4.5
   b. 8
   c. 45
   d. 80

8. If the average woman burns 8.2 calories per minute while riding a bicycle, how many calories will she burn if she rides for 35 minutes?
   a. 286
   b. 287
   c. 387
   d. 984

9. If Raindrop Roofing gave an estimate of $6,000 to repair the Kleins' roof, and Kendra's Contracting gave an estimate that was $\frac{3}{5}$ of the estimate by Raindrop Roofing, how much was the estimate given by Kendra's Contracting?
   a. $1,200
   b. $2,000
   c. $3,000
   d. $3,600

10. Thirty percent of the students at a middle school are involved in the vocal and instrumental music programs. If 15% of the musicians are in the choir, what percentage of the whole school is in the choir?
   a. 4.5%
   b. 9.0%
   c. 15%
   d. 30%

Use the following information to answer questions 11 and 12.

Basic cable television service, which includes 16 channels, costs $15.00 a month. The initial labor fee to install the service is $25.00. A $65.00 deposit is required, but will be refunded within two years if the customer's bills are paid in full. Other cable services may be added to the basic service: the movie channel service is $9.40 a month; the news channels are $7.50 a month; the arts channels are $5.00 a month; the sports channels are $4.80 a month.

11. A customer's cable television bill totaled $20.00 a month. Using the preceding passage, what portion of the bill was for basic cable service?
   a. 25%
   b. 33%
   c. 50%
   d. 75%

12. A customer's first bill after having cable television installed totaled $112.50. This customer chose basic cable and one additional cable service. Which additional service was chosen?
   a. the news channels
   b. the movie channels
   c. the arts channels
   d. the sports channels

13. Out of 100 shoppers polled, 80 said they buy fresh fruit every week. How many shoppers out of 30,000 could be expected to buy fresh fruit every week?

a. 2,400
b. 6,000
c. 22,000
d. 24,000

Use the following information to answer questions 14 and 15.

Songs Downloaded

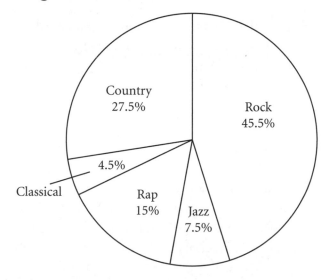

14. If a total of 400 songs were downloaded, how many of the songs were country music?

a. 11
b. 18
c. 30
d. 110

15. Based on the graph, which types of music represent exactly half of the songs downloaded?

a. rock and jazz
b. classical and rock
c. rap, classical, and country
d. jazz, classical, and rap

16. Last year, 220 people bought cars from a certain dealer. Of those, 60% reported that they were completely satisfied with their new cars. How many people reported being unsatisfied with their new car?

a. 22
b. 55
c. 88
d. 132

17. Of 1,125 university students, 135 speak fluent Spanish. What percentage of the student body speaks fluent Spanish?

a. 5%
b. 8.3%
c. 12%
d. 13.6%

18. A rectangular community garden needs fencing to keep deer from eating the vegetables. If 200 linear feet of fencing is needed to enclose the garden space, which of the following could be the length and width dimensions of the garden?

a. 100 feet long and 100 feet wide
b. 100 feet long and 2 feet wide
c. 80 feet long and 20 feet wide
d. 50 feet long and 40 feet wide

19. A piece of ribbon 3 feet 4 inches long was divided into 5 equal parts. How long was each part?

a. 1 foot 2 inches
b. 10 inches
c. 8 inches
d. 6 inches

20. A middle school cafeteria has three different options.

For $2, a student can get either a sandwich or two cookies.

For $3, a student can get a sandwich and one cookie.

For $4, a student can get either two sandwiches, or a sandwich and two cookies.

If Jimae has $6 to pay for lunch for her and her brother, which of the following is NOT a possible combination?
- **a.** three sandwiches and one cookie
- **b.** two sandwiches and two cookies
- **c.** one sandwich and four cookies
- **d.** three sandwiches and no cookies

21. A circular table is going to be covered with tile. If the diameter of the table is 10 feet, approximately how many square feet of tile must be purchased to cover the table?
- **a.** 10 square feet
- **b.** 16 square feet
- **c.** 25 square feet
- **d.** 79 square feet

22. Mr. Beard's temperature is 98° Fahrenheit. What is his temperature in degrees Celsius? $C = \frac{5}{9}(F - 32)$
- **a.** 29.3
- **b.** 36.7
- **c.** 37.6
- **d.** 31.1

23. All of the rooms on the main floor of an office building are rectangular, with 8-foot-high ceilings. Keira's office is 9 feet wide by 11 feet long. What is the combined surface area of the four walls of her office, including any windows and doors?

- **a.** 99 square feet
- **b.** 160 square feet
- **c.** 320 square feet
- **d.** 716 square feet

24. A recipe serves four people and calls for $1\frac{1}{2}$ cups of broth. If you want to serve six people, how much broth do you need?
- **a.** 1 cup
- **b.** 2 cups
- **c.** $2\frac{1}{3}$ cups
- **d.** 3 cups

25. Plattville is 80 miles west and 60 miles north of Quincy. How long is a direct route from Plattville to Quincy?
- **a.** 100 miles
- **b.** 120 miles
- **c.** 140 miles
- **d.** 160 miles

26. A builder has 27 cubic feet of concrete to pave a sidewalk whose length is 6 times its width. The concrete must be poured 6 inches deep. How long is the sidewalk?
- **a.** 9 feet
- **b.** 12 feet
- **c.** 15 feet
- **d.** 18 feet

27. Which of the following brands is the least expensive per ounce?

BRAND	W	X	Y	Z
Price	0.21	0.48	0.56	0.96
Weight in ounces	6	15	20	32

- **a.** W
- **b.** X
- **c.** Y
- **d.** Z

28. Belicia drives a compact car that gets, on average, 28 miles per gallon of gas. If she must drive 364 miles from Los Angeles to San Francisco, and gas costs on average $4.85 per gallon, approximately how much will she spend on gas?
   a. $63.00
   b. $72.75
   c. $97.00
   d. $136.00

29. A cook spends $540 on silverware. If a place setting includes one knife, one fork, and two spoons, and if knives cost twice as much as forks or spoons, how much did he spend on forks?
   a. $90
   b. $108
   c. $135
   d. $180

30. An office uses two dozen pencils and $3\frac{1}{2}$ reams of paper each week. If pencils cost five cents each and a ream of paper costs $7.50, how much does it cost to supply the office for a week?
   a. $7.55
   b. $26.25
   c. $27.45
   d. $38.25

Part 2: Word Knowledge

Time: 11 minutes

Select the choice that best matches the underlined word.

1. Specious most nearly means
   a. special.
   b. wide open.
   c. misleading.
   d. aimless.

2. The attorney wanted to expedite the process.
   a. accelerate
   b. evaluate
   c. reverse
   d. justify

3. The student gave a plausible explanation for his lateness, so it was excused by the teacher.
   a. unbelievable
   b. credible
   c. insufficient
   d. apologetic

4. Concurrent most nearly means
   a. incidental.
   b. simultaneous.
   c. apprehensive.
   d. substantial.

5. Impromptu most nearly means
   a. tactless.
   b. passive.
   c. rehearsed.
   d. spontaneous.

6. <u>Rescind</u> most nearly means
   a. withdraw.
   b. increase.
   c. oppose.
   d. divide.

7. He based his conclusion on what he <u>inferred</u> from the evidence, not on what he actually observed.
   a. intuited
   b. imagined
   c. surmised
   d. implied

8. <u>Saturate</u> most nearly means
   a. deprive.
   b. construe.
   c. soak.
   d. verify.

9. <u>Synopsis</u> most nearly means
   a. summary.
   b. abundance.
   c. stereotype.
   d. configuration.

10. <u>Hyperbole</u> most nearly means
   a. sincerity.
   b. exaggeration.
   c. understatement.
   d. indignation.

11. <u>Delineate</u> most nearly means
   a. reverse.
   b. count.
   c. battle.
   d. describe.

12. <u>Proponent</u> most nearly means
   a. advocate.
   b. delinquent.
   c. idealist.
   d. critic.

13. <u>Intrepid</u> most nearly means
   a. belligerent.
   b. consistent.
   c. timid.
   d. fearless.

14. <u>Statute</u> most nearly means
   a. replica.
   b. ordinance.
   c. collection.
   d. hypothesis.

15. Those who had a stake in the verdict were <u>aggrieved</u> by the negative outcome.
   a. enraged
   b. indifferent
   c. suspicious
   d. wary

16. Mindy's father found her lies <u>disconcerting</u>.
   a. upsetting
   b. delightful
   c. simple
   d. enlightening

17. <u>Refrain</u> most nearly means
   a. desist.
   b. secure.
   c. glimpse.
   d. persevere.

18. One of the duties of a captain is to <u>delegate</u> responsibility.
   a. analyze
   b. respect
   c. criticize
   d. assign

19. <u>Spurious</u> most nearly means
   a. prevalent.
   b. false.
   c. melancholy.
   d. actual.

20. The spokesperson must <u>articulate</u> the philosophy of an entire department.
   a. trust
   b. refine
   c. verify
   d. express

21. <u>Appease</u> most nearly means
   a. please.
   b. anger.
   c. annoy.
   d. calm.

22. The hospital was an <u>expansive</u> facility.
   a. obsolete
   b. meager
   c. spacious
   d. costly

23. <u>Urbane</u> most nearly means
   a. foolish.
   b. vulgar.
   c. sophisticated.
   d. sentimental.

24. <u>Rationale</u> most nearly means
   a. explanation.
   b. regret.
   c. denial.
   d. anticipation.

25. Although Ivan had failed another test, he seemed <u>apathetic</u> about it.
   a. upset
   b. indifferent
   c. curious
   d. enthusiastic

26. <u>Accolade</u> most nearly means
  a. disbelief.
  b. impression.
  c. praise.
  d. happiness.

27. <u>Verisimilitude</u> most nearly means
  a. deceit.
  b. fanaticism.
  c. similarity.
  d. realism.

28. <u>Umbrage</u> most nearly means
  a. protection.
  b. offense.
  c. transition.
  d. gathering.

29. She approaches her hobby with <u>alacrity</u>.
  a. eagerness
  b. sadness
  c. bitterness
  d. unconcern

30. They didn't want to get bogged down in the <u>minutiae</u> of the project.
  a. microcosm
  b. regiment
  c. details
  d. pattern

31. <u>Penury</u> most nearly means
  a. destitution.
  b. punishment.
  c. judgment.
  d. agony.

32. <u>Forbearance</u> most nearly means
  a. poverty.
  b. strength.
  c. patience.
  d. ancestry.

33. <u>Asperity</u> most nearly means
  a. harshness.
  b. pettiness.
  c. complexity.
  d. fortune.

34. <u>Decorum</u> most nearly means
  a. shy.
  b. decoration.
  c. coarse.
  d. etiquette.

35. As he read about the tragedy, he was struck with <u>consternation</u>.
  a. dismay
  b. constellation
  c. reservation
  d. disbelief

Part 3:
Paragraph Comprehension

Time: 13 minutes

Read the passages and answer the questions that follow.

Hearsay evidence, which is the secondhand reporting of a statement, is allowed in court only when the truth of the statement is irrelevant. Hearsay that depends on the statement's truthfulness is inadmissible because the witness does not appear in court and swear an oath to tell the truth. Because his or her demeanor when making the statement is not visible to the jury, the accuracy of the statement cannot be tested under cross-examination, and to introduce it would be to deprive the accused of the constitutional right to confront the accuser. Hearsay is admissible, however, when the truth of the statement is unimportant. If, for example, a defendant claims to have been unconscious at a certain time, and a witness claims that the defendant actually spoke to her at that time, this evidence would be admissible because the truth of what the defendant actually said is irrelevant.

1. The main purpose of the passage is to
   a. explain why hearsay evidence abridges the rights of the accused.
   b. question the probable truthfulness of hearsay evidence.
   c. argue that rules about the admissibility of hearsay evidence should be changed.
   d. specify which use of hearsay evidence is inadmissible and why.

2. Which of the following is NOT a reason given in the passage for the inadmissibility of hearsay evidence?
   a. Rumors are not necessarily credible.
   b. The person making the original statement was not under oath.
   c. The jury should be able to watch the gestures and facial expressions of the person making the statement.
   d. The person making the statement cannot be cross-examined.

3. How does the passage explain the proper use of hearsay evidence?
   a. by listing a set of criteria
   b. by providing a hypothetical example
   c. by referring to the Constitution
   d. by citing case law

4. The passage suggests that the criterion used for deciding that most hearsay evidence is inadmissible was most likely
   a. the unreliability of most hearsay witnesses.
   b. the importance of physical evidence to corroborate witness testimony.
   c. concern for discerning the truth in a fair manner.
   d. doubt about the relevance of hearsay testimony.

During the next ten months, all bus operators with two or more years of service will be required to have completed twenty hours of refresher training on one of the Vehicle Maneuvering Training Bus simulators.

Instructors who have used this new technology report that trainees develop skills more quickly than with traditional training methods. The new refresher training system reinforces defensive driving skills and safe driving habits. Drivers can also check their reaction times and hand-eye coordination.

5. All bus operators are required to do which of the following?
   a. receive training in defensive driving and operating a computer
   b. complete ten months of refresher driver training
   c. train new drivers on how to operate a simulator
   d. complete twenty hours of training on a simulator

6. The main purpose of the refresher training course on the simulator is to
   a. make sure that all bus operators are maintaining proper driving habits.
   b. give experienced bus operators an opportunity to learn new driving techniques.
   c. help all bus operators to develop hand-eye coordination.
   d. reduce the city's operating budget.

The city has distributed standardized recycling containers to all households with directions that read: "We would prefer that you use this new container as your primary recycling container. Additional recycling containers may be purchased from the city."

7. According to the directions, each household
   a. may only use one recycling container.
   b. must use the new recycling container.
   c. should use the new recycling container.
   d. must buy a new recycling container.

8. According to the directions, which of the following is true about the new containers?
   a. The new containers are better than other containers.
   b. Households may use only the new containers for recyclable items.
   c. The new containers hold more than the old hold.
   d. The new containers are standardized.

After a snow or ice fall, the city streets are treated with ordinary rock salt. In some areas, the salt is combined with calcium chloride, which is more effective in below-zero temperatures and which melts ice better. This combination of salt and calcium chloride is also less damaging to foliage along the roadways.

9. In deciding whether to use ordinary rock salt or the salt and calcium chloride on a particular street, which of the following is NOT a consideration?
   a. the temperature at the time of treatment
   b. the plants and trees along the street
   c. whether there is ice on the street
   d. whether the street is a main or secondary road

10. According to the snow treatment directions, which of the following is true?
   a. If the temperature is below zero, salt and calcium chloride is effective in treating snow- and ice-covered streets.
   b. Crews must wait until the snow or ice stops falling before salting streets.
   c. The city always salts major roads first.
   d. If the snowfall is light, the city will not salt the streets as this would be a waste of the salt supply.

On February 3, 1956, Autherine Lucy became the first African-American student to attend the University of Alabama, although the dean of women refused to allow Autherine to live in a university dormitory. White students rioted in protest of her admission, and the federal government had to assume command of the Alabama National Guard in order to protect her. Nonetheless, on her first day in class, Autherine bravely took a seat in the front row. She remembers being surprised that the professor of the class appeared not to notice she was even in class. Later she would appreciate his seeming indifference, as he was one of only a few professors to speak out in favor of her right to attend the university.

11. This passage is most likely from a book called
   a. *Twentieth-Century United States History.*
   b. *A Collection of Favorite Children's Stories.*
   c. *A History of the Civil War.*
   d. *How to Choose the College That Is Right for You.*

12. According to the passage, Autherine Lucy
   a. lived in a dormitory.
   b. sat in the front row of her class.
   c. became a lawyer.
   d. majored in history.

Photojournalists who cover tragic events, such as terrorist attacks, extreme poverty, and death, are susceptible to stress disorders. As a result, newsroom managers must be on the lookout for signs of such a condition among their staff. Although studies have shown that most photojournalists are resilient to stress disorders, witnessing automobile carnage and human-induced trauma are most difficult to overcome. The more exposure a photojournalist has to death and injury, the more likely he or she is to develop stress disorders.

13. What is the main idea of the passage?
   a. Newsroom managers must be on the lookout for signs of stress disorders among their staff.
   b. Witnessing a terrorist attack will most likely cause a photojournalist to experience stress disorders.
   c. The more exposure a photojournalist has to death and injury, the more likely he or she is to develop stress disorders.
   d. Photojournalists who cover tragic events could develop stress disorders because of the extreme trauma they witness.

14. According to the passage, under which of the following circumstances should a newsroom manager be most alert to a photojournalist's state of mind?

  a. after witnessing extreme poverty

  b. when the photojournalist returns from covering a traumatic story

  c. when taking part in assembling relief funds for tragic events

  d. after exposure to a tragedy caused by humans

15. According to the passage, which of the following would be the most advantageous action a newsroom manager could take to avoid stress disorders among her staff?

  a. Rotate the photojournalists who are exposed to traumatic events.

  b. Give extra time off to photojournalists who cover war.

  c. Have psychotherapists travel with photojournalists.

  d. Advise photojournalists to seek help after they cover traumatic events.

Part 4:
Mathematics Knowledge

Time: 24 minutes

1. In the figure below, angle *POS* measures 90°. What is the measure of angle *ROQ*?

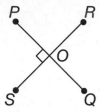

  a. 45°

  b. 90°

  c. 180°

  d. 270°

2. $4\frac{1}{5} + 1\frac{2}{5} + 3\frac{3}{10} =$

  a. $8\frac{9}{10}$

  b. $9\frac{1}{5}$

  c. $8\frac{4}{5}$

  d. $8\frac{6}{20}$

3. $\frac{4}{5}$ is equivalent to which of the following?

  a. 0.45

  b. $\frac{5}{4}$

  c. 8%

  d. 80%

4. What is the decimal equivalent of $\frac{1}{3}$, rounded to the nearest hundredth?

  a. 0.13

  b. 0.33

  c. 0.50

  d. 0.67

5. $4\frac{1}{3} + 3\frac{2}{5} - 2\frac{14}{15} =$

   a. $4\frac{4}{5}$

   b. $5\frac{1}{5}$

   c. $10\frac{2}{3}$

   d. $51\frac{1}{7}$

6. Which of the following is equal to 20,706?

   a. $200 + 70 + 6$

   b. $2,000 + 700 + 6$

   c. $20,000 + 70 + 6$

   d. $20,000 + 700 + 6$

7. What are the missing integers on this number line?

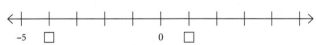

   a. −4 and 1

   b. −6 and 1

   c. −4 and −1

   d. 4 and 9

8. Which of the following is divisible by 3, 7, and 8?

   a. 21

   b. 24

   c. 56

   d. 168

9. What is another way to write $4 \times 4 \times 4$?

   a. 3×4

   b. 8×4

   c. 4^3

   d. 3^4

10. Which of these is equivalent to 35°C? ($F = \frac{9}{5}C + 32$)

   a. 105°F

   b. 95°F

   c. 63°F

   d. 31°F

11. What is the volume of a pyramid that has a rectangular base 5 feet by 3 feet and a height of 8 feet? ($V = \frac{1}{3}lwh$)

   a. 16 feet

   b. 60 feet

   c. 40 feet

   d. 120 feet

12. How many inches are there in $3\frac{1}{3}$ yards?

   a. 108

   b. 120

   c. 160

   d. 144

13. $\frac{13}{4} =$

   a. 3.40

   b. 4.25

   c. 3.75

   d. 3.25

14. 125% is equivalent to
  a. 0.125.
  b. 1.25.
  c. 12.5.
  d. 125.

15. Triangle *ABC* is an isosceles triangle, with a base length of 14 inches. If its perimeter is 3 feet, what is the length of each of the legs of triangle *ABC*?
  a. 36 inches
  b. 18 inches
  c. 22 inches
  d. 11 inches

16. Which value of *x* will make the following number sentence true?
$$x + 25 = 13$$
  a. −13
  b. −11
  c. −12
  d. 38

17. How many faces does a cube have?
  a. 4
  b. 6
  c. 2
  d. 12

18. What is the length of a rectangle if its width is 9 feet and its area is 117 square feet?
  a. 1.3 feet
  b. 6.5 feet
  c. 26 feet
  d. 13 feet

19. A square is a special case of all of the following geometric figures EXCEPT a
  a. parallelogram.
  b. rectangle.
  c. rhombus.
  d. trapezoid.

20. What is the value of *x* in the figure below?

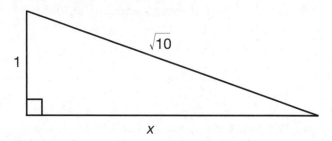

  a. 2
  b. 3
  c. $\sqrt{11}$
  d. 9

21. $5\frac{2}{3}$ is closest to
  a. 5.23.
  b. 5.33.
  c. 0.523.
  d. 5.67.

22. If the following figure is a regular decagon with a center at *Q*, what is the measure of the indicated angle?

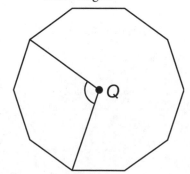

a. 36°
b. 45°
c. 90°
d. 108°

23. Negative 2.07 is equal to
  a. $-2\frac{7}{10}$.
  b. $-2\frac{7}{100}$.
  c. $-2\frac{7}{1,000}$.
  d. -2.7.

24. 62.5% is equal to
  a. $\frac{1}{16}$.
  b. $\frac{5}{8}$.
  c. $6\frac{1}{4}$.
  d. $6\frac{2}{5}$.

25. A line intersects two parallel lines in the following figure. If $\angle P$ measures 40°, what is the measure of $\angle Q$?

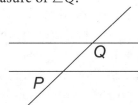

a. 40°
b. 50°
c. 80°
d. 140°

Answers

Part 1: Arithmetic Reasoning

1. This is a decimal problem.
  b. Since Ellen has $36.00, divide the price per lily by $36.00 in order to see how many lilies she can purchase. $\frac{\$36.00}{\$1.80} = 20$, so Ellen can buy 20 lilies at the market. Choice **a** is incorrect because you divided by $2—don't round up the divisor before dividing. Choice **c** is incorrect because it would have required each to cost $1.50. Choice **d** is incorrect because it would have required each to cost $1.00.

2. This is a geometry problem.
  c. The volume of the aquarium can be found by using the formula $V = l \times w \times h$. Since the length is 12 inches, the width is 5 inches, and the height is 10 inches, multiply $V = 12 \times 5 \times 10$ to get a volume of 600 cubic inches. Choice **a** is incorrect because you computed surface area, not volume. Choice **b** is incorrect because you computed perimeter of the base and multiplied *that* by the height. Choice **d** is incorrect because you used 12 inches for both the length and height.

3. This is a decimal problem.
  c. The value of the handbag ($150) must be included in the total. Choice **a** is incorrect because you didn't count the value of the handbag in the total. Choice **b** is incorrect because you didn't carry the one to the tenths place when adding the dollar values. Choice **d** is incorrect because it is $100 too much.

4. This is a decimal problem.

　d. Both choices **a** and **b** can be ruled out because there is no way to determine how many tickets are for adults or for children. Choice **c** can be ruled out because the price of group tickets is not given.

5. This is a decimal problem.

　d. Since the 15-year-old is older than 12, her admission cost will be the same as the adult ticket price. The tickets for the 12- and 11-year-old children will be at the reduced rate. Therefore, the Saturday evening movie would cost $7.50 × (2 tickets) + $5.00 × (2 tickets) = $25.00. The Saturday matinee movie would cost $5.50 × (2 tickets) + $3.00 × (2 tickets) = $17.00. Since $25.00 − $17.00 = $8.00, the Reaves would save $8.00 by going to the 3:30 p.m. matinee. Choice **a** is incorrect because this is the cost of the Saturday evening movie. Choice **b** is incorrect because this is a wrong estimate of the cost of the Saturday evening movie, obtained by using one too few adult tickets. Choice **c** is incorrect because this is the cost of the Saturday matinee movie.

6. This is a decimal problem.

　a. The adult price on Saturday afternoon is $5.50; the child's price is $3.00. Choice **b** is incorrect because you mistakenly used the costs for *non-matinee* show times. Choice **c** is incorrect because you mistakenly used the costs for *non-matinee* show times and then proceeded to subtract in the wrong order. Choice **d** is incorrect because this is the average cost of two such tickets, not the difference in the price.

7. This is a decimal problem.

　d. This problem is solved by dividing 60 by 0.75. Choice **a** is incorrect because you multiplied 60 by 0.075. Choice **b** is incorrect because you used 6 instead of 60. Choice **c** is incorrect because you multiplied 60 by 0.75 when you should have divided by 0.75.

8. This is an averages problem.

　b. This is a simple multiplication problem that is solved by multiplying 35 times 8.2. Choice **a** is incorrect because you didn't carry the one in the first step of the multiplication. Choice **c** is incorrect because this is too large; you didn't handle the hundreds place correctly when multiplying. Choice **d** is incorrect because this is nearly the number of calories burned in *2 hours*, not 35 minutes.

9. This is a fractions problem.

　d. Raindrop Roofing gave an estimate of $6,000 and Kendra's Contracting had an estimate that was $\frac{3}{5}$ of that, so $6,000 is multiplied by $\frac{3}{5}$: $\frac{\$6,000}{1} \times \frac{3}{5} = \frac{\$18,000}{5} = \$3,600$. Choice **a** is incorrect because this is $\frac{1}{5}$, not $\frac{3}{5}$, of $6,000. Choice **b** is incorrect because this is $\frac{1}{3}$, not $\frac{3}{5}$, of $6,000. Choice **c** is incorrect because this is $\frac{1}{2}$, not $\frac{3}{5}$, of $6,000.

10. This is a percents problem.

　a. In this question, you need to find 15% of the 30% of students that are in the music program. To find 15% of 30%, change the percents to decimal form and multiply. Since 30% = 0.30 and 15% = 0.15, multiply (0.30)(0.15) = 0.045. As a decimal, this is equivalent to 4.5%, which is **a**. Choice **b** is incorrect because you multiplied (0.30)(0.30), not (0.30)(0.15). Choice **c** is incorrect because you didn't account for the fact that this percent was taken of only a portion (namely 30%) of the entire student body. Choice **d** is incorrect because you didn't account for the fact that only 15% of this portion of the student body was in the choir.

11. This is a percents problem.

    d. The basic cable service fee of $15.00 is 75% of $20.00. Choice **a** is incorrect because this would imply that the monthly bill was ($15.00)(4) = $60.00. Choice **b** is incorrect because this would imply that the monthly bill was ($15.00)(3) = $45.00. Choice **c** is incorrect because this would imply that the monthly bill was ($15.00)(2) = $30.00.

12. This is a decimal problem.

    a. The labor fee ($25.00) plus the deposit ($65.00) plus the basic service ($15.00) equals $105.00. The difference between the total bill, $112.50, and $105.00 is $7.50, the cost of the news channels. Choice **b** is incorrect because you mistakenly computed the difference as $9.40. Choice **c** is incorrect because you mistakenly computed the difference as $5.00. Choice **d** is incorrect because you mistakenly computed the difference as $4.80.

13. This is a percents problem.

    d. Eighty out of 100 is 80%. Eighty percent of 30,000 is 24,000. Choice **a** is incorrect because you mistakenly used 8 instead of 80 when setting up the problem. Choice **b** is incorrect because this is the number you would expect to NOT buy fresh fruit each week. Choice **c** is incorrect because you multiplied incorrectly; (30,000)(0.80) = 24,000.

14. This is a percents problem.

    d. 27.5% of 400 is 110. Choice **a** is incorrect because you mistakenly used 0.0275 instead of 0.275 for 27.5%. Choice **b** is incorrect because this is the number of classical CDs sold. Choice **c** is incorrect because this is the number of jazz CDs sold.

15. This is a percents problem.

    b. Rock is 45.5%; when we add 4.5% for classical, the total is 50%. Choice **a** is incorrect because this sums to 53%, not 50%. Choice **c** is incorrect because this sums to 47%, not 50%. Choice **d** is incorrect because this sums to 27%, not 50%.

16. This is a percents problem.

    c. If 60% of the people were satisfied with their new car, 40% were unsatisfied; 40% of 220 is 88. Choice **a** is incorrect because this is 10% of the number who bought cars, not 40%. Choice **b** is incorrect because this is 25% of the number who bought cars, not 40%. Choice **d** is incorrect because this is the number of people who report being *satisfied* with their new car.

17. This is a percents problem.

    c. Divide 135 Spanish-speaking students by 1,125 total students to arrive at 0.12 or 12%. Choice **a** is incorrect because this would require the size of the student body to be 2,700, not 1,125. Choice **b** is incorrect because you divided in the wrong order. Choice **d** is incorrect because you divided the number of students fluent in Spanish by the number *not* fluent in Spanish; you should be dividing by the number of students in the entire student body.

18. This is a geometry problem.

    c. Since the garden needs 200 feet of linear fencing to enclose it, the distance around the garden (the perimeter) is 200 feet. The formula for calculating the perimeter of a rectangle is (2 × length) + (2 × width). (2 × 80) + (2 × 20) = 200, so the dimensions of the garden could be 80 feet long and 20 feet wide. Choice **a** is incorrect because you didn't count the length and width each twice in the perimeter calculation. Choice **b** is incorrect because you computed area, not perimeter. Choice **d** is incorrect because the perimeter would be 180 feet, not 200 feet.

19. This is a fractions problem.

c. Three feet 4 inches equals 40 inches; 40 divided by 5 is 8. Choice **a** is incorrect because this would require there to be (14 in.)(5) = 70 in. of ribbon to begin with. Choice **b** is incorrect because you divided into 4 equal parts, not 5. Choice **d** is incorrect because you converted "3 feet 4 inches" to inches incorrectly—you should have gotten 40, not 30.

20. This is an algebra problem.

a. It will cost $3 for a sandwich and a cookie. To get two additional sandwiches, it would cost another $4. Therefore, it would cost $7 to get three sandwiches and a cookie. Since she has only $6 to spend, this combination is not possible. Choice **b** is incorrect because this *is* possible and would cost $6. Choice **c** is incorrect because this *is* possible and would cost $6. Choice **d** is incorrect because this *is* possible and would cost $6.

21. This is a geometry problem.

d. In order to know how many square feet of tile are needed to cover the table, the area of the table must be calculated. The area of a circle is calculated with the formula $A = \pi r^2$. The diameter of the table is 10 feet and therefore the radius is 5 feet (half the diameter). The area of the tabletop will be $\pi \times 5^2 = 3.14 \times 25 = 78.5$ feet. The closest approximation of 78.5 is 79 square feet. Choice **a** is incorrect because you didn't compute the area correctly. Remember, r is the radius in the formula $A = \pi r^2$. Choice **b** is incorrect because you didn't square the radius. Choice **c** is incorrect because you forgot to multiply by π.

22. This is a fractions problem.

b. Use the formula beginning with the operation in parentheses: 98 − 32 = 66. Then multiply 66 by $\frac{5}{9}$, first multiplying 66 by 5 to get 330; 330 divided by 9 is 36.66667, which is rounded up to 36.7. Choice **a** is incorrect because you used $\frac{4}{9}$ instead of $\frac{5}{9}$ in the formula. Choice **c** is incorrect because you mixed up the tenths and ones digits—they should be switched. Choice **d** is incorrect because you mistakenly computed the difference 98 − 32 as 56, not 66.

23. This is a geometry problem.

c. Each 9-foot-wide wall has an area of 9 × 8 or 72 square feet. There are two such walls, so those two walls combined have an area of 72 × 2 or 144 square feet. Each 11-foot-wide wall has an area of 11 × 8 or 88 square feet, and again there are two such walls: 88 × 2 = 176. To find the total surface area, add 144 and 176 to get 320 square feet. Choice **a** is incorrect because this is the area of the floor. Choice **b** is incorrect because this is half of the surface area; you need to account for all four walls. Choice **d** is incorrect because you added the area of four *floors* to the area of four walls.

24. This is a fractions problem.

a. $1\frac{1}{2}$ cups equals $\frac{3}{2}$ cups. The ratio is 6 people to 4 people, which is equal to the ratio of x to $\frac{3}{2}$. By cross multiplying, we get $6(\frac{3}{2})$ equals $4x$, or 9 equals $4x$. Dividing both sides by 4, we get $\frac{9}{4}$, or $2\frac{1}{4}$ cups. Choice **b** is incorrect because you divided incorrectly. Choice **c** is incorrect because you set up the wrong proportion. Choice **d** is incorrect because this would imply the original recipe served 3 people, not 4.

25. This is a geometry problem.

a. The distance between Plattville and Quincy is the hypotenuse of a right triangle with side lengths of 80 and 60. The length of the hypotenuse equals the square root of $(80^2 + 60^2)$, which equals the square root of $(6,400 + 3,600)$, which equals the square root of 10,000, which equals 100 miles. Choice **b** is incorrect because you made an arithmetic error when using the Pythagorean theorem. Choice **c** is incorrect because this is not a *direct* route; it is the sum of two separate routes. Choice **d** is incorrect because this route is longer than the given non-direct route, which cannot happen.

26. This is a geometry problem.

    d. The volume of concrete is 27 cubic feet. Volume is length times width times depth, or $(l)(w)(d)$, so $(l)(w)(d) = 27$. We're told that the length l is 6 times the width w, so l equals $6w$. We're also told that the depth is 6 inches, or 0.5 feet. Substituting what we know about the length and depth into the original equation and solving for w, we get $(l)(w)(d) = (6w)(w)(0.5) = 27$. $3w^2 = 27$; $w^2 = 9$, so $w = 3$. To get the length, we remember that l equals $6w$, so l equals $(6)(3)$, or 18 feet. Choice **a** is incorrect because you interpreted the length as $6 + w$, not $6w$. Choice **b** is incorrect because the length is 6 times the width, not 4 times the width. Choice **c** is incorrect because the length is 6 times the width, not 5 times the width.

27. This is a fractions problem.

    c. Find the price per ounce of each brand, as follows: Brand W is $\frac{21}{6}$ or 3.5 cents per ounce; Brand X is $\frac{48}{15}$ or 3.2 cents per ounce; Brand Y is $\frac{56}{20}$ or 2.8 cents per ounce; Brand Z is $\frac{96}{32}$ or 3.0 cents per ounce. It is then easy to see that choice **c**, Brand Y, at 2.8 cents per ounce, is the least expensive. Choices **a**, **b**, and **d** are incorrect, as illustrated in the preceding list of prices per ounce.

28. This is a decimals problem.

    a. The first calculation needed to be made is to figure out how many gallons of gas Belicia's car will consume in the 364-mile trip. The car gets 28 miles per gallon of gas, so divide 364 by 28 to calculate this: $\frac{364 \text{ miles}}{28 \text{ miles per gallon}} = 13$ gallons of gas needed. Since gas costs $4.85 per gallon, calculate the total cost by multiplying 13 gallons of gas by $4.85. $13 \times \$4.85 = \$63.05$. Choice **b** is

incorrect because you divided 364 miles by 28 miles per gallon incorrectly to get 15. Choice **c** is incorrect because you divided 364 miles by 28 miles per gallon incorrectly to get 20. Choice **d** is incorrect because you multiplied $4.85 by 28 gallons.

29. This is an algebra problem.

    b. $K + F + S = \$540$. Also, $K = 2F$ and $S = 2F$, which changes the original equation to $2F + F + 2F = 540$, so $5F = 540$ and $F = \$108$. Choice **a** is incorrect because you incorrectly expressed the total cost as 6 times the number of forks, not 5 times the number of forks. Choice **c** is incorrect because you incorrectly expressed the total cost as 4 times the number of forks, not 5 times the number of forks. Choice **d** is incorrect because you assumed that the forks, spoons, and knives all cost the same amount, and that there were the same number of each of them.

30. This is a decimal problem.

    c. First find the total price of the pencils: (24 pencils)($0.05) = $1.20. Then find the total price of the paper: (3.5 reams)($7.50) = $26.25. Next, add the two totals together: $1.20 + $26.25 = $27.45. Choice **a** is incorrect because this is the cost of 1 ream of paper and 1 pencil. Choice **b** is incorrect because this is just the cost of the paper. Choice **d** is incorrect because this is the cost for 5 reams of paper and 15 pencils.

Part 2: Word Knowledge

1. c. If something is *specious*, it is deliberately deceitful or *misleading*. Choice **a**, *special*, may look like *specious*, but that does not mean the words have the same meaning. *Special* means unusual in a positive way. Choice **b**, *wide open*, does not have the same meaning as *specious* either. Choice **d**, *aimless*, means wandering or lacking direction.

2. a. To *expedite* a process is to hurry it up or *accelerate* it. Choice **b**, *evaluate*, means to assess. Choice **c**, *reverse*, means to go back, which is indicated by its prefix *re-*, meaning again. Choice **d**, *justify*, means to support.

3. b. If something is *plausible*, it is believable or *credible*, which explains why the teacher would have excused the lateness. Choice **a**, *unbelievable*, has the opposite meaning of *credible*, and an unbelievable excuse wouldn't likely be accepted by a teacher. Nor would an *insufficient*, or inadequate, excuse, which is why choice **c** is incorrect. Choice **d**, *apologetic*, means sorry, and it is less likely that a teacher would sooner accept an apologetic excuse than a plausible one.

4. b. *Concurrent* means happening at the same time, which is also the definition of *simultaneous*. Choice **a**, *incidental*, means minor. Choice **c**, *apprehensive*, means reluctant. Choice **d**, *substantial*, means large.

5. d. *Impromptu* means without preparation, which is also the definition of *spontaneous*. *Impromptu* contains the prefix *im-*, meaning without, and since the word *rehearsed*, or practiced, does not indicate a lack of anything, choice **c** can be eliminated. Choice **a**, *tactless*, means lacking care. Choice **b**, *passive*, means inactive.

6. a. To *rescind* is to cancel or *withdraw* an offer, which can be inferred from its prefix *re-*, meaning again or back. Choices **b**, *increase* (to make larger), **c**, *oppose* (to be against), and **d**, *divide* (to split) do not indicate a movement back.

7. c. To *infer* something is to *surmise* it or deduce it from the evidence. Although choice **a**, *intuited*, shares a prefix with *inferred*, it means to conclude based on a feeling rather than concrete evidence. Choice **b**, *imagined*, means to picture something in one's mind, not to make a conclusion based on evidence. Choice **d**, *implied*, means suggested, and it does not make sense within the context of this sentence.

8. c. To *saturate* is to fill or load to capacity, which is also the meaning of *soak*. Choice **a**, *deprive*, means to take away, which can be inferred from its prefix *de-*, which means to remove. Choice **b**, *construe*, means interpret. Choice **d**, *verify*, means to check facts, which can be inferred from its root word *ver-*, indicating truth.

9. a. A *synopsis* is an abbreviated version, as is a *summary*. Choice **b**, *abundance*, means a great deal. Choice **c**, *stereotype*, means a clichéd or prejudiced concept. Choice **d**, *configuration*, means arrangement.

10. b. A *hyperbole* is an extravagant statement, as is an *exaggeration*. Choice **a**, *sincerity*, means honesty. Choice **c**, *understatement*, means the opposite of *hyperbole*, which can be inferred from its prefix, *under-*, meaning less. Choice **d**, *indignation*, means annoyance.

11. d. To *delineate* is to explain something in detail or *describe* it. Choice **a**, *reverse*, means to go back, which can be inferred from its prefix *re-*, meaning again or back. Choice **b**, *count*, means to sum. Choice **c**, *battle*, means to fight.

12. a. Like an *advocate*, a *proponent* is a supporter of something, which is indicated by its prefix *pro-*, meaning favoring. Choice **b**, *delinquent*, means offending. Choice **c**, *idealist*, means optimistic. Choice **d**, *critic*, means someone who is the opposite of a *proponent*.

13. d. An *intrepid* person approaches a challenge without fear. Choice **a**, *belligerent*, means warlike. Choice **b**, *consistent*, means constant. Choice **c**, *timid*, is the opposite of *intrepid*.

14. b. A *statute* is a law, as is an *ordinance*. Choice **a**, *replica*, means copy, which can be inferred from its prefix, *re-*, meaning again. Choice **c**, *collection*, means a set of related objects. Choice **d**, *hypothesis*, means a theory.

15. a. One could be *aggrieved*, or *enraged*, *by* a verdict, whereas one could be *suspicious* or *wary* (choices **c** and **d**), *of* it. Someone who has a stake in a verdict would be interested in it, so choice **b**, meaning uninterested, can be ruled out.

16. a. If something is *disconcerting*, it is disturbing or *upsetting*. Choice **b**, *delightful*, means pleasant, which would not describe lies being told by one's daughter. Choice **c**, *simple*, means plain. Choice **d**, *enlightening*, means informative, and a lie is the opposite of informative.

17. a. To *refrain* is to hold back, or *desist*, from doing something. Choice **b**, *secure*, means safe. Choice **c**, *glimpse*, means see briefly. Choice **d**, *persevere*, means continue.

18. d. To *delegate* a task is to *assign* it or to appoint another to do it. A captain would not likely be responsible for *analyzing* or examining responsibility, so choice **a** is incorrect. One might *respect* responsibility (choice **b**), but this would not likely be a captain's duty, nor would *criticizing* a responsibility (choice **c**).

19. b. Something that is *spurious* is not genuine, or *false*. Choice **a**, *prevalent*, means common. Choice **c**, *melancholy*, means sad. Choice **d**, *actual*, means real, which is the opposite of *spurious*.

20. d. To *articulate* something is to *express* it with words, which is the main job of a spokesperson. A spokesperson would not be responsible for *trusting* (choice **a**), *refining* or changing (choice **b**), or *verifying* or checking the facts of (choice **c**) a department's philosophy.

21. d. To *appease* is to soothe or *calm* someone down. Choice **a**, *please*, may look similar to *appease*, but the two words do not share the same meaning. Choices **b**, *anger*, and **c**, *annoy*, mean the opposite of *appease*.

22. c. The prefix *ex-* means out, so one can conclude that *expansive* means *spacious* or spread out. Choices **a**, *obsolete* (meaning out-of-date), **b**, *meager* (meaning weak), and **d**, *costly* (meaning expensive) all fit the sentence's context, but none of them indicate something that is spread out or *expansive*.

23. c. To be *urbane* is to show refined manners or be *sophisticated*. Choices **a**, *foolish*, and **b**, *vulgar* (meaning crass), have opposite meanings of *urbane*. Choice **d**, *sentimental*, means romantic or nostalgic.

24. a. A *rationale* is a reason or *explanation* for doing something. Choice **b**, *regret*, means to be sorry. Choice **c**, *denial*, means refusal. Choice **d**, *anticipation*, means expectation.

25. b. The word *although* indicates that Ivan did not have the expected reaction to his failed test. One would expect a student to be upset about a failed test, but Ivan was *apathetic* or *indifferent* about it. Therefore, choice **a**, *upset*, is incorrect. Choice **c**, *curious*, means interested, which does not make sense in the context of this sentence. Although Ivan was not upset about the failed test, it is not likely he would be *enthusiastic*, or excited, about it, so choice **d** is incorrect.

26. c. An *accolade* is a great compliment, or *praise*. Choice **a**, *disbelief*, means a lack of belief, which can be concluded from its prefix *dis-*, meaning not. Choice **b**, *impression*, means idea or image. Choice **d**, *happiness*, means the state of being happy.

27. d. *Verisimilitude* is the appearance of being true, or *realism*, which can be concluded from its root word *veri-*, meaning true. Choice **a**, *deceit*, means lie, which is the opposite of *verisimilitude*. Choice **b**, *fanaticism*, means extreme passion. Choice **c**, *similarity*, means sameness.

28. b. To take *umbrage* is to feel resentment about something or take *offense* to it. Choice **a**, *protection*, means defense. Choice **c**, *transition*, means a change, which can be inferred from its prefix, *trans-*, meaning across. Choice **d**, *gathering*, means assembling.

29. a. *Alacrity* is enthusiasm and *eagerness*, which is how someone might approach a hobby she or he enjoys doing. One probably would not bother with a hobby if it stirred feelings of *sadness* (choice **b**), *bitterness* (choice **c**), or *unconcern* (choice **d**).

30. c. *Minutiae* are the finer points or *details* that might prevent someone from progressing with a project efficiently. Choice **a** may seem similar to *minutiae* because both the prefix *micro-* and the root word *minut-* mean *small*, but the root word *-cosm* means world, so *microcosm* means small world. Choice **b**, *regiment*, means division. Choice **d**, *pattern*, means model.

31. a. *Penury* is pennilessness, or *destitution*. Choice **b**, *punishment*, may look similar to *penury*, but the two words do not share the same meaning. Choice **c**, *judgment*, means an analysis or verdict. Choice **d**, *agony*, means extreme pain.

32. c. *Forbearance* means *patience*, willingness to wait, or tolerance. Choice **a**, *poverty*, means poor. Choice **b**, *strength*, means power. Choice **d**, *ancestry*, means history.

33. a. *Asperity* is rigor, severity, or *harshness*. Choice **b**, *pettiness*, means small-mindedness. Choice **c**, *complexity*, means difficulty. Choice **d**, *fortune*, means wealth.

34. d. *Decorum* is having good manners, respect, or *etiquette*. Choice **b**, *decoration* (meaning adornment), may look similar to *decorum*, but the two words do not share the same meaning. Choice **a**, *shy*, means timid. Choice **c**, *coarse*, means harsh or rough.

35. a. *Consternation* is concern or *dismay*, which is an emotion one might feel after reading about a tragedy. Choice **b**, *constellation*, may look similar to *consternation*, but it means a pattern of stars. Choice **c**, *reservation*, means hesitation, which is not as expected an emotion to feel after reading about a tragedy as *dismay* is. One might experience *disbelief* after reading about a tragedy, but *disbelief* and *consternation* do not share the same meaning, so choice **d** is incorrect.

Part 3: Paragraph Comprehension

1. d. This is a main idea question. Although the last sentence expands on the main point, the rest of the passage explains why hearsay evidence is only admissible when it doesn't matter whether the statement is true. Choice **a** deals with only one idea mentioned in the passage. Choice **b** is incorrect because the passage never questions the truthfulness of hearsay evidence. Choice **c** is incorrect because the passage only presents facts and does not express a personal argument.

2. a. This is a facts and details question, and choice **a** is correct because the idea that *rumors are not necessarily credible* does not appear in the passage. Choice **b** appears in the second sentence of the passage, *Hearsay that depends on the statement's truthfulness is inadmissible because the witness does not appear in court and swear an oath to tell the truth.* Choices **c** and **d** appear in the third sentence: *Because his or her demeanor when making the statement is not visible to the jury, the accuracy of the statement cannot be tested under cross-examination.*

3. b. This is a facts and details question, and the answer appears in the final sentence of the passage: *If, for example, a defendant claims to have been unconscious at a certain time, and a witness claims that the defendant actually spoke to her at that time, this evidence would be admissible because the truth of what the defendant actually said is irrelevant.* The words *for example* indicate a hypothetical example is to follow. Choice **a** is incorrect because the passage does not contain any lists. Choice **c** is incorrect because there is no mention of the Constitution in the passage. Choice **d** is incorrect because the passage does not cite case law.

4. c. This is an inference question, which is indicated by indefinite words such as *suggests* and *most likely*. The passage mentions the truthfulness of testimony several times. The statement that introducing hearsay would *deprive the accused of the constitutional right to confront the accuser* implies that to do so would be unfair to the accused. The passage does not question the reliability of most hearsay witnesses (choice **a**), nor does it question the relevance of hearsay testimony (choice **d**). Choice **b** is incorrect because the importance of physical evidence is not discussed in this passage.

5. d. This is a facts and details question, and the answer appears in the opening sentence: *During the next ten months, all bus operators with two or more years of service will be required to have completed twenty hours of refresher training on one of the Vehicle Maneuvering Training Bus simulators.* There is no mention of operating a computer in the passage, so choice **a** is incorrect. The first sentence of the passage mentions that bus operators will have to complete the refresher

training course *During the next ten months,* but it does not say that the course lasts ten months, so choice **b** is incorrect. The sentence also explains that *all bus operators with two or more years of service* must complete the training course, not new operators, so choice **c** is incorrect.

6. a. This is a facts and details question, and the answer appears in the second sentence in the second paragraph: *The new refresher training system reinforces defensive driving skills and safe driving habits.* Choice **c** is mentioned in the final sentence of the passage, but it is not presented as the main purpose of the refresher training course. Although choices **b** and **d** are possible benefits of the program, these are not mentioned in the passage.

7. c. This is an inference question; the directions indicate that the city *prefers,* but does not require, use of the new container, so choice **b** is incorrect. In addition, it appears the city charges residents only for additional containers, which eliminates choice **d**. Choice **a** is incorrect because the passage does not indicate anything about the number of recycling containers households are allowed to use.

8. d. This is a facts and details question, which is expressed in the opening sentence: *The city has distributed standardized recycling containers to all households. . . .* The passage never indicates the quality (choice **a**) or size (choice **c**) of the new containers. That the city prefers households use the new containers, but does not require that they do, contradicts choice **b**.

9. d. This is a facts and details question; the directions mention nothing about main or secondary roads. Choice **a** is mentioned in the second sentence, which discusses the effectiveness of the salt and calcium chloride combination in *below-zero temperatures*. Choice **b** is mentioned in the final sentence, which mentions that the salt and calcium chloride combination is *less damaging to foliage along the roadways*. The passage states that the salt and calcium chloride is used to melt ice, so choice **c** is incorrect.

10. a. This is a facts and details question, and the answer appears in the second sentence of the passage: *In some areas, the salt is combined with calcium chloride, which is more effective in below-zero temperatures and which melts ice better.* Choices **b**, **c**, and **d** are not mentioned in the passage at all.

11. a. This is an inference question since the passage never states the name of the book that contains it. The passage discusses an important event in twentieth-century U.S. history, so choice **a** is the most likely answer. The passage states that the events it describes happened in 1956; this rules out choice **c**. The purpose of the passage is to explain a historical event, not tell a children's story (choice **b**) or explain the best way to choose a college (choice **d**).

12. b. This is a facts and details question, and the answer appears in the third sentence: *Nonetheless, on her first day in class, Autherine bravely took a seat in the front row.* Choice **a** is contradicted in the first sentence, which states that *the dean of women refused to allow Autherine to live in a university dormitory*. The passage does not discuss Lucy's later profession (choice **c**) or major (choice **d**).

13. d. This is a main idea question, which is expressed in the topic sentence: *Photojournalists who cover tragic events, such as terrorist attacks, extreme poverty, and death, are suscep-*

tible to stress disorders. Choices **a** and **c** are details in the passage, not the main idea of the passage. Choice **b** is incorrect because the passage states that witnessing a terrorist attack *might* cause stress disorders, not that it will *most likely* cause stress disorders.

14. d. This is an inference question, and the answer is suggested in the opening sentence, which mentions several tragedies caused by humans: *terrorist attacks, extreme poverty, and death.* Choice **a** is incorrect because extreme poverty is only one of the circumstances mentioned in the passage. Choice **b** is incorrect because the passage does not indicate precisely *when* stress disorders are first noticeable. Collecting relief funds is not an issue discussed in the passage, so choice **c** is incorrect.

15. a. This is an inference question. The more trauma photojournalists witness, the more likely they are to develop stress disorders, so it would be most advantageous for newsroom managers to rotate the photojournalists who are exposed to traumatic events, ensuring that no one photojournalist is exposed more than others. Although overexposure to war would possibly cause a stress disorder, war is not mentioned in the passage, so choice **b** is incorrect. There is no evidence in the passage to support choices **c** and **d**.

Part 4: Mathematics Knowledge

1. This is a geometry problem.

b. $\overline{PQ}$ and $\overline{RS}$ are intersecting lines. The fact that $\angle POS$ is a 90-degree angle means that $\overline{PQ}$ and $\overline{RS}$ are perpendicular, indicating that all the angles formed by their intersection, including $\angle ROQ$, measure 90°. Choice **a** is incorrect because this is half of the correct measure. Choice **c** is incorrect because this is double the correct measure. Choice **d** is incorrect because this is 360° minus the measure of $\angle ROQ$.

2. This is a fractions problem.

   a. Incorrect answers include adding both the numerator and the denominator and not converting fifths to tenths properly. Choice **b** is incorrect because you also multiplied the numerator of $\frac{3}{10}$ by 2 when converting all fractions to tenths, but this fraction is already in terms of tenths. Choice **c** is incorrect because you did not convert fifths to tenths properly. Choice **d** is incorrect because you added the fractions incorrectly; you need to get a common denominator.

3. This is a percents problem.

   d. To convert a fraction to a percent, change the denominator to 100 with multiplication. (Multiply the denominator and the numerator by the same number, so that you do not change the value of the original fraction.) For example, $\frac{4}{5} \times \frac{20}{20} = \frac{80}{100}$, which is equivalent to 80%. Another way to consider this problem is to change it to a decimal first by dividing the numerator, 4, by the denominator, 5: $4.00 \div 5 = 0.80 = 80\%$. Choice **a** is incorrect because $0.45 = \frac{45}{100}$, which does not simplify to $\frac{4}{5}$. Choice **b** is incorrect because this is the reciprocal of $\frac{4}{5}$, and is not equal to it. Choice **c** is incorrect because $8\% = 0.08 = \frac{8}{100}$, which does not simplify to $\frac{4}{5}$.

4. This is a decimals problem.

   b. Divide the numerator by the denominator: $1.000 \div 3 = 0.33\overline{3}$. Round the answer to the hundredths place (two decimal places) to get the answer 0.33. Choice **a** is incorrect because this equals $\frac{13}{100}$, which is not equal to $\frac{1}{3}$. Choice **c** is incorrect because this equals $\frac{1}{2}$, not $\frac{1}{3}$. Choice **d** is incorrect because this is approximately equal to $\frac{2}{3}$, not $\frac{1}{3}$.

5. This is a fractions problem.

   a. First, consider the addition: $4\frac{1}{3} + 3\frac{2}{5}$. In order to add or subtract fractions, they must have common denominators. Since both of the denominators (3 and 5), are factors of 15, use 15 as your common denominator.
   $\frac{1}{3} \times \frac{5}{5} = \frac{5}{15}$, so $4\frac{1}{3} = 4\frac{5}{15}$
   $\frac{2}{5} \times \frac{3}{3} = \frac{6}{15}$, so $3\frac{2}{5} = 3\frac{6}{15}$
   Then, add the mixed numbers with common denominators:
   $4\frac{5}{15} + 3\frac{6}{15} = 7\frac{11}{15}$
   Then, $7\frac{11}{15} - 2\frac{14}{15}$ must be calculated. Since the numerator of the first fraction, 11, is smaller than the numerator of the second fraction, 14, borrow one whole number from the 7 in $7\frac{11}{15}$, changing it to 6, and add $\frac{15}{15}$ to $\frac{11}{15}$ to get $\frac{26}{15}$. Therefore, $7\frac{11}{15} = 6\frac{26}{15}$. Lastly, $6\frac{26}{15} - 2\frac{14}{15} = 4\frac{12}{15} = 4\frac{4}{5}$. Choice **b** is incorrect because you did not subtract the fractional parts correctly; it should be $\frac{11}{15} - \frac{14}{15}$, not $\frac{14}{15} - \frac{11}{15}$. Choice **c** is incorrect because you added all three fractions. Choice **d** is incorrect because this is too large since you are subtracting a quantity from a sum that is approximately 8.

6. This is a decimals problem.

   d. Choice **a** is incorrect because it reads 276. Choice **b** is incorrect because it reads 2,706. Choice **c** is incorrect because it reads 20,076.

7. This is a decimals problem.

   a. The first box is one greater than −5; the second is one greater than 0. Choice **b** is incorrect because the first box is to the right of −5 by one unit, so it should be −4. Choice **c** is incorrect because the second box is to the right of 0 by one unit, so it should be 1. Choice **d** is incorrect because you are not using the position of 0 on the number line as a reference point.

8. This is an algebra problem.

  d. 168 is the only number that can be divided by 3, 7, and 8. $168 \div 3 = 56$, $168 \div 7 = 24$, $168 \div 8 = 21$. Choice **a** is incorrect because 8 does not divide evenly into this number. Choice **b** is incorrect because 7 does not divide evenly into this number. Choice **c** is incorrect because 3 does not divide evenly into this number.

9. This is an algebra problem.

  c. The meaning of 4^3 is 4 times itself 3 times. Choice **a** is incorrect because this does not mean the product of three 4s. Choice **b** is incorrect because this equals $2 \times 4 \times 4$, not $4 \times 4 \times 4$. Choice **d** is incorrect because this equals $3 \times 3 \times 3 \times 3$.

10. This is a fractions problem.

  b. Use 35 for C; $F = (\frac{9}{5} \times 35) + 32$. Therefore, $F = 63 + 32$, or $95°$. Choice **a** is incorrect because you added incorrectly; you mistakenly carried a one to the tens position. Choice **c** is incorrect because you forgot to add 32. Choice **d** is incorrect because you subtracted 32 instead of adding it.

11. This is a geometry problem.

  c. $5(3)(8) = 120$; $120 \div 3 = 40$. Choice **a** is incorrect because you added the dimensions instead of multiplying them, and disregarded the $\frac{1}{3}$ in the formula. Choice **b** is incorrect because you used $\frac{1}{2}$ instead of $\frac{1}{3}$ in the formula. Choice **d** is incorrect because you forgot to multiply by $\frac{1}{3}$.

12. This is a fractions problem.

  b. To solve this problem, you must first convert yards to inches. There are 36 inches in a yard; $36(3\frac{1}{3}) = 120$. Choice **a** is incorrect because you converted 3 yards to inches, not $3\frac{1}{3}$ yards. Choice **c** is incorrect because you assumed that 1 yard equals 48 inches, not 36 inches. Choice **d** is incorrect because you assumed that 1 yard equals 48 inches, and converted 3 yards to inches, not $3\frac{1}{3}$ yards.

13. This is a decimals problem.

  d. To change a fraction into decimal, divide the numerator by the denominator: $13 \div 4 = 3.25$. Another way to consider this problem is to change $\frac{13}{4}$ into a mixed fraction by dividing 13 by 4 to get 3, with $\frac{1}{4}$ left over: $\frac{13}{4} = 3\frac{1}{4} = 3.25$. Choice **a** is incorrect because this equals $3\frac{2}{5} = \frac{17}{5}$, not $\frac{13}{4}$. Choice **b** is incorrect because this equals $4\frac{1}{4} = \frac{17}{4}$, not $\frac{13}{4}$. Choice **c** is incorrect because this equals $3\frac{3}{4} = \frac{15}{4}$, not $\frac{13}{4}$.

14. This is a percents problem.

  b. Percent means "out of 100." In order to turn a percent into a decimal, divide it by 100: $125\% = \frac{125}{100} = 1.25$. (When dividing a number by a power of 10 such as 10, 100, or 1,000, simply move the decimal point of the numerator one place to the left for every zero in the denominator.) Choice **a** is incorrect because you moved the decimal point 3 places to the left, not 2. Choice **c** is incorrect because you moved the decimal point only 1 place to the left, not 2. Choice **d** is incorrect because you didn't move the decimal point 2 places to the left.

15. This is a geometry problem.

  d. An isosceles triangle has two equal legs and one base. The perimeter of the triangle is 3 feet, which is equivalent to 36 inches (12 inches in every foot). The base is 14 inches, so the sum of the two legs is 36 inches − 14 inches = 22 inches. Since both legs are of equal length, $22 \div 2 = 11$ inches for each leg. Choice **a** is incorrect because this is the perimeter of the triangle, not the length of a leg. Choice **b** is incorrect because if both legs were 18 inches long, there could be no base because the perimeter of the entire triangle is 36 inches. Choice **c** is incorrect because this is the sum of the lengths of both legs.

16. This is an algebra problem.

c. Subtract 25 from both sides to get $x = -12$. Choice **a** is incorrect because $-13 + 25 = 12$, not 13. Choice **b** is incorrect because $-11 + 25 = 14$, not 13. Choice **d** is incorrect because you added 25 to both sides instead of subtracting it.

17. This is a geometry problem.

b. A cube has four sides and two bases (a top and a bottom), which means that it has six faces. Choice **a** is incorrect because you forgot the top and bottom. Choice **c** is incorrect because the number of faces does not equal the number of bases. Choice **d** is incorrect because this is the number of edges, not faces.

18. This is a geometry problem.

d. To solve this problem, you should use the formula $A = lw$, or $117 = 9l$. Next, you must divide 117 by 9 to find the answer. Choice **a** is incorrect because you mistakenly divided by 90. Choice **b** is incorrect because you divided the correct length by 2. Choice **c** is incorrect because you doubled the length.

19. This is a geometry problem.

d. A square is a special case of all of these figures except the trapezoid. A square is not a trapezoid because a trapezoid has only two sides parallel. Choice **a** is incorrect because a square is a parallelogram because its opposite sides are parallel. Choice **b** is incorrect because a square is a rectangle because it is a quadrilateral with 90-degree angles. Choice **c** is incorrect because a square is a rhombus because it is a parallelogram with all sides equal in length.

20. This is a geometry problem.

b. The Pythagorean theorem states that the square of the length of the hypotenuse of a right triangle is equal to the sum of the squares of the other two sides, so we know that $1^2 + x^2 = (\sqrt{10})^2$, so that $1 + x^2 = 10$, and so, $x^2 = 10 - 1 = 9$, so $x = 3$. Choice **a** is incor-

rect because if this were true, $1^2 + 2^2 = 5$, so that the hypotenuse would have length $\sqrt{5}$, not $\sqrt{10}$. Choice **c** is incorrect because you used the Pythagorean theorem assuming that $\sqrt{10}$ was the length of one of the legs, not the hypotenuse. Choice **d** is incorrect because you forgot to take the square root.

21. This is a decimals problem.

d. $\frac{2}{3} = 0.6666$ repeating, so $5\frac{2}{3}$ is equivalent to 5.6666 repeating, or about 5.67. Choice **a** is incorrect because you are not treating the fraction $\frac{2}{3}$ correctly; it is not equal to 0.23. Choice **b** is incorrect because $\frac{1}{3}$ is approximately 0.33 while $\frac{2}{3}$ is approximately 0.67. Choice **c** is incorrect because this is the furthest away from $5\frac{2}{3}$ because its whole part is 0.

22. This is a geometry problem.

d. If the figure is a regular decagon, it can be divided into ten equal sections by lines passing through the center. Two such lines form the indicated angle, which includes three of the ten sections: $\frac{3}{10}$ of $360° = 108°$. Choice **a** is incorrect because this would correspond to the angle of one sector, not three. Choice **b** is incorrect because this would be the angle for one sector if the figure had 8 sides, not 10. Choice **c** is incorrect because this would be the angle for two sectors if the figure had 8 sides, not 10.

23. This is an algebra problem.

b. The 7 is in the hundredths place, therefore, 0.07 is equal to $\frac{7}{100}$ and $2.07 = 2\frac{7}{100}$. "Negative 2.07" is equal to $-2\frac{7}{100}$. Choice **a** is incorrect because $\frac{7}{10} = 0.7$, not 0.07. Choice **c** is incorrect because $\frac{7}{1,000} = 0.007$, not 0.07. Choice **d** is incorrect because -2.07 does not equal -2.7 because 0.7 is not equal to 0.07.

24. This is a percents problem.

b. 62.5% is $\frac{62.5}{100}$. You should multiply both the numerator and denominator by 10 to move the decimal point, resulting in $\frac{625}{1,000}$, and then factor both the numerator and denominator to find out how far you can reduce the fraction; $\frac{625}{1,000} = \frac{5 \times 5 \times 5 \times 5}{5 \times 5 \times 5 \times 8}$. If you cancel the three 5s that are in both the numerator and denominator, you will get $\frac{5}{8}$. Choice **a** is incorrect because this equals 6.25%, not 62.5%. Choice **c** is incorrect because this equals 625%, not 62.5%. Choice **d** is incorrect because this equals 640%, not 62.5%.

25. This is a geometry problem.

d. A line that intersects two parallel lines forms supplementary angles on either side of it. Supplementary angles are angles whose measures add up to 180°; 180 − 40 = 140. Choice **a** is incorrect because $\angle P$ and $\angle Q$ are not congruent. Choice **b** is incorrect because $\angle P$ and $\angle Q$ are supplementary, not complimentary, angles. Choice **c** is incorrect because angle Q is obtuse and supplementary to P; since 40° + 80° ≠ 180°, this choice is not correct.

SCORING

Write your raw score (the number you got right) for each test in the following blanks. Then turn to Chapter 3 to find out how to convert these raw scores into the scores the armed services use.

1. Arithmetic Reasoning: _____ right out of 30
2. Word Knowledge: _____ right out of 35
3. Paragraph Comprehension: _____ right out of 15
4. Mathematics Knowledge: _____ right out of 25

Here are the steps you should take, depending on your AFQT score on the first practice test:

- **If your AFQT is below 29,** you need more help in reading and/or math. You should spend plenty of time reviewing the lessons and practice questions found in this book.

- **If your AFQT is 29–31,** be sure to focus on your weakest subjects in the review lessons and practice questions that are found in this book.
- **If your AFQT is above 31,** review the areas that give you trouble, and then take the second practice test in Chapter 12 to make sure you are able to get a passing score again.

6 ▶ MATH REVIEW

CHAPTER SUMMARY

This chapter gives you some important tips for dealing with math questions and reviews some of the most commonly tested concepts. If you need to learn or review important math skills, this chapter is for you.

Two subtests of the ASVAB—Arithmetic Reasoning and Mathematics Knowledge—cover math skills. Arithmetic Reasoning is basically math word problems. Mathematics Knowledge tests your knowledge of math concepts, principles, and procedures. You don't have to do a lot of calculation in the Mathematics Knowledge subtest; you need to know basic terminology (like *sum* and *perimeter*), formulas (such as the area of a square), and computation rules. Both subtests cover the subjects you probably studied in school. This chapter reviews concepts you will need for both Arithmetic Reasoning and Mathematics Knowledge. Chapter 7 gives you more of these types of problems for extra practice.

Math Strategies

- **Don't work in your head.** Use your test book or scratch paper to take notes, draw pictures, and calculate. Although you might think that you can solve math questions more quickly in your head, that's a good way to make mistakes. Write out each step.

- **Read a math question in parts, rather than straight through from beginning to end.** As you read each part, stop to think about what it means and make notes or draw a picture to represent that part.
- **When you get to the actual question, circle it.** This will keep you more focused as you solve the problem.
- **Glance at the answer choices for clues.** If they are fractions, you probably should do your work in fractions; if they are decimals, you should probably work in decimals; and so on.
- **Make a plan of attack to help you solve the problem.**
- **If a question stumps you, try one of the *backdoor* approaches explained in the next section.** These are particularly useful for solving word problems.
- **When you get your answer, reread the circled question to make sure you have answered it.** This helps avoid the careless mistake of answering the wrong question.
- **Check your work after you get an answer.** Test takers get a false sense of security when they get an answer that matches one of the multiple-choice answers. Here are some good ways to check your work *if you have time:*
  - Ask yourself whether your answer is reasonable, whether it makes sense.
  - Plug your answer back into the problem to make sure the problem holds together.
  - Do the question a second time, but use a different method.
- **Approximate when appropriate.** For example:
  - $5.98 + $8.97 is a little less than $15. (Add: $6 + $9.)
  - 0.9876×5.0342 is close to 5. (Multiply: 1×5.)
- **Skip hard questions and come back to them later.** Mark them in your test book so you can find them quickly.

Backdoor Approaches for Answering Tough Questions

Many word problems are actually easier to solve by backdoor approaches. The two techniques that follow are time-saving ways to solve multiple-choice word problems that you don't know how to solve with a straightforward approach. The first technique, *nice numbers*, is useful when there are unknowns (like x) in the text of the word problem, making the problem too abstract for you. The second technique, *working backward*, presents a quick way to substitute numeric answer choices back into the problem to see which one works.

Nice Numbers

1. When a question contains unknowns, like x, plug nice numbers in for the unknowns. A nice number is easy to calculate with and makes sense in the problem.
2. Read the question with the nice numbers in place. Then solve it.
3. If the answer choices are all numbers, the choice that matches your answer is the right one.
4. If the answer choices contain unknowns, substitute the same nice numbers into all the answer choices. The choice that matches your answer is the right one. If more than one answer matches, do the problem again with different nice numbers. You will have to check only the answer choices that have already matched.

Example

Judi went shopping with p dollars in her pocket. If s shirts cost d dollars, what is the maximum number of shirts Judi could buy with the money in her pocket?

a. psd
b. $\frac{ps}{d}$
c. $\frac{pd}{s}$
d. $\frac{ds}{p}$

To solve this problem, let's try these nice numbers: p = \$100, s = 2; d = \$25. Now reread it with the numbers in place:

> Judi went shopping with *\$100* in her pocket. If *2* shirts cost *\$25*, what is the maximum number of shirts Judi could buy with the money in her pocket?

Since 2 shirts cost \$25, that means that 4 shirts cost \$50, and 8 shirts cost \$100. So our answer is 8. Let's substitute the nice numbers into all four answers:

  a. $100 \times 2 \times 25 = 5,000$

  b. $\frac{100 \times 2}{25} = 8$

  c. $\frac{100 \times 25}{2} = 1,250$

  d. $\frac{25 \times 2}{100} = \frac{1}{2}$

The answer is **b** because it is the only one that matches our answer of 8.

Working Backward

You can frequently solve a word problem by plugging the answer choices back into the text of the problem to see which one fits all the facts stated in the problem. The process is faster than you think because you will probably have to substitute only one or two answers to find the right one.

This approach works only when:

- All the answer choices are numbers.
- You are asked to find a simple number, not a sum, product, difference, or ratio.

Here's What to Do

1. Look at all the answer choices and begin with the one in the middle of the range. For example, if the answers are 14, 8, 2, 20, and 25, begin by plugging 14 into the problem.
2. If your choice doesn't work, eliminate it. Determine whether you need a bigger or smaller answer.
3. Plug in one of the remaining choices.
4. If none of the answers works, you may have made a careless error. Begin again or look for your mistake.

Example
Juan ate $\frac{1}{3}$ of the jelly beans. Maria then ate $\frac{3}{4}$ of the remaining jelly beans, which left 10 jelly beans. How many jelly beans were there to begin with?

 a. 60
 b. 80
 c. 90
 d. 120

Starting with the middle answer, let's assume there were 90 jellybeans to begin with:

Since Juan ate $\frac{1}{3}$ of them, that means he ate 30 ($\frac{1}{3} \times 90 = 30$), leaving 60 of them ($90 - 30 = 60$). Maria then ate $\frac{3}{4}$ of the 60 jelly beans, or 45 of them ($\frac{3}{4} \times 60 = 45$). That leaves 15 jelly beans ($60 - 45 = 15$).

The problem states that there were 10 jelly beans left, and we wound up with 15 of them. That indicates that we started with too big a number. Thus, 90 and 120 are incorrect. With only two choices left, let's use common sense to decide which one to try. The next lower answer is only a little smaller than 90 and may not be small enough. So, let's try 60:

Since Juan ate $\frac{1}{3}$ of them, that means he ate 20 ($\frac{1}{3} \times 60 = 20$), leaving 40 of them ($60 - 20 = 40$). Maria then ate $\frac{3}{4}$ of the 40 jelly beans, or 30 of them ($\frac{3}{4} \times 40 = 30$). That leaves 10 jelly beans ($40 - 30 = 10$).

The result of 10 jelly beans agrees with the problem, so the correct answer is **a**.

Word Problems

Many of the math problems on tests are word problems. A word problem can include any kind of math, including simple arithmetic, fractions, decimals, percentages, algebra, and geometry.

The hardest part of any word problem is translating English into math. When you read a problem, you can frequently translate it word for word from English statements into mathematical statements. At other times, however, a key word in the word problem hints at the mathematical operation to be performed. Here are the translation rules:

EQUALS key words: *is, are, has*	
ENGLISH	**MATH**
Bob **is** 18 years old.	$b = 18$
There **are** seven hats.	$h = 7$
Judi **has** five cats.	$c = 5$

ADDITION key words: *sum; more, greater, or older than; total; all together*	
ENGLISH	**MATH**
The **sum** of two numbers is 10.	$x + y = 10$
Karen has $5 **more** than Sam.	$k = 5 + s$
The base is 3" **greater than** the height.	$b = 3 + h$
Judi is two years **older than** Tony.	$j = 2 + t$
The **total** of three numbers is 25.	$a + b + c = 25$
How much do Joan and Tom have **all together**?	$j + t = ?$

SUBTRACTION key words: *difference, fewer, less or younger than, remain, left over*	
ENGLISH	**MATH**
The **difference** between two numbers is 17.	$x - y = 17$
Mike has five **fewer*** books than twice the number Jan has.	$m = 2j - 5$
Jay is two years **younger** than Brett.	$j = b - 2$
After Carol ate three apples, *r* apples **remained**.	$r = a - 3$

***Note:** Notice that the order of subtraction is flipped when "fewer than" is used: "8 less than 10" translates to "10 − 8," not "8 − 10."

MULTIPLICATION key words: *of, product, times*	
ENGLISH	**MATH**
Twenty percent **of** Matthew's baseball caps are red.	$0.20 \times m$
Half **of** the boys will be there.	$\frac{1}{2} \times b$
The **product** of two numbers is 12.	$a \times b = 12$

DIVISION key word: *per*	
ENGLISH	**MATH**
Add 15 drops **per** teaspoon.	$\frac{15 \text{ drops}}{\text{teaspoon}}$
Her car gets 22 miles **per** gallon.	$\frac{22 \text{ miles}}{\text{gallon}}$

GLOSSARY OF TERMS

Denominator   the bottom number in a fraction. *Example:* 2 is the denominator in $\frac{1}{2}$.

Difference   subtract. The difference of two numbers means subtract one number from the other.

Divisible by   a number is divisible by a second number if that second number divides *evenly* into the original number. *Example:* 10 is divisible by 5 (10 ÷ 5 = 2, with no remainder). However, 10 is not divisible by 3. (See *multiple of*)

Even integers   integers that are divisible by 2, like . . . –4, –2, 0, 2, 4. . . . (See *integer*)

Integers   numbers along the number line, like . . . –3, –2, –1, 0, 1, 2, 3. . . . Integers include the whole numbers and their opposites. (See *whole number*)

Multiple of   a number is a multiple of a second number if that second number can be multiplied by an integer to get the original number. *Example:* 10 is a multiple of 5 (10 = 5 × 2); however, 10 is not a multiple of 3. (See *divisible by*)

Negative number   a number that is less than zero, like . . . –1, –18.6, $-\frac{3}{4}$. . . .

Numerator   the top part of a fraction. *Example:* 1 is the numerator of $\frac{1}{2}$.

Odd integers   integers that aren't divisible by 2, like . . . –5, –3, –1, 1, 3. . . .

Positive number   a number that is greater than zero, like . . . 2, 42, $\frac{1}{2}$, 4.63. . . .

Prime numbers   integers that are divisible only by 1 and themselves, like . . . 2, 3, 5, 7, 11. . . . All prime numbers are odd, except for the number 2. The number 1 is not considered prime.

Product   multiply. The product of two numbers is the answer when the numbers are multiplied together.

Quotient   the answer you get when you divide. *Example:* 10 divided by 5 is 2; the quotient is 2.

Real numbers   all the numbers you can think of, like . . . 17, –5, $\frac{1}{2}$, –23.6, 3.4329, 0. . . . Real numbers include the integers, fractions, and decimals. (See *integer*)

Remainder   the number left over after division. *Example:* 11 divided by 2 is 5, with a remainder of 1.

Sum   the sum of two numbers is the answer when the numbers are added together.

Whole numbers   counting numbers that do not have decimals, like . . . 0, 1, 2, 3. . . . All whole numbers are positive.

Distance Formula:
Distance = Rate × Time

The key words are words that imply movement, like *plane, train, boat, car, walk, run, climb,* or *swim.* In these cases, use $d = r \times t$ (distance = rate × time), making sure that your units are the same. (You cannot use minutes and hours in the same equation—you must convert all items into the same unit. For example, 90 minutes equal 1.5 hours.)

■ How far did the plane travel in four hours if it averaged 300 miles per hour?

$d = r \times t$

$d = 300 \times 4$

$d = 1,200$ miles

■ Ben walked 20 miles in four hours. What was his average speed?

$d = r \times t$

$20 = r \times 4$

5 miles per hour $= r$

Solving a Word Problem Using the Translation Table

Remember the problem at the beginning of this chapter about the jelly beans?

Juan ate $\frac{1}{3}$ of the jelly beans. Maria then ate $\frac{3}{4}$ of the remaining jelly beans, which left 10 jelly beans. How many jelly beans were there to begin with?

a. 60
b. 80
c. 90
d. 120

We solved it by *working backward.* Now, let's solve it using our translation rules.

Assume Juan started with J jelly beans. Eating $\frac{1}{3}$ of them means eating $\frac{1}{3} \times J$ jelly beans. Maria ate a fraction of the remaining jelly beans, which means we

must subtract to find out how many are left after Juan ate some: $J - \frac{1}{3} \times J = \frac{2}{3} \times J$. Maria then ate $\frac{3}{4}$, leaving $\frac{1}{4}$ of the $\frac{2}{3} \times J$ jelly beans, or $\frac{1}{4} \times \frac{2}{3} \times J$ jelly beans. Multiplying out $\frac{1}{4} \times \frac{2}{3} \times J$ gives $\frac{1}{6} J$ as the number of jelly beans left. The problem states that there were 10 jelly beans left, meaning that we set $\frac{1}{6} \times J$ equal to 10: $\frac{1}{6} \times J$ = 10.

Solving this equation for J gives $J = 60$. Thus, the right answer is **a** (the same answer we got when we *worked backward*). As you can see, both methods—working backward and translating from English to math—work. You should use whichever method is more comfortable for you.

Practice Word Problems

You will find word problems using fractions, decimals, and percentages in those sections of this chapter. For now, practice using the translation table on problems that just require you to work with basic arithmetic. Answers are found on pages 99–100.

1. Joan went shopping with $100.00 and returned home with $18.42. How much money did she spend?
   a. $81.58
   b. $72.68
   c. $72.58
   d. $71.58

2. Mark invited ten friends to a party. Each friend brought three guests. How many people came to the party, excluding Mark?
   a. 3
   b. 10
   c. 30
   d. 40

3. If Jennifer uses her cell phone approximately 2.5 hours a day for her new travel business Monday through Friday, and 2.5 hours a day for personal calls on Saturdays and Sundays, how many minutes will she use in April, which has 30 days?
  a. 2,500 minutes
  b. 3,000 minutes
  c. 3,500 minutes
  d. 4,500 minutes

4. Mr. Wallace is writing a budget request to upgrade his personal computer system. He wants to purchase a hard drive, which will cost $100, two new software programs at $350 each, a color printer for $249, and an additional color cartridge for $25. What is the total amount Mr. Wallace should write on his budget request?
  a. $724
  b. $974
  c. $1,049
  d. $1,074

Fraction Review

Problems involving fractions may be straightforward calculation questions, or they may be word problems. Typically, they ask you to add, subtract, multiply, divide, or compare fractions.

Working with Fractions
A fraction is a part of something.

Example
Let's say that a pizza was cut into eight equal slices and you ate three of them. The fraction $\frac{3}{8}$ tells you what part of the pizza you ate. The following pizza shows this: three of the eight pieces (the ones you ate) are shaded.

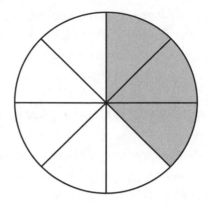

THREE KINDS OF FRACTIONS	
Proper fraction	The numerator is less than the denominator: $\frac{1}{2}, \frac{2}{3}, \frac{4}{9}, \frac{8}{13}$ The value of a proper fraction is less than 1.
Improper fraction	The numerator is greater than or equal to the denominator: $\frac{3}{2}, \frac{5}{3}, \frac{14}{9}, \frac{12}{12}$ The value of an improper fraction is 1 or more.
Mixed number	A fraction written to the right of a whole number: $3\frac{1}{2}, 4\frac{2}{3}, 12\frac{3}{4}, 24\frac{3}{4}$ The value of a mixed number is more than 1: it is the sum of the whole number plus the fraction.

Changing Improper Fractions into Mixed or Whole Numbers
Sometimes, you'll need to turn an improper fraction into a mixed number. To change an improper fraction, say $\frac{13}{2}$, into a mixed number, follow these steps:

1. Divide the denominator (2) into the numerator (13) to get the whole number portion (6) of the mixed number:

$$2{\overline{\smash{\big)}\,13}}$$
$$\underline{12}$$
$$1$$

with 6 above.

2. Write the remainder of the division (1) over the old denominator (2):
$$6\frac{1}{2}$$

3. Check: Change the mixed number back into an improper fraction (see the following section). If you end up with your original improper fraction, your answer is correct.

Changing Mixed Numbers into Improper Fractions

You must change mixed numbers into improper fractions when multiplying or dividing. To change a mixed number, say $2\frac{3}{4}$, into an improper fraction, follow these steps:

1. Multiply the whole number (2) by the denominator (4):

   $2 \times 4 = 8$

2. Add the result (8) to the numerator (3):

   $8 + 3 = 11$

3. Put the total (11) over the denominator (4):

   $\frac{11}{4}$

4. Check: Reverse the process by changing the improper fraction into a mixed number. If you get the number you started with, your answer is right.

Reducing Fractions

Reducing a fraction means writing it in its *lowest terms,* that is, with the smallest possible numerator and denominator. For instance, 50¢ is $\frac{50}{100}$ of a dollar, or $\frac{1}{2}$ of a dollar. In fact, if you have 50¢ in your pocket, you say that you have half a dollar. Reducing a fraction does not change its value.

Follow these steps to reduce a fraction:

1. Find a whole number that divides *evenly* into both numbers that make up the fraction.
2. Divide that number into the numerator, and replace the numerator with the quotient (the answer you got when you divided).
3. Do the same thing to the denominator.
4. Repeat the first three steps until you can't find a number that divides evenly into both the

numerator and the denominator of the fraction.

For example, let's reduce $\frac{8}{24}$. We could do it in two steps $\frac{8 \div 4}{24 \div 4} = \frac{2}{6}$; then $\frac{2 \div 2}{6 \div 2} = \frac{1}{3}$. Or we could do it in a single step $\frac{8 \div 8}{24 \div 8} = \frac{1}{3}$.

Shortcut: When the numerator and denominator both end in zeros, cross out the same number of zeros in both numbers to begin the reducing process. For example $\frac{300}{4,000}$ reduces to $\frac{3}{40}$ when you cross out two zeros in both numbers. This trick works because you're dividing both numbers by a power of ten, like 10; 100; 1,000; and so on.

Whenever you do arithmetic with fractions, reduce your answer. On a multiple-choice test, don't panic if your answer isn't listed. Try to reduce it and then compare it to the choices.

Reduce these fractions to lowest terms:

5. $\frac{3}{12} =$

6. $\frac{14}{35} =$

7. $\frac{24}{42} =$

Raising Fractions to Higher Terms

Before you can add and subtract fractions, you have to know how to raise a fraction to higher terms. This is actually the opposite of reducing a fraction.

Follow these steps to raise $\frac{2}{3}$ to 24ths:

1. Divide the old denominator (3) into the new one (24):

   $\frac{24}{3} = 8$

2. Multiply the answer (8) by the old numerator(2):

   $2 \times 8 = 16$

3. Put the answer (16) over the new denominator (24):

$$\frac{16}{24}$$

4. Check: Reduce the new fraction to see if you return to the original one:

$$\frac{16 \div 8}{24 \div 8} = \frac{2}{3}$$

Raise these fractions to higher terms:

8. $\frac{5}{12} = \frac{}{24}$

9. $\frac{2}{9} = \frac{}{27}$

10. $\frac{2}{5} = \frac{}{500}$

Adding Fractions

In order to add and subtract fractions, they must have the same denominator. If the fractions have the same denominators, just add the numerators together and write the total over the denominator.

Examples: $\frac{2}{9} + \frac{4}{9} = \frac{6}{9}$ Reduce the $\frac{6}{9}$ to $\frac{2}{3}$.

$\frac{5}{8} + \frac{7}{8} = \frac{12}{8}$ Change $\frac{12}{8}$ to a mixed number: $1\frac{4}{8}$; then reduce: $1\frac{1}{2}$.

There are a few extra steps to add mixed numbers with the same denominators, such as $2\frac{3}{5} + 1\frac{4}{5}$:

1. Add the fractions:
$$\frac{3}{5} + \frac{4}{5} = \frac{7}{5}$$

2. Change the improper fraction into a mixed number:
$$\frac{7}{5} = 1\frac{2}{5}$$

3. Add the whole numbers:
$$2 + 1 = 3$$

4. Add the results of steps 2 and 3:
$$1\frac{2}{5} + 3 = 4\frac{2}{5}$$

Finding the Least Common Denominator

If the fractions you want to add don't have the same denominator, you will have to raise some or all of the fractions to higher terms so that they do have a **common denominator**. All the original denominators divide evenly into the common denominator. If it is the smallest number into which they all divide evenly, it is called the **least common denominator (LCD)**.

Here are a few tips for finding the LCD, the smallest number that all the denominators evenly divide into:

■ See if all the denominators divide evenly into the biggest one.
■ Write out a multiplication table of the largest denominator until you find a number that all the others divide into evenly.
■ When all else fails, multiply all the denominators together.

Example
$\frac{2}{3} + \frac{4}{5}$

1. Find the LCD. Multiply the denominators:
$$3 \times 5 = 15$$

2. Raise each fraction to 15ths:
$$\frac{2}{3} = \frac{10}{15}$$
$$+ \frac{4}{5} = \frac{12}{15}$$

3. Add as usual: $\frac{22}{15}$

4. Optional: Write as a mixed number: $1\frac{7}{15}$.

Try these addition problems:

11. $\frac{3}{4} + \frac{1}{6} =$

12. $\frac{7}{8} + \frac{2}{3} + \frac{3}{4} =$

13. $4\frac{1}{3} + 2\frac{3}{4} + \frac{1}{6} =$

Subtracting Fractions

Like addition, fractions must have the same denominators before subtracting. If the fractions have the same denominators, just subtract the numerators and write the difference over the denominator.

Example

$$\frac{4}{9} - \frac{3}{9} = \frac{4-3}{9} = \frac{1}{9}$$

If the fractions you want to subtract don't have the same denominator, you will have to raise some or all of the fractions to higher terms so that they all have the same denominator, or LCD. If you forgot how to find the LCD, just read the section on adding fractions with different denominators.

Example

$$\frac{5}{6} - \frac{3}{4}$$

1. Raise each fraction to 12ths because 12 is the LCD, the smallest number that 6 and 4 both divide into evenly:

   $$\frac{5}{6} = \frac{10}{12}$$

   $$-\frac{3}{4} = \frac{9}{12}$$

2. Subtract as usual:

   $$\frac{1}{12}$$

Subtracting mixed numbers with the same denominator is similar to adding mixed numbers.

Example

$$4\frac{3}{5} - 1\frac{2}{5}$$

1. Subtract the fractions: $\frac{3}{5} - \frac{2}{5} = \frac{1}{5}$
2. Subtract the whole numbers: $4 - 1 = 3$
3. Add the results of steps 1 and 2: $\frac{1}{5} + 3 = 3\frac{1}{5}$

Sometimes, there is an extra "borrowing" step when you subtract mixed numbers with the same denominators, say $7\frac{3}{5} - 2\frac{4}{5}$:

1. You can't subtract the fractions the way they are because $\frac{4}{5}$ is bigger than $\frac{3}{5}$. So you borrow 1 from the 7, making it 6, and change that 1 to $\frac{5}{5}$ because 5 is the denominator:

   $$7\frac{3}{5} = 6\frac{3}{5} + \frac{5}{5}$$

2. Add the numbers from step 1:

   $$6\frac{3}{5} + \frac{5}{5} = 6\frac{8}{5}$$

3. Now you have a different version of the original problem:

   $$6\frac{8}{5} - 2\frac{4}{5}$$

4. Subtract the fractional parts of the two mixed numbers:

   $$\frac{8}{5} - \frac{4}{5} = \frac{4}{5}$$

5. Subtract the whole number parts of the two mixed numbers:

   $$6 - 2 = 4$$

6. Add the results of the last 2 steps together:

   $$4 + \frac{4}{5} = 4\frac{4}{5}$$

Try these subtraction problems:

14. $\frac{4}{5} - \frac{2}{3} =$

15. $\frac{7}{8} - \frac{1}{4} - \frac{1}{2} =$

16. $10\frac{1}{3} - 6\frac{5}{7} =$

Now, let's put what you have learned about adding and subtracting fractions to work in some real-life problems:

17. Manuel drove $3\frac{1}{2}$ miles to work. Then he drove $4\frac{3}{4}$ miles to the store. When he left there, he drove 2 miles to the dry cleaner. Then he drove $3\frac{2}{3}$ miles back to work for a meeting. Finally, he drove $3\frac{1}{2}$ miles home. How many miles did he travel in total?

   a. $17\frac{5}{12}$

   b. $16\frac{5}{12}$

   c. $15\frac{7}{12}$

   d. $15\frac{5}{12}$

18. Before leaving the warehouse, a truck driver noted that the mileage gauge registered $4{,}357\frac{4}{10}$ miles. When he arrived at the delivery location, the mileage gauge then registered $4{,}400\frac{1}{10}$ miles. How many miles did he drive from the warehouse to the delivery location?

   a. $42\frac{3}{10}$

   b. $42\frac{7}{10}$

   c. $43\frac{7}{10}$

   d. $47\frac{2}{10}$

Multiplying Fractions

Multiplying fractions is actually easier than adding them. All you do is multiply the numerators and then multiply the denominators.

Examples

$\frac{2}{3} \times \frac{5}{7} = \frac{2 \times 5}{3 \times 7} = \frac{10}{21}$

$\frac{1}{2} \times \frac{3}{5} \times \frac{7}{4} = \frac{1 \times 3 \times 7}{2 \times 5 \times 4} = \frac{21}{40}$

Sometimes you can *cancel* before multiplying. Canceling is a shortcut that makes the multiplication go faster because you're multiplying with smaller numbers. It's very similar to reducing: if there is a number that divides evenly into both the numerator and the

denominator, do that division before multiplying. If you forget to cancel, you can reduce it in the end.

Example

$\frac{5}{6} \times \frac{9}{20}$

1. Cancel a 3 in both the 6 and the 9: $6 \div 3 = 2$ and $9 \div 3 = 3$.

$\frac{5}{6} \times \frac{\overset{3}{\cancel{9}}}{20}$
$\quad_{2}$

2. Cancel a 5 in both the 5 and the 20: $5 \div 5 = 1$ and $20 \div 5 = 4$.

$\frac{\overset{1}{\cancel{5}}}{2} \times \frac{3}{\underset{4}{\cancel{20}}}$

3. Multiply across the new numerators and denominators:

$\frac{1}{2} \times \frac{3}{4} = \frac{1 \times 3}{2 \times 4} = \frac{3}{6} = \frac{1}{2}$

Try these multiplication problems:

19. $\frac{4}{15} \times \frac{25}{8} =$

20. $\frac{2}{3} \times \frac{4}{7} \times \frac{3}{5} =$

21. $\frac{3}{4} \times \frac{8}{9} =$

To multiply a fraction by a whole number, first rewrite the whole number as a fraction with a denominator of 1.

Example

$5 \times \frac{2}{3} = \frac{5}{1} \times \frac{2}{3} = \frac{10}{3}$

(Optional: Convert $\frac{10}{3}$ to a mixed number: $3\frac{1}{3}$.)

To multiply with mixed numbers, you must change them to improper fractions before multiplying.

Example

$4\frac{2}{3} \times 5\frac{1}{2}$

1. Convert $4\frac{2}{3}$ to an improper fraction:

$4\frac{2}{3} = \frac{4 \times 3 + 2}{3} = \frac{14}{3}$

2. Convert $5\frac{1}{2}$ to an improper fraction:

$$5\frac{1}{2} = \frac{5 \times 2 + 1}{2} = \frac{11}{2}$$

3. Cancel and multiply the fractions:

$$\frac{\overset{7}{\cancel{14}}}{3} \times \frac{11}{\underset{1}{\cancel{2}}} = \frac{77}{3}$$

4. Optional: Convert the improper fraction to a mixed number:

$$\frac{77}{3} = 25\frac{2}{3}$$

Now, try these multiplication problems with mixed numbers and whole numbers:

22. $4\frac{1}{3} \times \frac{2}{5} =$

23. $4\frac{5}{6} \times 12 =$

24. $3\frac{3}{4} \times 4\frac{2}{5} =$

Here are a few more real-life problems to test your skills:

25. After driving $\frac{2}{3}$ of the 15 miles to work, Mr. Stone stopped to make a phone call. How many miles had he driven when he made his call?
   a. 5
   b. $7\frac{1}{2}$
   c. 10
   d. 12

26. Alrecho used $\frac{5}{7}$ of his savings on his first two years of college. If his original savings totaled $14,000, how much did he use during his first two years?
   a. $5,000
   b. $5,700
   c. $7,000
   d. $10,000

27. Technician Chin makes $14.00 an hour. When she works more than 8 hours a day, she gets overtime pay of $1\frac{1}{2}$ times her regular hourly wage for the extra hours. How much did she earn for working 11 hours in one day?
   a. $77
   b. $154
   c. $175
   d. $210

Dividing Fractions

To divide one fraction by a second fraction, invert the second fraction (that is, flip the numerator and denominator) and then multiply.

Example
$\frac{1}{2} \div \frac{3}{5}$

1. Invert the second fraction ($\frac{3}{5}$) to find its reciprocal: $\frac{5}{3}$.
2. Change the division sign ($\div$) to a multiplication sign ($\times$).
3. Multiply the first fraction by the reciprocal of the second fraction: $\frac{1}{2} \times \frac{5}{3} = \frac{1 \times 5}{2 \times 3} = \frac{5}{6}$

To divide a fraction by a whole number, first change the whole number to a fraction by putting it over 1. Then follow the division steps.

Example
$\frac{3}{5} \div 2 = \frac{3}{5} \div \frac{2}{1} = \frac{3}{5} \times \frac{1}{2} = \frac{3 \times 1}{5 \times 2} = \frac{3}{10}$

When the division problem has a mixed number, convert it to an improper fraction and then divide as usual.

Example
$2\frac{3}{4} \div \frac{1}{6}$

1. Convert $2\frac{3}{4}$ to an improper fraction:

$$2\frac{3}{4} = \frac{2 \times 4 + 3}{4} = \frac{11}{4}$$

2. Find the reciprocal of $\frac{6}{1}:\frac{1}{6}$

3. Change ÷ to ×, cancel, and multiply:

$$\frac{\overset{}{\cancel{11}}}{\underset{2}{\cancel{4}}} \times \frac{\overset{3}{\cancel{6}}}{1} = \frac{11 \times 3}{2 \times 1} = \frac{33}{2}$$

4. Optional: Convert to a mixed number: $16\frac{1}{2}$.

Here are a few division problems to try:

28. $\frac{1}{3} \div \frac{2}{3} =$

29. $2\frac{3}{4} \div \frac{1}{2} =$

30. $\frac{3}{5} \div 3 =$

31. $3\frac{3}{4} \div 2\frac{1}{3} =$

Let's wrap this up with some real-life problems:

32. If four friends evenly split $6\frac{1}{2}$ pounds of candy, how many pounds of candy does each friend get?
    a. $\frac{8}{13}$
    b. $1\frac{5}{8}$
    c. $1\frac{1}{2}$
    d. $1\frac{5}{13}$

33. If Terry has a cord that is $23\frac{1}{4}$ inches long and he needs to divide it into $\frac{3}{4}$-inch segments for a school project, how many $\frac{3}{4}$-inch pieces of rope will he have when finished?
    a. 23 pieces
    b. 26 pieces
    c. 31 pieces
    d. 34 pieces

34. Ms. Goldbaum earned $36.75 for working $3\frac{1}{2}$ hours. What was her hourly wage?
    a. $10.00
    b. $10.50
    c. $10.75
    d. $12.00

Decimals

A decimal is a special kind of fraction. You use decimals every day when you deal with money—$10.35 is a decimal that represents 10 dollars and 35 cents. The decimal point separates the dollars from the cents. Because there are 100 cents in one dollar, 1¢ is $\frac{1}{100}$ of a dollar, or $0.01.

Each decimal digit to the right of the decimal point has a name:

Examples

$0.1 = 1$ tenth $= \frac{1}{10}$

$0.02 = 2$ hundredths $= \frac{2}{100}$

$0.003 = 3$ thousandths $= \frac{3}{1,000}$

$0.0004 = 4$ ten-thousandths $= \frac{4}{10,000}$

When you add zeros after the right-most decimal place, you don't change the value of the decimal. For example, 6.17 is the same as all of these:

6.170
6.1700
6.17000000000000000

If there are digits on both sides of the decimal point (like 10.35), the number is called a **mixed decimal**. If there are non-zero digits only to the right of the decimal point (like 0.53), the number is called a **decimal**. A whole number (like 15) is understood to have a decimal point at its right (15.). Thus, 15 is the same as 15.0, 15.00, 15.000, and so on.

Changing Fractions to Decimals

To change a fraction to a decimal, divide the denominator into the numerator after you put a decimal point and a few zeros to the right of the numerator. When you divide, bring the decimal point up into your answer.

Example
Change $\frac{3}{4}$ to a decimal.

1. Add a decimal point and two zeros to the top number (3):

   3.00

2. Divide the bottom number (4) into 3.00:
   Bring the decimal point up into the answer:

$$\begin{array}{r} 0.75 \\ 4\overline{)3.00} \\ -2\,8 \\ \hline 20 \\ -20 \\ \hline 0 \end{array}$$

3. The quotient (result of the division) is the answer:

   0.75

Some fractions may require you to add many decimal zeros in order for the division to come out evenly. In fact, when you convert a fraction like $\frac{2}{3}$ to a decimal, you can keep adding decimal zeros to the top number forever because the division will never come out evenly. As you divide 3 into 2, you will keep getting 6s:

$$2 \div 3 = 0.6666666666 \text{ etc.}$$

This is called a **repeating decimal** and it can be written as $0.\overline{666}$ or as $0.66\frac{2}{3}$. You can approximate it as 0.67, 0.667, 0.6667, and so on.

Changing Decimals to Fractions

To change a decimal to a fraction, write the digits of the decimal as the numerator and write the decimal's name as the denominator. Then reduce the fraction, if possible.

Example
0.018

1. Write 18 as the numerator:

   $\underline{18}$

2. Three places to the right of the decimal means *thousandths,* so write 1,000 as the denominator:

$$\frac{18}{1,000}$$

3. Reduce by dividing 2 into the top and bottom numbers:

$$\frac{18 \div 2}{1,000 \div 2} = \frac{9}{500}$$

Now, change these decimals or mixed decimals to fractions:

35. $0.005 =$

36. $3.48 =$

37. $123.456 =$

Comparing Decimals

Because decimals are easier to compare when they have the same number of digits after the decimal point, tack zeros onto the end of the shorter decimals. Then, all you have to do is compare the numbers as if the decimal points weren't there:

Example
Compare 0.08 and 0.1.

1. Tack one zero at the end of 0.1: 0.10
2. To compare 0.10 to 0.08, just compare 10 to 8.
3. Since 10 is larger than 8, 0.1 is larger than 0.08.

Adding and Subtracting Decimals

To add or subtract decimals, stack them so their decimal points are aligned. You may want to tack on zeros at the end of shorter decimals so you can keep all your digits lined up evenly. Remember, if a number doesn't have a decimal point, then put one at the right end of the number.

Example
$1.23 + 57 + 0.038 =$

1. Line up the numbers like this:

$$
\begin{array}{r}
1.230 \\
57.000 \\
+0.038 \\
\hline
\end{array}
$$

2. Add. 58.268

Example

$1.23 - 0.038 =$

1. Line up the numbers like this:

$$
\begin{array}{r}
1.230 \\
-0.038 \\
\hline
\end{array}
$$

2. Subtract. 1.192

Try these addition and subtraction problems:

38. $0.007 + 7.7 + 700 =$

39. $0.005 + 8 + 0.3 =$

40. $3.48 - 2.573 =$

41. $123.456 - 122 =$

42. A park ranger drove 3.7 miles to the state park. He then walked 1.6 miles around the park to make sure everything was all right. He got back into the car, drove 2.75 miles to check on a broken light, and then drove 2 miles back to the ranger station. How many miles did he drive in total?
   a. 8.45
   b. 8.8
   c. 10
   d. 10.05

43. Over the course of one year, the price for a stock dropped from $101.53 per share to $78.97 per share. How much did this stock's shares drop in price?
   a. $23.44
   b. $22.56
   c. $33.56
   d. $13.44

Multiplying Decimals

To multiply decimals, ignore the decimal points and just multiply the numbers. Then, count the total number of decimal digits (the digits to the *right* of the decimal point) in the numbers you are multiplying. Starting on the right side of your answer, count backward to the left one space for each of the decimal digits, and then put the decimal point to the left of those digits. For example, if you have three decimal digits, count back three spaces and then insert the decimal into your answer.

Example

215.7×2.4

1. Multiply 2,157 times 24:

$$
\begin{array}{r}
2,157 \\
\times\ 24 \\
\hline
8,628 \\
+\ 4,314 \\
\hline
51,768 \\
\end{array}
$$

2. Because there are a total of two decimal digits in 215.7 and 2.4, count off two places from the right in 51,768, placing the decimal point to the *left* of the last two digits: 517.68.

If your answer doesn't have enough digits, tack zeros on to the left of the answer.

Example

0.03×0.006

1. Multiply 3 times 6: $\qquad 3 \times 6 = 18$
2. You need five decimal digits in your
   answer, so tack on three zeros: $\qquad$ 00018
3. Put the decimal point at the front
   of the number (which is five digits
   from the right): $\qquad$ 0.00018

You can practice multiplying decimals with these:

44. $0.05 \times 0.6 =$

45. $0.053 \times 6.4 =$

46. $38.1 \times 0.0184 =$

47. Gas costs $5.12 per gallon in Lone Pine, California. If Jessie puts 8.5 gallons in her car, how much will that cost?
   a. $40.60
   b. $42.50
   c. $43.52
   d. $44.60

48. Nuts cost $3.50 per pound. Approximately how much will 4.25 pounds of nuts cost?
   a. $12.25
   b. $12.88
   c. $14.50
   d. $14.88

Dividing Decimals

To divide a decimal by a whole number, set up the division, and immediately bring the decimal point straight up into the answer. Then, divide as you would normally divide whole numbers.

Example

$0.256 \div 8$

$$
\begin{array}{r}
.032 \\
8\overline{)0.256} \\
-0 \\
\hline
25 \\
-24 \\
\hline
16 \\
-16 \\
\hline
0
\end{array}
$$

To divide any number by a decimal, you must perform an extra step before you can divide. Move the decimal point to the very right of the number you are dividing by, counting the number of places you are moving it. Then, move the decimal point the same number of places to the right in the number you are dividing into. In other words, first change the problem to one in which you are dividing by a whole number.

Example: $0.06\overline{)1.218}$

1. Because there are two decimal digits in 0.06, move the decimal point two places to the right in both numbers and move the decimal point straight up into the answer:

$$0.06\overline{)1.21.8}$$

2. Divide using the new numbers:

$$
\begin{array}{r}
20.3 \\
6\overline{)121.8} \\
-12 \\
\hline
01 \\
-00 \\
\hline
18 \\
-18 \\
\hline
0
\end{array}
$$

Under certain conditions, you must tack on zeros to the right of the last decimal digit in the number you are dividing into:

- If there aren't enough digits for you to move the decimal point to the right.
- If the answer doesn't come out evenly when you do the division.
- If you are dividing a whole number by a decimal. Then you will have to tack on the decimal point as well as some zeros.

Try your skills on these division problems:

49. $7\overline{)9.8}$ =

50. $0.0004\overline{)0.0512}$ =

51. $0.5\overline{)28.6}$ =

52. $0.14\overline{)196}$ =

53. If Mary Lou paid $11.00 for 4 pounds of grapes, how much did the grapes cost per pound?
  a. $2.75
  b. $2.65
  c. $2.80
  d. $2.85

54. Mary walked a total of 18.6 miles in 4 days. On average, how many miles did she walk each day?
  a. 4.15
  b. 4.60
  c. 4.65
  d. 22.60

Percents

Percent literally means "out of 100." The root *cent* means 100: a *century* is 100 years, there are 100 *cents* in a dollar, and so on. Thus, 17% means 17 parts out of 100. It is easy to compare fractions when they are both out of 100, which is why percents are so useful. For example, 17% is the same as $\frac{17}{100}$. Because fractions can also be expressed as decimals, 17% is also equivalent to 0.17, which is 17 hundredths.

You encounter percents every day. Sales tax, interest, and discounts are just a few common examples.

If you're shaky on fractions, you may want to review the fraction section again before reading further.

Changing a Decimal to a Percent and Vice Versa

To change a decimal to a percent, move the decimal point two places to the right and tack on a percent sign (%) at the end. If the decimal point moves to the end of the number, you can eliminate it. If there aren't enough places to move the decimal point, add zeros on the right before moving the decimal point.

To change a percent to a decimal, drop off the percent sign and move the decimal point two places to the left. If there aren't enough places to move the decimal point, add zeros on the left before moving the decimal point.

Try changing these decimals to percents:

55. 0.45 =

56. 0.008 =

57. 0.0875 =

Now, change these percents to decimals:

58. 12% =

59. $87\frac{1}{2}$% =

60. 250% =

Changing a Fraction to a Percent and Vice Versa

To change a fraction to a percent, there are two techniques. Each is illustrated by changing the fraction $\frac{1}{4}$ to a percent:

Technique 1: Multiply the fraction by 100%.

Multiply $\frac{1}{4}$ by 100%: $\frac{1}{\cancel{4}_1} \times \frac{\cancel{100\%}^{25}}{1} = 25\%$.

Technique 2: Divide the denominator into the numerator; then, move the decimal point two places to the right and tack on a percent sign (%).

Divide 4 into 1 and move the decimal point two places to the right:

$$4\overline{)1.00} \quad\quad 0.25 = 25\%$$
$$0.25$$

To change a percent to a fraction, remove the percent sign and write the number over 100. Then, reduce if possible.

Example
Change 4% to a fraction.

1. Remove the % and write the fraction 4 over 100: $\frac{4}{100}$
2. Reduce: $\frac{4 \div 4}{100 \div 4} = \frac{1}{25}$

Example
Change $16\frac{2}{3}$% to a fraction.

1. Remove the % and write the fraction $16\frac{2}{3}$ over 100: $\frac{16\frac{2}{3}}{100}$
2. Since a fraction means "numerator divided by denominator," rewrite the fraction as a division problem: $16\frac{2}{3} \div 100$
3. Change the mixed number ($16\frac{2}{3}$) to an improper fraction ($\frac{50}{3}$): $\frac{50}{3} \div \frac{100}{1}$
4. Flip the second fraction ($\frac{100}{1}$) and multiply:
$$\frac{\cancel{50}^1}{3} \times \frac{1}{\cancel{100}_2} = \frac{1}{6}$$

Try changing these fractions to percents:

61. $\frac{1}{8}$ =

62. $\frac{5}{4}$ =

63. $\frac{7}{12}$ =

Now, change these percents to fractions:

64. 95% =

65. $37\frac{1}{2}$% =

66. 125% =

Sometimes it is more convenient to work with a percentage as a fraction or a decimal. Rather than have to *calculate* the equivalent fraction or decimal, consider memorizing the following equivalence table. Not only will this increase your efficiency on the math test, but it will also be practical for real-life situations.

CONVERSION TABLE		
DECIMAL	**%**	**FRACTION**
0.25	25%	$\frac{1}{4}$
0.50	50%	$\frac{1}{2}$
0.75	75%	$\frac{3}{4}$
0.10	10%	$\frac{1}{10}$
0.20	20%	$\frac{1}{5}$
0.40	40%	$\frac{2}{5}$
0.60	60%	$\frac{3}{5}$
0.80	80%	$\frac{4}{5}$
$0.33\overline{3}$	$33\frac{1}{3}\%$	$\frac{1}{3}$
$0.66\overline{6}$	$66\frac{2}{3}\%$	$\frac{2}{3}$

Percent Word Problems

Word problems involving percents come in three main varieties:

- Find a percent of a whole.
    Example: What is 30% of 40?
- Find what percent one number is of another.
    Example: 12 is what percent of 40?
- Find the whole when the percent of it is given.
    Example: 12 is 30% of what number?

While each variety has its own approach, there is a single shortcut formula you can use to solve each of these:

$$\frac{is}{of} = \frac{\%}{100}$$

The **is** is the number that usually follows or is just before the word *is* in the question. The **of** is the number that usually follows the word *of* in the question. The **%** is the number that is in front of the % or *percent* in the question.

Or you may think of the shortcut formula as:

$$\frac{part}{whole} = \frac{\%}{100}$$

To solve each of the three varieties, let's use the fact that the **cross-products** are equal. The cross-products are the products of the numbers diagonally across from each other. Remembering that *product* means *multiply*, here's how to create the cross-products for the percent shortcut:

$$\frac{part}{whole} = \frac{\%}{100}$$

$$part \times 100 = whole \times \%$$

Here's how to use the shortcut with cross-products:

- Find a percent of a whole.
    What is 30% of 40?
    30 is the % and 40 is the *of* number:
    $$\frac{is}{40} = \frac{30}{100}$$
    Cross multiply and solve for *is*:
    $$is \times 100 = 40 \times 30$$
    $$is \times 100 = 1,200$$
    $$\mathbf{12} \times 100 = 1,200$$
    Thus, **12 is** 30% of 40.
- Find what percent one number is of another number.
    12 is what percent of 40?
    12 is the *is* number and 40 is the *of* number:
    $$\frac{12}{40} = \frac{\%}{100}$$
    Cross multiply and solve for %:
    $$12 \times 100 = 40 \times \%$$
    $$1,200 = 40 \times \%$$
    $$1,200 = 40 \times \mathbf{30}$$
    Thus, 12 is **30% of** 40.

- Find the whole when the percent of it is given.

  12 is 30% of what number?

  12 is the *is* number and 30 is the %:

  $$\frac{12}{of} = \frac{30}{100}$$

  Cross-multiply and solve for the *of* number:

  $$12 \times 100 = of \times 30$$
  $$1{,}200 = of \times 30$$
  $$1{,}200 = \mathbf{40} \times 30$$

  Thus, 12 is 30% **of 40**.

A common type of percentage question involves finding the percentage of *increase* or *decrease* between two numbers. When solving such questions, it is helpful to use the following formula:

$$percent\ of\ change = \frac{amount\ of\ change}{original\ amount}$$

To find the *amount of change*, find the difference between the original number and the new number by using subtraction. Put this answer over the *original amount*. After that number is turned into a percentage, it will be your *percent of change*.

Example

If attendance of a class drops from 50 students in the fall semester to 40 students in the spring semester, find the percent of decrease in the class enrollment.

1. Find the amount of change:

   $$50 - 40 = 10\ students$$

2. Divide the amount of change by the original amount:

   $$\frac{10\ students}{50\ students} = \frac{10}{50}$$

3. Turn that fraction into a percentage:

   $$\frac{10}{50} = \frac{20}{100} = 20\%$$

4. Therefore, the class enrollment dropped by 20%.

Note that if the class enrollment were to rise from 40 students to 50 students, that would not be a 20% increase. Although the amount of change would still be 10 students, the original amount would be 40 students (instead of 50 students), which would change your answer:

1. Amount of change:

   $$50 - 40 = 10\ students$$

2. Divide the amount of change by the original amount:

   $$\frac{10\ students}{40\ students} = \frac{10}{40}$$

3. Turn that fraction into a percentage:

   $$\frac{10}{40} = \frac{1}{4} = 25\%$$

4. Therefore, the class enrollment would have a percentage increase of 25%.

Find a percent of a whole:

67. 1% of 25 =

68. 18.2% of 50 =

69. 42.5% of 200 =

70. 125% of 60 =

Find what percent one number is of another number:

71. 10 is what % of 20?

72. 16 is what % of 24?

73. 12 is what % of 4?

Find the whole when the percent of it is given:

74. 15% of what number is 15?

75. $37\frac{1}{2}$% of what number is 3?

76. 200% of what number is 20?

Now, try your percent skills on some real-life problems:

77. Last Monday, 20% of 140 staff members were absent. How many employees were absent that day?
  a. 14
  b. 28
  c. 112
  d. 126

78. 40% of Vero's postal service employees are women. If there are 80 women in Vero's postal service, how many men are employed there?
  a. 32
  b. 112
  c. 120
  d. 160

79. There are 780 students at Cliffside Park High School. If 273 of them play at least one sport, what percentage of Cliffside Park High School students plays sports?
  a. 27.3%
  b. 2.85%
  c. 30%
  d. 35%

80. Sam's Shoe Store put all of its merchandise on sale for 20% off. If Jason saved $10 by purchasing one pair of shoes during the sale, what was the original price of the shoes?
  a. $12
  b. $20
  c. $40
  d. $50

Averages

An average, also called an **arithmetic mean**, is a number that *typifies* a group of numbers, a measure of central tendency. You come into contact with averages on a regular basis: your bowling average, the average grade on a test, the average number of hours you work per week.

To calculate an average, add the numbers being averaged and divide that total by the number of items.

Example
What is the average of 6, 10, and 20?

Add the three numbers together and divide by 3:
$$\frac{6 + 10 + 20}{3} = \frac{36}{3} = 12$$

Shortcut
Here's a shortcut for some average problems:

- Look at the numbers being averaged. If they are equally spaced, such as 5, 10, 15, 20, and 25, then the average is the number in the middle, or 15 in this case.
- If there is an even number of equally spaced numbers, say 10, 20, 30, and 40, then there is no middle number. In this case, the average is halfway between the two middle numbers. In this case, the average is halfway between 20 and 30, or 25.

- If the numbers are almost evenly spaced, you can probably estimate the average without going to the trouble of actually computing it. For example, the average of 10, 20, and 32 is just a little more than 20, the middle number.

Sometimes you will be asked to find a **weighted average**, which is an average made when some data points occur more frequently than other data points.

Example

Mr. Beasley gave a test in his English class. Five students scored 72, two students scored 78, and three students scored 86. What was the average score for this test?

1. First, you must calculate the total number of data points, which in this question would be the number of students:

    There were 10 students in this class (5 + 3 + 2 = 10).

2. Second, you must calculate the weighted sum of the data by multiplying each data point by the number of times it occurred. In this case, it will be the number of students who scored a particular mark multiplied by their test scores:

    Five students scored 72 = (5 × 72) = 360 points.

    Two students scored 78 = (2 × 78) = 156 points.

    Three students scored 86 = (3 × 86) = 258 points.

    The total number of points was 360 + 156 + 258 = 801.

Then, divide the total number of points by the total number of students:

$$\frac{801 \text{ points}}{10 \text{ students}} = \text{test average of } 80.1$$

Try these average questions:

81. Bob's bowling scores for the last five games were 180, 182, 184, 186, and 188. What was his average bowling score?
   a. 182
   b. 183
   c. 184
   d. 185

82. Conroy averaged 30 miles an hour for the two hours he drove in town and 60 miles an hour for the two hours he drove on the highway. What was his average speed in miles per hour?
   a. 18
   b. $22\frac{1}{2}$
   c. 45
   d. 60

83. A developer wants to cut down the trees on a lot to build condos, but must first calculate the average tree age to determine whether this will be permissible. If there are 12 trees that are 80 years old and 8 trees that are 24 years old, what is the closest approximation of the average age of these trees?
   a. 52 years
   b. 58 years
   c. 60 years
   d. 64 years

Angle   two rays with a common endpoint called a vertex. There are four types of angles:

       Acute: less than 90°

       Obtuse: more than 90°

       Right: 90°

       Straight: 180°

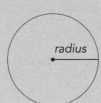

Circle   set of all points that are the same distance from the center.

       Area = πr^2

       Circumference = $2\pi r$

       ($\pi \approx 3.14$; r = radius)

radius

Circumference   distance around a circle. (See *circle*)

Diameter   a line through the center of a circle. The diameter is twice the length of the radius. (See *circle, radius*)

Line   extends endlessly in both directions. It is referred to by a letter next to it or by two points on it. Thus, the line below may be referred to as line *l* or as $\overleftrightarrow{AB}$.

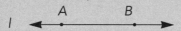

Parallel lines   two lines in the same plane that do not intersect.   *l* _____

       l | | *m*   *m* _____

Perimeter   distance around a figure, such as a triangle or a rectangle. Also known as the sum of length of all sides. The perimeter of a circle is called its *circumference*.

Perpendicular lines   two lines in the same plane that intersect to form four right angles.

Point   has a location but no size or dimension. It is referred to by a letter close to it, like this: • *A*

Radius   line segment from the center to any point on a circle. The radius is half the diameter. (See *circle, diameter*)

Rectangle   four-sided figure with a right angle and both pairs of opposite sides parallel (which implies that all four sides are right angles and that opposite sides are equal in length).

   Area = *length × width*
   Perimeter = 2 × *length* + 2 × *width*

Square   rectangle with four equal sides. (See *rectangle*)

   Area = (*side*)^2
   Perimeter = 4 × *side*

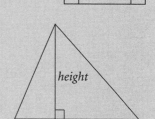

Triangle   three-sided figure.

   Area = $\frac{1}{2}$(*base × height*)
   Perimeter = sum of the lengths of all three sides
   Angles: The sum of the three angles of a triangle is always 180°.

height

base

Geometry

Typically, there are very few geometry problems in the math sections. The problems that are included tend to cover the basics: lines, angles, triangles, rectangles, squares, and circles. You may be asked to find the area or perimeter of a particular shape, or the size of an angle. The arithmetic involved is pretty simple, so all you really need are a few definitions and formulas.

Practice Problems in Geometry

Try your hand at these sample problems:

84. What is the area (in square inches) of a triangle with base 10 inches and height 8 inches?
   a. 80
   b. 40
   c. 20
   d. 10

85. Find the perimeter of a triangle with sides of length 3, 4, and 5 units.
   a. 60 units
   b. 20 units
   c. 12 units
   d. 9 units

86. If the perimeter of a square tabletop is 32 feet, what is the area of this tabletop?
   a. 8 square feet
   b. 16 square feet
   c. 64 square feet
   d. it cannot be determined with the information given

87. The length of a rectangle is twice its width. If the perimeter of the rectangle is 30 units, what is the width of the rectangle?
   a. 30 units
   b. 20 units
   c. 15 units
   d. 5 units

88. A circular opening has a diameter of $8\frac{1}{2}$ inches. What is the radius in inches of a circular disk that will fit exactly into the opening?

   a. 17
   b. 8.5
   c. 8
   d. 4.25

89. The radius of a hoop is 10 inches. If you roll the hoop along a straight path through 6 complete revolutions, approximately how far will it roll, in inches? (Use a value of 3.14 for π.)

   a. 31.4
   b. 62.8
   c. 188.4
   d. 376.8

Algebra

Algebra questions do not appear on every test. However, when they do, they typically cover the material you learned in pre-algebra or in the first few months of your high school algebra course. Popular topics for algebra questions include:

- solving equations
- positive and negative numbers
- algebraic expressions

What Is Algebra?

Algebra is a way to express and solve problems using numbers and symbols. These symbols, called *unknowns* or *variables,* are letters of the alphabet that are used to represent numbers.

For example, let's say you are asked to find out what number, when added to 3, gives you a total of 5. Using algebra, you could express the problem as $x + 3 = 5$. The variable x represents the number you are trying to find.

Here's another example, but this one uses only variables. To find the distance traveled, multiply the rate of travel (speed) by the amount of time traveled: $d = r \times t$. The variable d stands for *distance,* r stands for *rate,* and t stands for *time.*

In algebra, the variables may take on different values. In other words, they *vary,* and that's why they're called *variables.*

Operations

Algebra uses the same operations as arithmetic: addition, subtraction, multiplication, and division. In arithmetic, we might say $3 + 4 = 7$, while in algebra we would talk about two numbers whose values we don't know that add up to 7, or $x + y = 7$. Here's how each operation translates to algebra:

ALGEBRAIC OPERATIONS	
The sum of two numbers	$x + y$
The difference of two numbers	$x - y$
The product of two numbers	$x \times y$ or $x \cdot y$ or xy
The quotient of two numbers	$x \div y$ or $\frac{x}{y}$

Equations

An equation is a mathematical sentence stating that two quantities are equal. For example:

$$2x = 10$$
$$x + 5 = 8$$

The idea is to find a replacement for the unknown that will make the sentence true. That's called *solving* the equation. Thus, in the first example, $x = 5$ because $2 \times 5 = 10$. In the second example, $x = 3$ because $3 + 5 = 8$.

Sometimes you can solve an equation by inspection, as with the previous examples. Other equations may be more complicated and require a step-by-step solution, for example:

$$\frac{n + 2}{4} + 1 = 3$$

The general approach is to consider an equation like a balance scale, with both sides equally balanced. Essentially, whatever you do to one side, you must also do to the other side to maintain the balance. Thus, if you were to add 2 to the left side, you would also have to add 2 to the right side.

Let's apply this *balance* concept to our previous complicated equation. Remembering that if we want to solve it for *n*, we must somehow rearrange it so the *n* is isolated on one side of the equation. Its value will then be on the other side. Looking at the equation, you can see that *n* has been increased by 2, then divided by 4, and ultimately added to 1. Therefore, we will undo these operations to isolate *n*.

Begin by subtracting 1 from both sides of the equation:

$$\begin{array}{rcl} \frac{n+2}{4} + 1 & = & 3 \\ -1 & & -1 \\ \hline \frac{n+2}{4} & = & 2 \end{array}$$

Next, multiply both sides by 4:

$$4 \times \frac{n+2}{4} = 2 \times 4$$
$$n + 2 = 8$$

Finally, subtract 2 from both sides:

$$\begin{array}{rcl} n + 2 & = & 8 \\ -2 & & -2 \\ \hline n & = & 6 \end{array}$$

This isolates *n* and solves the equation.

Notice that each operation in the original equation was undone by using the inverse operation. That is, addition was undone by subtraction, and division was undone by multiplication. In general, each operation can be undone by its *inverse*:

ALGEBRAIC INVERSES	
OPERATION	**INVERSE**
Addition	Subtraction
Subtraction	Addition
Multiplication	Division
Division	Multiplication

After you solve an equation, check your work by plugging the answer back into the original equation to make sure it balances. Let's see what happens when we plug 6 in for *n:*

$$\begin{array}{rcl} \frac{6+2}{4} + 1 & = & 3 \\ \frac{8}{4} + 1 & = & 3 \\ 2 + 1 & = & 3 \\ 3 & = & 3 \end{array}$$

Solve each equation for *x*:

90. $x + 5 = 12$

91. $27 = -13 + 4x$

92. $\frac{1}{4}x = 7$

Positive and Negative Numbers

Positive and negative numbers, also known as *signed* numbers, are best shown as points along the number line:

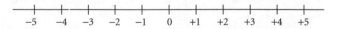

Numbers to the left of 0 are *negative* and those to the right are *positive*. Zero is neither negative nor positive. If a number is written without a sign, it is assumed to be *positive*. Notice that when you are on the negative side of the number line, numbers with bigger values are actually smaller. For example, –5 is *less than* –2. You come into contact with negative numbers more often than you might think; for example, very cold temperatures are recorded as negative numbers.

As you move to the right along the number line, the numbers get larger. Mathematically, to indicate that one number, say 4, is *greater than* another number, say –2, the *greater than* sign (>) is used:

$$4 > -2$$

On the other hand, to say that –2 is *less than* 4, we use the *less than* sign, (<):

$$-2 < 4$$

Arithmetic with Positive and Negative Numbers

The following table illustrates the rules for doing arithmetic with signed numbers. Notice that when a negative number follows an operation (as it does in the second example), it is enclosed in parentheses to avoid confusion.

RULE	EXAMPLE
ADDITION	
■ If both numbers have the same sign, just add them. The answer has the same sign as the numbers being added.	$3 + 5 = 8$ $-3 + (-5) = -8$
■ If both numbers have different signs, subtract the smaller number from the larger. The answer has the same sign as the larger number.	$-3 + 5 = 2$ $3 + (-5) = -2$
■ If both numbers are the same but have opposite signs, the sum is zero.	$3 + (-3) = 0$
SUBTRACTION	
■ Change the sign of the number to be subtracted, then add as above.	$3 - 5 = 3 + (-5) = -2$ $-3 - 5 = -3 + (-5) = -8$ $-3 - (-5) = -3 + 5 = 2$
MULTIPLICATION	
■ Multiply the numbers together. If both numbers have the same sign, the answer is positive; otherwise, it is negative.	$3 \times 5 = 15$ $-3 \times (-5) = 15$ $-3 \times 5 = -15$ $3 \times (-5) = -15$
■ If one or both numbers are zero, the answer is zero.	$3 \times 0 = 0$
DIVISION	
■ Divide the numbers. If both numbers have the same sign, the answer is positive; otherwise, it is negative.	$15 \div 3 = 5$ $-15 \div (-3) = 5$ $15 \div (-3) = -5$ $-15 \div 3 = -5$
■ If the top number is zero, the answer is zero.	$0 \div 3 = 0$
■ A number cannot be divided by zero.	$3 \div 0 =$ INVALID

When more than one arithmetic operation appears, you must know the correct sequence in which to perform the operations. For example, do you know what to do first to calculate $2 + 3 \times 4$? You're right if you said multiply. The correct answer is 14. If you add first, you will get the wrong answer of 20. The correct sequence of operations is:

1. **P**arentheses
2. **E**xponents
3. **M**ultiplication & **D**ivision (in order from left to right)
4. **A**ddition & **S**ubtraction (in order from left to right)

This saying can help you remember the order of operations:

Please **E**xcuse **M**y **D**ear **A**unt **S**ally

It is important to remember that multiplication and division are done in order from left to right, and that sometimes multiplication will come *after* division. The same is true of addition and subtraction.

Example
$24 \div 8 \times 10$
$(24 \div 8) \times 10$ [not $24 \div (8 \times 10)$]
$3 \times 10 = 30$

If the multiplication of 8×10 had been done first, the answer would have worked out to $24 \div 80$, which is not equal to 30, and is incorrect.

Even when signed numbers appear in an equation, the step-by-step solution works exactly as it does for positive numbers. You just have to remember the arithmetic rules for negative numbers. For example, let's solve $14x + 2 = 5$.

1. Subtract 2 from both sides:
$$-14x + 2 = -5$$
$$\underline{\quad -2 \qquad -2 \quad}$$
$$-14x = -7$$

2. Divide both sides by -14:
$$-14x \div -14 = -7 \div -14$$
$$x = \tfrac{1}{2}$$

Now, try these problems with signed numbers. Solve for x.

93. $1 - 3 \times (-4) = x$

94. $-3x + 6 = -18$

95. $\frac{x}{-4} + 3 = -7$

Algebraic Expressions

An algebraic expression is a group of numbers, unknowns, and arithmetic operations, like $3x - 2y$. This one may be translated as, "3 times some number minus 2 times another number." To *evaluate* an algebraic expression, replace each variable with its value. For example, if $x = 5$ and $y = 4$, we would evaluate $3x - 2y$ as follows:

$$3(5) - 2(4) = 15 - 8 = 7$$

Evaluate these expressions:

96. $4a + 3b$; $a = 2$ and $b = -1$

97. $-10j - r + 3jr$; $j = -7$ and $r = 4$

98. $-2x - \frac{1}{2}y + 4z$; $x = 5$, $y = -4$, and $z = 6$

99. The volume of a cylinder is given by the formula $V = \pi r^2 h$, where r is the radius of the base and h is the height of the cylinder. What is the volume of a cylinder with a base radius of 3 and a height of 4? (Leave π in your answer.)

100. If $x = 3$, what is the value of $3x - x$?

Answers

Word Problems
1. a.
2. d.
3. d.
4. d.

Fractions
5. $\frac{1}{4}$
6. $\frac{2}{5}$
7. $\frac{4}{7}$
8. 10
9. 6
10. 200
11. $\frac{11}{12}$
12. $\frac{55}{24}$ or $2\frac{7}{24}$
13. $\frac{29}{4}$ or $7\frac{1}{4}$
14. $\frac{2}{15}$
15. $\frac{1}{8}$
16. $\frac{76}{21}$ or $3\frac{13}{21}$
17. a.
18. b.
19. $\frac{5}{6}$
20. $\frac{8}{35}$
21. $\frac{2}{3}$
22. $\frac{26}{15}$ or $1\frac{11}{15}$
23. $\frac{58}{1}$ or 58
24. $\frac{33}{2}$ or $16\frac{1}{2}$
25. c.
26. d.
27. c.
28. $\frac{1}{2}$
29. $\frac{11}{2}$ or $5\frac{1}{2}$
30. $\frac{1}{5}$

31. $\frac{45}{28}$ or $1\frac{17}{28}$
32. b.
33. c.
34. b.

Decimals
35. $\frac{5}{1,000}$ or $\frac{1}{200}$
36. $3\frac{12}{25}$
37. $123\frac{456}{1,000}$ or $123\frac{57}{125}$
38. 707.707
39. 8.305
40. 0.907
41. 1.456
42. d.
43. b.
44. 0.03
45. 0.3392
46. 0.70104
47. c.
48. d.
49. 1.4
50. 128
51. 57.2
52. 1,400
53. a.
54. c.

Percents
55. 45%
56. 0.8%
57. 8.75% or $8\frac{3}{4}$%
58. 0.12
59. 0.875
60. 2.5
61. 12.5% or $12\frac{1}{2}$%
62. 125%
63. $58.\overline{3}$% or $58\frac{1}{3}$%
64. $\frac{19}{20}$
65. $\frac{3}{8}$

66. $\frac{5}{4}$ or $1\frac{1}{4}$

67. $\frac{1}{4}$ or 0.25

68. 9.1

69. 85

70. 75

71. 50%

72. $66.66\overline{6}$ or $66.66\frac{2}{3}\%$

73. 300%

74. 100

75. 8

76. 10

77. b.

78. c.

79. d.

80. d.

Averages

81. c.

82. c.

83. b.

Geometry

84. b.

85. c.

86. c.

87. d.

88. d.

89. d.

Algebra

90. 7

91. 10

92. 28

93. 13

94. 8

95. 40

96. 5

97. -18

98. 16

99. 36π

100. 6

MATH PRACTICE

CHAPTER SUMMARY

This chapter gives you an opportunity for more practice with math.

I f you feel like you could use some more practice with fractions, decimals, ratios, percentages, and word problems, try the questions or exercises in this chapter. The answers are given at the end. If there is a specific type of math question that gives you trouble, go back to Chapter 6 and review the rules. Remember, the more math exercises you do, the closer you are to mastering the two math sections of the ASVAB that count toward the Armed Forces Qualifying Test score—Arithmetic Reasoning and Mathematics Knowledge.

Arithmetic Reasoning

1. ⓐ ⓑ ⓒ ⓓ
2. ⓐ ⓑ ⓒ ⓓ
3. ⓐ ⓑ ⓒ ⓓ
4. ⓐ ⓑ ⓒ ⓓ
5. ⓐ ⓑ ⓒ ⓓ
6. ⓐ ⓑ ⓒ ⓓ

7. ⓐ ⓑ ⓒ ⓓ
8. ⓐ ⓑ ⓒ ⓓ
9. ⓐ ⓑ ⓒ ⓓ
10. ⓐ ⓑ ⓒ ⓓ
11. ⓐ ⓑ ⓒ ⓓ
12. ⓐ ⓑ ⓒ ⓓ

13. ⓐ ⓑ ⓒ ⓓ
14. ⓐ ⓑ ⓒ ⓓ
15. ⓐ ⓑ ⓒ ⓓ
16. ⓐ ⓑ ⓒ ⓓ
17. ⓐ ⓑ ⓒ ⓓ

Mathematics Knowledge

18. ⓐ ⓑ ⓒ ⓓ
19. ⓐ ⓑ ⓒ ⓓ
20. ⓐ ⓑ ⓒ ⓓ
21. ⓐ ⓑ ⓒ ⓓ
22. ⓐ ⓑ ⓒ ⓓ
23. ⓐ ⓑ ⓒ ⓓ
24. ⓐ ⓑ ⓒ ⓓ
25. ⓐ ⓑ ⓒ ⓓ

26. ⓐ ⓑ ⓒ ⓓ
27. ⓐ ⓑ ⓒ ⓓ
28. ⓐ ⓑ ⓒ ⓓ
29. ⓐ ⓑ ⓒ ⓓ
30. ⓐ ⓑ ⓒ ⓓ
31. ⓐ ⓑ ⓒ ⓓ
32. ⓐ ⓑ ⓒ ⓓ
33. ⓐ ⓑ ⓒ ⓓ

34. ⓐ ⓑ ⓒ ⓓ
35. ⓐ ⓑ ⓒ ⓓ
36. ⓐ ⓑ ⓒ ⓓ
37. ⓐ ⓑ ⓒ ⓓ
38. ⓐ ⓑ ⓒ ⓓ
39. ⓐ ⓑ ⓒ ⓓ
40. ⓐ ⓑ ⓒ ⓓ

Arithmetic Reasoning

1. Derek earns $64.00 per day and spends $4.00 per day on transportation. What fraction of Derek's daily earnings does he spend on transportation?

  a. $\frac{1}{32}$

  b. $\frac{15}{16}$

  c. $\frac{1}{16}$

  d. $\frac{1}{8}$

2. A bread recipe calls for $6\frac{1}{2}$ cups of flour, but Leonard has only $5\frac{1}{3}$ cups. How much more flour does Leonard need?

  a. $\frac{2}{3}$ cup

  b. $\frac{5}{6}$ cup

  c. $1\frac{1}{6}$ cups

  d. $1\frac{1}{4}$ cups

3. Over a period of four days, Roberto drove a total of 956.58 miles. What is the average number of miles Roberto drove each day?

  a. 239.145

  b. 239.250

  c. 249.145

  d. 239.445

4. Finer Fabric International sells a total of $880,600.00 in fabrics during the course of the year. If 32% of the company's sales went to pay for labor to make those fabrics, how much money did Finer Fabric International spend on this labor?

  a. $28,179.20

  b. $32,000.00

  c. $281,792.00

  d. $598,808.00

5. The cost of milk at Jonesy Smith Grocery rose from $2.50 to $2.80 over the course of several months. What was the percentage increase in the cost of milk?

  a. 12%

  b. 30%

  c. 10.7%

  d. 8%

6. On a state road map, one inch represents 20 miles. Denise wants to travel from Garden City to Marshalltown, which is a distance of $4\frac{1}{4}$ inches on the map. How many miles will Denise travel?

  a. 45

  b. 80

  c. 85

  d. 90

7. In the freshman class, the ratio of in-state students to out-of-state students is 15 to 2. If there are 750 in-state students in the class, how many out-of-state students are there?

  a. 100

  b. 115

  c. 150

  d. 5,625

8. At the Greene County Summer Fair, Brad sold the following pieces of artwork: a sculpture for $80, an oil painting for $168, an ink drawing for $52, and a photograph for $52. What was the average (mean) price for the pieces of artwork he sold?

  a. $52

  b. $66

  c. $88

  d. $124

9. A bag contains 105 jelly beans: 23 white, 23 red, 14 purple, 26 yellow, and 19 green. What is the probability of selecting either a yellow or a green jelly bean?

   a. $\frac{3}{7}$

   b. $\frac{1}{6}$

   c. $\frac{4}{7}$

   d. $\frac{2}{5}$

10. A can contains 200 mixed nuts: almonds, cashews, and peanuts. If the probability of choosing an almond is $\frac{1}{10}$ and the probability of choosing a cashew is $\frac{1}{4}$, how many peanuts are in the can?

   a. 70

   b. 110

   c. 130

   d. 180

11. Tatum used a $100.00 bill to buy a chair for her office. The chair cost $60.00 plus an additional 8% tax. How much change did she receive after purchasing the chair with the $100.00 bill?

   a. $32.00

   b. $32.50

   c. $35.20

   d. $64.80

12. Colleen purchased a large bag of apples. She used $\frac{1}{2}$ of them to make applesauce. Of those she had left, she used $\frac{3}{4}$ to make an apple pie. When she was finished, she had only three apples left. How many apples were there to begin with?

   a. 21

   b. 24

   c. 27

   d. 48

13. Of the 80 employees working on the road construction crew, 35% worked overtime this week. How many employees did NOT work overtime?

   a. 28

   b. 45

   c. 52

   d. 56

14. If Lydia's height is $\frac{2}{a}$ of Francine's height and Francine is b inches tall, how tall is Lydia?

   a. $\frac{2}{ab}$ inches

   b. $2(ab)$ inches

   c. $\frac{ba}{2}$ inches

   d. $\frac{2b}{a}$ inches

15. A triangle has an area of 9 square inches. If its base is 3 inches, what is its height in inches?

   a. 3

   b. 4

   c. 6

   d. 12

16. What are the dimensions of a rectangular room with a perimeter of 42 feet if the long side is twice as long as the short side?

   a. 7 feet by 14 feet

   b. 8 feet by 16 feet

   c. 14 feet by 28 feet

   d. 12 feet by 24 feet

17. Celine has a fish tank in the shape of a cube. If the volume of her fish tank is 1,000 cubic inches, what is the area of one of the sides of Celine's fish tank?

   a. 10 square inches

   b. 100 square inches

   c. 333 square inches

   d. 666 square inches

Mathematics Knowledge

18. Name the fraction that indicates the shaded part of the figure below.

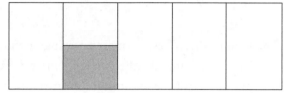

   a. $\frac{2}{5}$

   b. $\frac{1}{5}$

   c. $\frac{1}{6}$

   d. $\frac{1}{10}$

19. Four ounces is what fraction of a pound? (one pound = 16 ounces)

   a. $\frac{1}{3}$

   b. $\frac{2}{5}$

   c. $\frac{1}{4}$

   d. $\frac{1}{8}$

20. Which has the smallest value?

   a. $-\frac{1}{2}$

   b. -1

   c. 0

   d. $-\frac{7}{6}$

21. What is the decimal value of $\frac{5}{8}$?

   a. 0.58

   b. 0.625

   c. 0.875

   d. 6.25

22. Raise $\frac{5}{9}$ to 36ths.

   a. $\frac{18}{36}$

   b. $\frac{20}{36}$

   c. $\frac{24}{36}$

   d. $\frac{30}{36}$

23. $2\frac{4}{5} \div 7 =$

   a. $\frac{2}{5}$

   b. $\frac{98}{5}$

   c. $\frac{5}{2}$

   d. $\frac{8}{35}$

24. $4 - 1\frac{4}{5} =$

   a. $2\frac{1}{5}$

   b. $2\frac{4}{5}$

   c. $3\frac{3}{10}$

   d. $3\frac{1}{5}$

25. $\frac{5}{8} \times \frac{4}{15} =$

   a. $\frac{1}{6}$

   b. $\frac{1}{5}$

   c. $\frac{9}{23}$

   d. $\frac{75}{32}$

26. $\frac{1}{2} \times 16 \times \frac{3}{8} =$

   a. $\frac{1}{3}$

   b. $\frac{15}{16}$

   c. 3

   d. $\frac{20}{11}$

27. A cement truck must distribute $13\frac{3}{4}$ tons of cement evenly to five work sites. How many tons should it give to each work site?

   a. 2

   b. $2\frac{1}{4}$

   c. $2\frac{1}{2}$

   d. $2\frac{3}{4}$

28. What is 0.7849 rounded to the nearest hundredth?

   a. 0.8

   b. 0.78

   c. 0.785

   d. 0.79

29. 2.36 + 14 + 0.083 =
   a. 14.359
   b. 16.343
   c. 16.443
   d. 17.443

30. 1.5 − 0.188 =
   a. −0.38
   b. 1.222
   c. 1.23
   d. 1.312

31. 12 − 0.92 + 4.6 =
   a. 17.52
   b. 16.68
   c. 15.68
   d. 7.4

32. 2.39 × 10,000 =
   a. 239
   b. 2,390
   c. 23,900
   d. 239,000

33. 5 × 0.0063 =
   a. 0.0315
   b. 0.315
   c. 3.15
   d. 31.5

34. 45% is equal to what fraction?
   a. $\frac{4}{5}$
   b. $\frac{5}{8}$
   c. $\frac{25}{50}$
   d. $\frac{9}{20}$

35. 0.925 is equal to what percent?
   a. 925%
   b. 92.5%
   c. 9.25%
   d. 0.00925%

36. What is 12% of 60?
   a. 5
   b. 7.2
   c. 52.8
   d. 72

37. If 600 college freshman are entering Edenford University and 330 of them are female, what percentage of the incoming freshmen are male?
   a. 27%
   b. 40%
   c. 45%
   d. 55%

38. Katherine has written 42 pages of her doctorate thesis. If she has written 28% of her doctorate thesis, how many pages will her finished thesis be?
   a. 59 pages
   b. 150 pages
   c. 162 pages
   d. 1,176 pages

39. Which of the following is an obtuse angle?

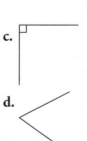

40. What is the perimeter of the polygon?

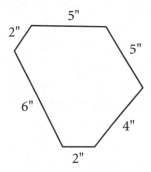

a. 24"
b. 25"
c. 27"
d. 32"

Answers

Arithmetic Reasoning

1. This is a fractions problem.

   c. The portion spent on transportation is $\frac{4.00}{64.00} = \frac{1}{16}$. Choice **a** is incorrect because that would correspond to $2 per day on transportation. Choice **b** is incorrect because this is the portion NOT spent on transportation. Choice **d** is incorrect because that would correspond to $8 per day on transportation.

2. This is a fractions problem.

   c. Raise the fractional parts to sixths and then subtract: $6\frac{1}{2} - 5\frac{1}{3} = 6\frac{3}{6} - 5\frac{2}{6} = 1\frac{1}{6}$. Choice **a** is incorrect because you would have only 6 cups after adding this amount of flour. Choice **b** is incorrect because you subtracted $5\frac{2}{3}$ from $6\frac{1}{2}$. Choice **d** is incorrect because this is slightly too much flour; this would be $6\frac{7}{12}$ cups, not $6\frac{1}{2}$ cups.

3. This is an averages problem.

   a. $956.58 ÷ 4 = $239.145. Choice **b** is incorrect because the decimal portion is wrong. Choice **c** is incorrect because the tenths digit is wrong. Choice **d** is incorrect because the tens digit is wrong.

4. This is a percents problem.

   c. Using 32% = 0.32, multiply to get ($880,600)(0.32) = $281,792.00. Choice **a** is incorrect because this is 3.2%, not 32%. Choice **b** is incorrect because you misinterpreted how to compute a percent. Choice **d** is incorrect because this is 68% of the amount and corresponds to the amount the company didn't spend on labor to make the fabrics.

5. This is a percents problem.

   a. Subtract the current amount minus the original amount to get $2.80 − $2.50 = $0.30. Then, divide this increase by the original amount to get $\frac{0.30}{2.50} = 0.12$. So, the percent increase is 12%. Choice **b** is incorrect because you forgot to divide the difference in price by the original amount. Choice **c** is incorrect because you divided the difference in price by the current amount instead of the original amount. Choice **d** is incorrect because you computed the difference in price as 0.20, not 0.30.

6. This is a fractions problem.

   c. $(4\frac{1}{4} \text{ in.}) \times \left(\frac{20 \text{ miles}}{1 \text{ in.}}\right) = (4\frac{1}{4} \times 20)$ miles $= (\frac{17}{4} \times 20)$ miles $= 85$ miles. Choice **a** is incorrect because this corresponds to $2\frac{1}{4}$ inches, not $4\frac{1}{4}$ inches. Choice **b** is incorrect because you converted $4\frac{1}{4}$ to $\frac{16}{4}$, not $\frac{17}{4}$. Choice **d** is incorrect because this corresponds to $4\frac{1}{2}$ inches, not $4\frac{1}{4}$ inches.

7. This is a fractions problem.

   a. Set up a proportion: $\frac{15}{2} = \frac{750}{p}$. Solve this for p by cross-multiplying and then dividing by the coefficient of p: $15p = 1{,}500$, so $p = 100$. Choice **b** is incorrect because you divided incorrectly. Choice **c** is incorrect because you used the ratio in-state to out-of-state as 15:3, not 15:2. Choice **d** is incorrect because you set up the proportion incorrectly—you flipped one of the fractions.

8. This is an averages problem.

   c. Add the amounts and divide by 4: $\frac{\$80 + \$168 + \$52 + \$52}{4} = \$88$. Choice **a** is incorrect because it is the mode, not the mean. Choice **b** is incorrect because it is the median, not the mean. Choice **d** is incorrect because this is only the average of the two highest priced pieces of art.

9. This is a fractions problem.

   a. There are $26 + 19 = 45$ ways to get either a yellow jelly bean or a green jelly bean. The total number of jelly beans in the bag is 105. So, the probability of getting yellow or green is $\frac{45}{105} = \frac{3}{7}$. Choice **b** is incorrect because you didn't compute the correct quotient. Choice **c** is incorrect because this is the probability of NOT getting yellow or green. Choice **d** is incorrect because there are unequal amounts of the different colors of jelly bean, but the computation leading to this choice assumes that all colors are equally likely to be chosen.

10. This is a fractions problem.

   c. The probability of choosing a peanut equals 1 *minus* the probability of choosing either an almond or a cashew. This equals $1 - (\frac{1}{4} + \frac{1}{10}) = \frac{26}{40} = \frac{13}{20}$. So, the total number of peanuts is $\frac{13}{20} \times 200 = 130$. Choice **a** is incorrect because this is the number of cashews and almonds. Choice **b** is incorrect because you computed the probability of getting a peanut as being $\frac{11}{20}$, not $\frac{13}{20}$. Choice **d** is incorrect because you didn't account for the number of cashews in the can.

11. This is a percents problem.

   c. The 8% tax is $(\$60)(0.08) = \$4.80$. The total bill is $\$60 + \$4.80 = \$64.80$. So, the change she gets back is $\$100 - \$64.80 = \$35.20$. Choice **a** is incorrect because you computed 8% tax on $100, not the cost of the item. Choice **b** is incorrect because you interchanged the digits in the ones and tenths places. Choice **d** is incorrect because this is the total cost, not the amount of change she gets back.

12. This is an algebra problem.

   b. Let x = the number of apples she has to begin with. Then, $\frac{1}{2}x$ = number of apples used for applesauce; $\frac{3}{4}(\frac{1}{2}x)$ number of apples used for pie; 3 = number of apples left over after making applesauce and pie. So, $x = \frac{1}{2}x + \frac{3}{4}(\frac{1}{2}x) + 3$. Solve for x, as follows:

$$x = \frac{1}{2}x + \frac{3}{8}x + 3$$
$$x = \frac{7}{8}x + 3$$
$$\frac{1}{8}x = 3$$
$$x = 24$$

Choice **a** is incorrect because you subtracted the 3 apples left over from the correct total. Choice **c** is incorrect because you added 3 apples to the total. Choice **d** is incorrect because this is twice too many apples. You likely added the fractions incorrectly.

13. This is a percents problem.

   c. First, compute 35% of 80: $(80)(0.35) = 28$. This is the number who *did* work overtime. Now, subtract this from 80 to conclude that 52 did NOT work overtime. Choice **a** is incorrect because this is the number who *did* work overtime. Choice **b** is incorrect because 35% of 80 is not 35; you computed 35% of 100. Choice **d** is incorrect because you used 30% instead of 35%.

14. This is an algebra problem.

   d. Multiply $\frac{2}{a}$ times b inches to get that $\frac{2b}{a}$ inches is Lydia's height. Choice **a** is incorrect because you divided $\frac{2}{a}$ by b; you should have multiplied these two quantities. Choice **b** is incorrect because you didn't treat the fraction $\frac{2}{a}$ correctly. Choice **c** is incorrect because you divided in the wrong order.

15. This is a geometry problem.

   c. Use the area formula $A = \frac{1}{2}(\text{base})(\text{height})$:

$$9 = \frac{1}{2}(3)(\text{height})$$
$$9 = \frac{3}{2}(\text{height})$$
$$9(\tfrac{2}{3}) = \text{height}$$
$$6 = \text{height}$$

Choice **a** is incorrect because you used the area formula incorrectly. Choice **b** is incorrect because you used $\frac{3}{4}$ instead of $\frac{1}{2}$ in the area formula. Choice **d** is incorrect because you used $\frac{1}{4}$ instead of $\frac{1}{2}$ in the area formula.

16. This is a geometry problem.

   a. Use w = length of the short side. Then, $2w$ = length of the longer side. Since the perimeter is 42, we have $2(w) + 2(2w) = 42$, which simplifies to $6w = 42$. Solving for w yields $w = 7$. So, the short side is 7 feet and the long side is 14 feet. Choice **b** is incorrect because the perimeter would be 48 feet, not 42 feet. Choice **c** is incorrect because you forgot to count the long side and short side each twice in the perimeter calculation. Choice **d** is incorrect because the perimeter would be 72 feet, not 42 feet.

17. This is a geometry problem.

   b. Use the formula $V = (\text{edge})^3$ to find the length of an edge: $1{,}000 = (\text{edge})^3$, so that taking the cube root of both sides, we see that an edge is 10 inches. So, the area of one of the sides is $(\text{edge})^2 = (10 \text{ in.})^2 = 100$ square inches. Choice **a** is incorrect because this is the length of an edge. Choice **c** is incorrect because you divided the volume by 3 instead of taking the cube root to find an edge. Choice **d** is incorrect because you divided the volume by 3 and multiplied by 2 to find the area—both computations are wrong.

33. This is a decimals problem.

    a. $(0.0063)(5) = 0.0315$. Choice **b** is incorrect because you moved the decimal point only three places instead of four after multiplying $63(5)$. Choice **c** is incorrect because you moved the decimal point only two places instead of four after multiplying $63(5)$. Choice **d** is incorrect because you moved the decimal point only one place instead of four after multiplying $63(5)$.

34. This is a percents problem.

    d. $45\% = \frac{45}{100} = \frac{9}{20}$. Choice **a** is incorrect because $\frac{4}{5}$ is equal to 0.80, which is 80%. Choice **b** is incorrect because $\frac{5}{8}$ is equal to 0.625, which is 62.5%. Choice **c** is incorrect because $\frac{1}{2}$ is equal to 0.50, which is 50%.

35. This is a percents problem.

    b. Move the decimal point two places to the right to get $0.925 = 92.5\%$. Choice **a** is incorrect because you moved the decimal point one too many places to the right. Choice **c** is incorrect because you moved the decimal point one too few places to the right. Choice **d** is incorrect because you moved the decimal point two places left instead of right.

36. This is a percents problem.

    b. 12% of $60 = (60)(0.12) = 7.2$. Choice **a** is incorrect because $12(5) = 60$, but this is not a correct interpretation of computing a percent. Choice **c** is incorrect because this is 88% of 60, not 12%. Choice **d** is incorrect because this is 120% of 60, not 12%; you mistakenly said $12\% = 1.2$ instead of 0.12.

37. This is a percents problem.

    c. There are $600 - 330 = 270$ male freshmen. So, the percentage is $\frac{270}{600} = \frac{9}{20} = 45\%$. Choice **a** is incorrect because you didn't divide 270 by the number of students (600); rather, you divided by 1,000. Choice **b** is incorrect because you converted the fraction incorrectly. Choice **d** is incorrect because this is the percentage of female freshmen.

38. This is a percents problem.

    b. Let $x =$ number of pages of the entire thesis. Then, 28% of x is 42, which can be written symbolically as $0.28x = 42$. So, $x = 150$. Choice **a** is incorrect because you used 72% (the percent left to go) in place of 28% in the computation. Choice **c** is incorrect because this is slightly too high and is likely the result of an arithmetic error. Choice **d** is incorrect because you incorrectly multiplied 28 times 42.

39. This is a geometry problem.

    b. This is the only one whose measure is between 90° and 180°. Choice **a** is incorrect because this is an acute angle. Choice **c** is incorrect because this is a right angle. Choice **d** is incorrect because this is an acute angle.

40. This is a geometry problem.

    a. Add the lengths of all sides: $2'' + 5'' + 5'' + 4'' + 2'' + 6'' = 24''$. Choices **b**, **c**, and **d** are incorrect because of arithmetic errors. Add all sides together.

8 ▶ WORD KNOWLEDGE REVIEW

CHAPTER SUMMARY

This chapter will help you improve your vocabulary skills so that you can score higher on the Word Knowledge section of the ASVAB.

The Word Knowledge subtest of the ASVAB is basically a vocabulary test. Combined with the Paragraph Comprehension score, Word Knowledge helps make up your Verbal Expression score—it is one of the four subtests that determine whether you will be allowed to enlist. Your ability to understand your training materials depends in part on your reading comprehension and vocabulary skills.

There are two different kinds of questions on the Word Knowledge subtest:

- **Synonyms**—identifying words that mean the same as the given words
- **Context**—determining the meaning of a word or phrase by noting how it is used in a sentence or paragraph

Synonym Questions

A word is a **synonym** of another word if it has the same or nearly the same meaning. Test questions will ask you to find the synonym of a word. If you're lucky, the word will be in the context of a sentence that helps you guess what the word means. If you're less lucky, you will get just the word, and then you have to figure out what the word means without any context.

Questions that ask for synonyms can be tricky because they require you to recognize the meaning of several words that may be unfamiliar—not only the words in the questions, but also those in the answer choices. Usually, the best strategy is to *look* at the structure of the word and to *listen* for its sound. See if a part of the word looks familiar. Think of other words you know that have similar key elements. How could those words be related?

Synonym Practice Questions

Try identifying the word parts and related words in these sample synonym questions. Circle the word that means the same or about the same as the underlined word. Answers and explanations appear right after the questions.

1. incoherent answer
   a. not understandable
   b. not likely
   c. undeniable
   d. challenging

2. ambiguous questions
   a. meaningless
   b. difficult
   c. simple
   d. vague

3. covered with debris
   a. good excuses
   b. transparent material
   c. scattered rubble
   d. protective material

4. inadvertently left
   a. mistakenly
   b. purposely
   c. cautiously
   d. carefully

5. exorbitant prices
   a. expensive
   b. unexpected
   c. reasonable
   d. outrageous

6. cantankerous mood
   a. silly
   b. irritable
   c. humorous
   d. shallow

7. belligerent attitude
   a. hostile
   b. reasonable
   c. instinctive
   d. friendly

Answers to Synonym Practice Questions

The explanations are important because they show you how to go about choosing a synonym if you don't know the word.

1. **a.** *Incoherent* means not understandable. To *cohere* means to connect. A *coherent* answer connects or makes sense. The prefix *in-* means not.

2. **d.** *Ambiguous* questions are *vague* or uncertain. The key part of this word is *ambi-*, which means two or both. An ambiguous question can be taken two ways.

3. **c.** *Debris* is scattered fragments and trash.

4. **a.** *Inadvertently* means by mistake. The key element in this word is the prefix *in-*, which usually means not, or the opposite of.

5. **d.** The key element here is *ex-*, which means out of or away from. *Exorbitant* literally means "out of orbit." An exorbitant price would be an *outrageous* one.

6. b. *Cantankerous* means *irritable*.

7. a. The key element in this word is the root *belli-*, which means warlike. The synonym choice, then, is *hostile*.

Context Questions

Context is the surrounding text in which a word is used. Most people use context to help them determine the meaning of an unknown word. A vocabulary question that gives you a sentence around the vocabulary word is usually easier to answer than one with little or no context. The surrounding text can help you as you look for synonyms for the specified words in the sentences.

The best way to take meaning from context is to look for key words in sentences or paragraphs that convey the meaning of the text. If nothing else, the context will give you a means to eliminate wrong answer choices that clearly don't fit. The process of elimination will often leave you with the correct answer.

Context Practice Questions

Try these sample questions. Circle the word that best describes the meaning of the italicized word in the sentence.

8. The maintenance workers were *appalled* by the filthy, cluttered condition of the building.
  a. horrified
  b. amused
  c. surprised
  d. dismayed

9. Even though she seemed rich, the defendant claimed to be *destitute*.
  a. wealthy
  b. ambitious
  c. solvent
  d. poor

10. Though she was *distraught* over losing her keys, the woman was calm enough to remember she had a spare set.
  a. punished
  b. distracted
  c. composed
  d. anguished

11. Their new house was *palatial* compared to their old, run-down apartment.
  a. adequate
  b. luxurious
  c. secure
  d. modern

Answers to Context Practice Questions

Check your answers and see whether you were able to pick out the key words that help to define the target word.

8. a. The key words *filthy* and *cluttered* signify horror rather than the milder emotions described by the other choices.

9. d. The key word here is *rich*, but this is a clue by contrast. The introductory *even though* signals that you should look for the opposite of the idea of having financial resources.

10. d. The key words here are *though* and *losing her keys*, signaling that you are looking for an opposite of *calm* in describing the woman. The only word strong enough to match the situation is *anguish*.

11. b. The key words here are *old* and *run-down*, but this is a clue by contrast. The words *compared to* signal that you should look for the opposite of such a description.

Be very careful not to be confused by the sound of words that may mislead you. Look at the word carefully, and pay attention to the structure and appearance of the word as well as its sound. You may be used to hearing English words spoken with an accent. The sounds of those words may be misleading in choosing a correct answer.

Word Parts

The best way to improve your vocabulary is to learn word parts: roots, which are the main part of the word; prefixes, which go before the root word; or suffixes, which go after. Any of these elements can carry meaning or change the use of a word in a sentence. For instance, the suffix *-s* or *-es* can change the meaning of a noun from singular to plural: *boy, boys.* The prefix *un-* can change the meaning of a root word to its opposite: *necessary, unnecessary.*

In the sections on **prefixes** and **suffixes** are some of the word elements seen most often in vocabulary tests. Simply reading them and their examples for five to ten minutes a day will give you the quick recognition you need to make a good association with the meaning of an unfamiliar word.

Prefixes

In order to be able to unlock the meaning of many words in our language, it is useful for you to understand what a prefix is. A prefix is a word part at the beginning of a word that changes or adds to the meaning of the root word in some way. By learning some common prefixes, you will learn to recognize many unfamiliar words. After you have completed the exercises in this chapter, you will become acquainted with the meanings suggested by some of the more common prefixes, which will improve your reading, speaking, and listening vocabularies.

antebellum *adj.*　　(an·ti·ˈbel·əm)
prefix: **ante-** means before
before the war
The event occurred during the _____ years of 1840–1861.

antipathy *noun*　　(an·ˈtip·ə·thē)
prefix: **anti-** means against
revulsion; any object of strong dislike
The child had an _____ toward snakes.

circumvent *verb*　　(sər·kəm·ˈvent)
prefix: **circum-** and **circ-** mean around
to go around; to catch in a trap; to gain superiority over; to prevent from happening
Police tried to _____ the riot by moving the crowd along.

consensus *noun*　　(kən·ˈsen·səs)
prefix: **con-** means with, together
agreement, especially in opinion
The committee reached a _____ about taxing soft drinks.

controversy *noun*　　(ˈkon·trə·ver·sē)
prefix: **contr-** means against
a discussion in which opposing views clash
There is a _____ about building nuclear power plants.

decimate *verb*   (ˊdes·i·māt)
prefix: **dec-** means ten
to destroy or kill a large portion of something; to
    take or destroy a tenth part of something
Caterpillars can _____ trees.

demote *verb*   (di·mōt)
prefix: **de-** means down, away from
to lower in grade or position
Upper ranked officers can _____ a lower ranked
    person.

distaste *noun*   (dis·ˊtāst)
prefix: **dis-** means not, opposite of
not savory, comfortable, or pleasing
A lazy person has a _____ for work.

euphemism *noun*   (ˊu·fə·mizm)
prefix: **eu-** means good, well
the use of a word or phrase that is considered less
    distasteful or offensive than another
"She was let go" is a _____ for "she was fired."

exorbitant *adj.*   (ek·ˊzor·bi·tənt)
prefix: **ex-** means out of, away from
going beyond what is reasonable and proper
The colonists rebelled against _____ taxes.

illegible *adj.*   (i·ˊlej·ə·bəl)
prefix: **il-** means not, opposite
not able to be read
The student had to rewrite the _____ paper.

intermittent *adj.*   (in·tər·ˊmit·ənt)
prefix: **inter-** means between
stopping and starting again at intervals
The weather forecaster predicted _____ showers.

malady *noun*   (mal·ˊəd·ē)
prefix: **mal-** means bad
a disease or disorder
His doctor said he had a serious _____.

precursor *noun*   (prē·ˊkər·sər)
prefix: **pre-** means before
a forerunner, a harbinger; one who, or that which
    goes before
Calmness is usually a _____ to a storm.

prognosis *noun*   (prog·ˊnō·sis)
prefix: **pro-** means before
a forecast, especially in medicine
The injured animal's _____ for recovery is good.

retrospect   (ˊret·rō·spekt)
prefix: **retro-** means back, again
1. *verb*
to think about the past
2. *noun*
looking back on or thinking about things past
In _____, the world leader wished he had acted
    differently.

subordinate   (sub·´or·din·it)
prefix: **sub-** means under
1. *adj.*
inferior to or placed below another in rank, power,
　　or importance
2. *noun*
a person or thing of lesser power or importance
　　than another
3. *verb*   (sub·´or·din·āt)
to treat as inferior or less important
The wise president treated her _____ with
　　respect.

synthesis *noun*   (´sin·thə·sis)
prefix: **syn-** or **sym-** means with or together
putting of two or more things together to form a
　　whole
In chemistry, the process of making a compound by
　　joining elements together is called _____.

transmute *verb*   (trans·´müt)
prefix: **trans-** means across
to change or alter
The music will gradually _____ into a crescendo.

tripod *noun*   (´trī·päd)
prefix: **tri-** means three
three-footed
The photographer set up his camera on the

　　_____.

Words in Context

The following exercise will help you figure out the
meaning of some words from the previous list. Circle
any context clues that help you figure out the meanings of the bold words.

In our country, the use of nuclear power as a
viable source of energy has been an ongoing
controversy. During the gas and oil shortages
of the 1970s, energy prices were **exorbitant**.
The federal government supported nuclear
power as a new energy source that would be
cost effective. Now, the president's National
Energy Policy Report lists nuclear power as a
safe and affordable alternative. Today, as in the
past, many people have voiced their **antipathy**
toward nuclear power plants, especially in the
wake of the 1979 partial meltdown of the Three
Mile Island nuclear power plant. At that time,
scientists scrambled to **circumvent** a total meltdown in a facility that was designed to be fail-
safe. There was great fear that the meltdown
would be complete, and **decimate** the area.
Now, the federal government is once again pro-
moting this alternative energy source.

Suffixes

Word endings that are added to the main part, or
root, of words are called **suffixes**. Suffixes are word
parts that signal how a word is being used in a sentence. You will note that each word in the list is a
particular part of speech (*noun, verb, adjective,* or
adverb). Suffixes often change the part of speech of
a word.

For example, take the word *deferment*. A *deferment* is a noun that means a postponement. If the
suffix (word ending -*ment*) is removed, the word
becomes *defer*, and it is used as a verb, meaning *to
postpone.*

As a *verb*, it appears as *defer*:
I will *defer* the payment until next month.

As a *noun*, it appears as it is:
The bank gave him a *deferment.*

As an *adjective*, it appears as *deferred*:
The *deferred* payment is due in one month.

The following table shows a list of common suffixes. They are divided into the parts of speech, or "jobs" they suggest for words. Note the examples given; then, add your own word(s) in the last column.

NOUN ENDINGS			
SUFFIX	MEANING	EXAMPLES	YOUR WORD
-tion	act or state of	retroaction, simulation	
-ment	quality	deportment, impediment	
-ist	one who	chauvinist, purist	
-ism	state or doctrine of	barbarism, materialism	
-ity	state of being	futility, civility	
-ology	study of	biology	
-escence	state of	adolescence	
-y, -ry	state of	mimicry, trickery	
ADJECTIVE ENDINGS			
SUFFIX	MEANING	EXAMPLES	YOUR WORD
-able	capable	perishable, flammable	
-ic	causing, making	nostalgic, fatalistic	
-ian	one who is or does	tactician, patrician	
-ile	pertaining to	senile, servile	
-ious	having the quality of	religious, glorious	
-ive	having the nature of	sensitive, divisive	
-less	without	regardless, feckless	
VERB ENDINGS			
SUFFIX	MEANING	EXAMPLES	YOUR WORD
-ize	to bring about	colonize, plagiarize	
-ate	to make	fumigate, annihilate	
-ify	to make	beautify, electrify	

agrarian *adj.*   (ə·ˈgrer·ē·ən)
suffix: **-ian** means *one who is or does*
having to do with agriculture or farming
The farmer loved his _____ life.

antagonist *noun*   (an·ˈta·gə·nist)
suffix: **-ist** means *one who*
one who contends with or opposes another
In the movie *Batman*, the Joker is Batman's _____.

bigotry *noun*   (ˈbig·ə·trē)
suffix: **-ry** means *state of*
unreasonable zeal in favor of a party, sect, or opin-
     ion; excessive prejudice
_____ can lead to malevolent actions.

consummate *verb*   (ˈkon·səm·māt)
suffix: **-ate** means *to make*
to complete; to carry to the utmost degree
The business executive needed to _____ the deal
     quickly.

copious *adj.*   (ˈcōp·ē·əs)
suffix: **-ious** means *having the quality of*
abundant; plentiful; in great quantities
A _____ amount of sunshine is predicted for the
     summer.

anthropomorphic *adj.*   (ˈan·thrəpə·morf·ik)
suffix: **-ic** means *causing*
resembling human form
Their concept of God is _____.

interment *noun*   (in·ˈtər·mənt)
suffix: **-ment** means *quality of*
the act or ritual of burying
The widow prepared for her husband's _____.

furtive *adj.*   (ˈfər·tiv)
suffix: **-ive** means *having the nature of*
done in a stealthy manner; sly and underhanded
The two criminals who were in cahoots gave each
     other _____ looks behind the detective's
     back.

laudable *adj.*   (ˈlaw·də·bəl)
suffix: **-able** means *capable of*
praiseworthy
Her dedication and ability to rehabilitate the injured
     is _____.

geology *noun*   (jē·ˈä·lə·jē)
suffix: **-ology** means *study of*
the study of the history of Earth and its life,
     especially as recorded in rocks
The _____ major traveled to Mt. Etna to exam-
     ine the effects of the volcano's most recent
     eruption.

minimize *verb*   (ˈmi·nə·mīz)
suffix: **-ize** means *to subject to an action*
to play down; to keep to a minimum
The man tried to _____ his involvement in the
     trial so that he would not be implicated in the
     scandal.

mutation *noun*   (mū·ˈtā·shən)
suffix: **-tion** means *action of, state of*
the act or process of changing
Scientists research gene _____ in fruit flies to
     see how genes change from one generation to
     the next.

incandescence *noun*   (in·kən·desˊ·ens)
suffix: **-escence** means *state of*
the state of being lit up
The candle's _____ helped me find my way in
     the dark.

parity *noun*   (ˈpar·i·tē)
suffix: **-ity** means *state of being*
the state or condition of being the same in power,
     value, or rank; equality
Women and minorities continue to fight for
     _____ in the workplace.

pragmatism *noun*   (´prag·mə·tizm)
suffix: **-ism** means *state or doctrine of*
faith in the practical approach
The man's _____ enabled him to run a successful
   business.

provocative *adj.*   (prō·´vok·ə·tiv)
suffix: **-ive** means *having the nature of*
something that stirs up an action
The _____ words of the environmental activist
   inspired many to volunteer for the community
   clean-up day.

puerile *adj.*   (´pyoor·əl)
suffix: **-ile** means *pertaining to*
childish, silly, immature
The teen's _____ actions at the party couldn't be
   ignored.

rectify *verb*   (´rek·ti·fī)
suffix: **-ify** means *to make*
to make right; to correct
The newspaper tried to _____ the mistake by
   correcting the misprint.

peerless *adj.*   (piər·´ləs)
suffix: **-less** means *without*
without match, unrivaled
She was _____ in her search for knowledge; no
   one was as informed as she.

venerate *verb*   (´ven·ə·rāt)
suffix: **-ate** means *to make*
to look upon with deep respect and reverence
Some cultures _____ their elders.

Words in Context

The following exercise will help you figure out the meaning of some words from the previous list by looking at context clues. Circle any context clues that help you figure out the meaning of the bold word.

The latest remake of *Planet of the Apes* develops the theme of **bigotry** in a world where apes are the dominant culture and humans are enslaved. **Parity** between the two species is unthinkable because the simians regard humans as inferior creatures. Leo, the central character, is the story's protagonist. He is a human astronaut who lands on a strange planet where apes **venerate** their own kind by offering praise and promotions for negative actions taken against humans. Leo's **antagonist**, General Thade, is the leader of the apes in this bizarre culture, and encourages the mistreatment of humans by apes. In General Thade's opinion, extermination of the humans is a **laudable** cause, and he mounts a full-scale campaign to exterminate humans from the planet.

HOW TO ANSWER VOCABULARY QUESTIONS

- The key to answering vocabulary questions is to notice and connect what you do know to what you may not recognize.
- **Know your word parts.** You can make a good guess at the meanings of words when you see a suggested meaning in a root word, prefix, or suffix.
- **Consider the context for clues about meaning.** Think of how the word makes sense in the sentence.
- **Don't be confused by words that sound like other words** but may have different meanings.

More Vocabulary Practice Questions

Here is another set of practice exercises with samples of each kind of question covered in this chapter. Answers are at the end of the exercise.

Select the word that means the same or nearly the same as the italicized word.

12. *congenial* company
   a. friendly
   b. dull
   c. tiresome
   d. angry

13. *fortuitous* meeting
   a. intimidating
   b. important
   c. lucky
   d. secret

14. *meticulous* record-keeping
   a. dishonest
   b. casual
   c. painstaking
   d. careless

15. *superficial* wounds
   a. life-threatening
   b. bloody
   c. severe
   d. surface

16. *impulsive* actions
   a. cautious
   b. sudden
   c. courageous
   d. cowardly

17. *tactful* comments
   a. polite
   b. rude
   c. angry
   d. confused

In the following examples, use the context to help choose the word that means the same or nearly the same as the italicized word.

18. Though relaxed about homework, the teacher was *adamant* about papers being on time.
   a. liberal
   b. casual
   c. inflexible
   d. pliable

19. The condition of the room after the party was *deplorable.*
   a. regrettable
   b. pristine
   c. festive
   d. tidy

20. Looking to ruin all that the group had accomplished, the *nefarious* character went ahead with his plans.
   a. strong
   b. wicked
   c. deceitful
   d. peaceful

Answers to Vocabulary Practice Questions

12. a.
13. c.
14. c.
15. d.
16. b.
17. a.
18. c.
19. a.
20. b.

CHAPTER
9 ▶ WORD KNOWLEDGE PRACTICE

CHAPTER SUMMARY

This chapter gives you the opportunity for more practice with Word Knowledge questions.

f you feel that you could use extra practice with synonym or context questions, complete the exercises in this chapter. The answers are given at the end. When you miss a question, look up that word in the dictionary, study the different parts of the word, and commit it to memory. It's a good idea to complete this chapter even if you feel you have strong vocabulary skills. You may learn a word or two—and that will help you pick up precious points on the Word Knowledge subtest of the ASVAB, which will count toward your Armed Forces Qualifying Test score.

Word Knowledge Practice

1.	ⓐ	ⓑ	ⓒ	ⓓ
2.	ⓐ	ⓑ	ⓒ	ⓓ
3.	ⓐ	ⓑ	ⓒ	ⓓ
4.	ⓐ	ⓑ	ⓒ	ⓓ
5.	ⓐ	ⓑ	ⓒ	ⓓ
6.	ⓐ	ⓑ	ⓒ	ⓓ
7.	ⓐ	ⓑ	ⓒ	ⓓ
8.	ⓐ	ⓑ	ⓒ	ⓓ
9.	ⓐ	ⓑ	ⓒ	ⓓ
10.	ⓐ	ⓑ	ⓒ	ⓓ
11.	ⓐ	ⓑ	ⓒ	ⓓ
12.	ⓐ	ⓑ	ⓒ	ⓓ

13.	ⓐ	ⓑ	ⓒ	ⓓ
14.	ⓐ	ⓑ	ⓒ	ⓓ
15.	ⓐ	ⓑ	ⓒ	ⓓ
16.	ⓐ	ⓑ	ⓒ	ⓓ
17.	ⓐ	ⓑ	ⓒ	ⓓ
18.	ⓐ	ⓑ	ⓒ	ⓓ
19.	ⓐ	ⓑ	ⓒ	ⓓ
20.	ⓐ	ⓑ	ⓒ	ⓓ
21.	ⓐ	ⓑ	ⓒ	ⓓ
22.	ⓐ	ⓑ	ⓒ	ⓓ
23.	ⓐ	ⓑ	ⓒ	ⓓ
24.	ⓐ	ⓑ	ⓒ	ⓓ

25.	ⓐ	ⓑ	ⓒ	ⓓ
26.	ⓐ	ⓑ	ⓒ	ⓓ
27.	ⓐ	ⓑ	ⓒ	ⓓ
28.	ⓐ	ⓑ	ⓒ	ⓓ
29.	ⓐ	ⓑ	ⓒ	ⓓ
30.	ⓐ	ⓑ	ⓒ	ⓓ
31.	ⓐ	ⓑ	ⓒ	ⓓ
32.	ⓐ	ⓑ	ⓒ	ⓓ
33.	ⓐ	ⓑ	ⓒ	ⓓ
34.	ⓐ	ⓑ	ⓒ	ⓓ
35.	ⓐ	ⓑ	ⓒ	ⓓ

Word Knowledge

Choose the word or phrase that is closest in meaning to the underlined word.

1. I would <u>characterize</u> the cowboy in that movie as a classic hero.
  a. describe
  b. treat
  c. watch
  d. display

2. Jeri viewed her neighbor's messy home as <u>repugnant</u>.
  a. advantageous
  b. suspect
  c. conventional
  d. offensive

3. Change had to be made, since the <u>ineffective</u> procedure was failing.
  a. former
  b. useless
  c. special
  d. questionable

4. The musicians' hard work and effort were <u>ostensible</u>, given their excellent performance.
  a. apparent
  b. commendable
  c. unrivaled
  d. bearable

5. <u>Austere</u> most nearly means
  a. tasteful.
  b. simple.
  c. resistant.
  d. dark.

6. <u>Parity</u> most nearly means
  a. equality.
  b. mimicry.
  c. style of belief.
  d. current trend.

7. <u>Pundit</u> most nearly means
  a. private joke.
  b. expert.
  c. diplomat.
  d. folk dance.

8. <u>Narcissistic</u> most nearly means
  a. having an addictive personality.
  b. having a narcotic effect.
  c. self-absorbed.
  d. witty.

9. <u>Mesmerize</u> most nearly means
  a. to reign over others.
  b. to record in prose.
  c. to memorialize.
  d. to fascinate.

10. <u>Prospectus</u> most nearly means
  a. published business plan.
  b. the outlook from a mountaintop.
  c. opening speech.
  d. professional playing field.

11. <u>Fiscal</u> most nearly means
  a. official.
  b. stated.
  c. financial.
  d. faithful.

12. The candidate for the position knew the <u>jargon</u> and had a pleasant demeanor.
  a. scientific specialty
  b. public policy issues
  c. language particular to the field
  d. unfriendly attitude

13. Surprisingly, the child had a <u>stoic</u> attitude
toward the hours of homework assigned to her.
   a. tainted
   b. uncomplaining
   c. angry
   d. self-defeating

14. <u>Belligerent</u> most nearly means
   a. warlike.
   b. flighty.
   c. easily tired.
   d. beautiful.

15. <u>Retrospect</u> most nearly means
   a. analytic.
   b. careful.
   c. hindsight.
   d. a magnifying instrument.

16. <u>Subsidy</u> most nearly means
   a. the punishment of a criminal offense.
   b. the aftermath of a storm.
   c. money given in support of a cause or
   industry.
   d. a vote directly by the people.

17. <u>Cryptic</u> most nearly means
   a. mysterious.
   b. evil.
   c. a spy code.
   d. a tomb.

18. There was an <u>audible</u> sigh of relief when the
rescuers brought the drowning man to the
surface.
   a. incredible
   b. able to be heard
   c. worthy of praise
   d. able to be seen

19. Before setting out on the long hike, we made
the <u>requisite</u> check for food and water supplies.
   a. required
   b. safe
   c. ample
   d. up-to-date

20. Her <u>vivacious</u> manner contrasted with the seriousness of her appearance.
   a. grave
   b. hostile
   c. joyous
   d. lively

21. He wanted to reread the recipe to <u>verify</u> the
ingredients before starting to cook.
   a. confirm
   b. total
   c. analyze
   d. measure

22. The <u>loquacious</u> dinner guest dominated the
conversation.
   a. intoxicated
   b. talkative
   c. silent
   d. greedy

23. The soap opera emphasized the <u>turmoil</u>, rather
than the humor, of family life.
   a. disorder
   b. humor
   c. activity
   d. sentiment

24. The <u>fluctuating</u> price of gas kept motorists
guessing.
   a. changing
   b. inexpensive
   c. costly
   d. reasonable

25. His <u>chronic</u> lateness was treated with humor by those who had known him for a long time.
   a. occasional
   b. constant
   c. unusual
   d. rare

26. <u>Abeyance</u> most nearly means
   a. obedience.
   b. reluctance.
   c. suspension.
   d. relief.

27. <u>Multifarious</u> most nearly means
   a. assorted.
   b. complex.
   c. impossible.
   d. bleak.

28. <u>Plaintive</u> most nearly means
   a. musical.
   b. uninteresting.
   c. loud.
   d. mournful.

29. Darcy found her mother's <u>inveterate</u> beliefs frustrating.
   a. kindly
   b. ingrained
   c. wise
   d. respectful

30. The prosecutor's <u>trenchant</u> closing statement deeply affected the jurors' verdict.
   a. effective
   b. polite
   c. long
   d. mild

31. After Yoshio was rescued, he recounted his <u>harrowing</u> experience to his family.
   a. traumatic
   b. mundane
   c. sensual
   d. joyful

32. <u>Arcane</u> most nearly means
   a. foreign.
   b. outdated.
   c. mysterious.
   d. active.

33. <u>Pernicious</u> most nearly means
   a. destructive.
   b. contagious.
   c. mild.
   d. fabricated.

34. The boarding school had very <u>stringent</u> rules.
   a. creative
   b. rigorous
   c. liberal
   d. amorous

35. <u>Ineluctable</u> most nearly means
   a. loose.
   b. anticipated.
   c. desirable.
   d. unavoidable.

Answers

1. a. To *characterize* someone means to *describe* that person, or to bring about (*-ize*) that person's character. Choice **b**, *treat*, means to care for or deal with, and one would not deal with a fictional character in a film directly. Choice **c**, *watch*, means to observe, and though an audience member would watch a film character, this word does not fit the context of the sentence. Choice **d**, *display*, means to show, which does not fit the context either.

2. d. Something that is *repugnant* is distasteful or *offensive*. Choice **a**, *advantageous*, means helpful or useful, which are not words that would describe a messy home. Neither are choice **b**, *suspect*, meaning suspicious, or choice **c**, *conventional*, meaning ordinary.

3. b. Something that is *ineffective* is *useless* or *not* (*in-*) *effective*. Choice **a**, *former*, means previous, and a procedure no longer in use would not require changing. Choice **c**, *special*, means particular in a positive way, and the word *failing* in the sentence indicates that the procedure is not positive. Choice **d**, *questionable*, means doubtful, which indicates a lack of certainty. The sentence states that the procedure is failing with certainty.

4. a. When something is *ostensible*, it is clear or *apparent*. Choice **b**, *commendable*, means praiseworthy. Choice **c**, *unrivaled*, means without peer or competition, which makes little sense in the context of the sentence. Choice **d**, *bearable*, means tolerable, and the word *excellent* in the sentence indicates that the musician's hard work and effort were not merely bearable.

5. b. *Austere* means *simple* or severe. Choice **a**, *tasteful*, means elegant or refined. Choice **c**, *resistant*, means opposed to. Choice **d**, *dark*, means devoid of light.

6. a. *Parity* means the state of being *equal* or fair. Choice **b**, *mimicry*, is the practice of copying. Choice **c**, *style of belief*, does not share the same meaning as *parity*. Choice **d**, *current trend*, refers to a fashion.

7. b. A *pundit* is an *expert* on a particular subject. Choice **a**, *private joke*, and choice **d**, *folk dance*, do not share the same meanings as *pundit*. Choice **c**, *diplomat*, is a government appointee responsible for negotiating with other countries.

8. c. The word *narcissistic* is derived from a Greek myth in which Narcissus falls in love with his own image. Someone who is *narcissistic* is one who is *self-absorbed*. Choice **a**, *having an addictive personality*, refers to someone who is not capable of moderation. Choice **b**, *having a narcotic effect*, refers to something that causes sleepiness. Choice **d**, *witty*, means cleverly humorous.

9. d. To *mesmerize* someone is to bring about a state of *fascination* in that person. Choice **a**, *to reign over others*, means to rule other people. Choice **b**, *to record in prose*, means to write something down without poetic style. Choice **c**, *to memorialize*, means to remember.

10. a. A *prospectus* is a *published business plan*. Choice **b**, *the outlook from a mountaintop*, does not share the same meaning as *prospectus* (though it might be a prospect), nor does choice **c**, *opening speech*, or choice **d**, *professional playing field*.

11. c. The words *fiscal* and *financial* both mean pertaining to money. Choice **a**, *official*, means authorized. Choice **b**, *stated*, means said explicitly. Choice **d**, *faithful*, means full of faith or loyal.

12. c. *Jargon* is *language particular to a field*. Choice **a**, *scientific specialty*, and choice **b**, *public policy issues*, do not share the same meaning as *jargon*, and since you do not know whether the candidate is applying to a scientific or political position, you cannot conclude that either of these choices are correct. Choice **d**, *unfriendly attitude*, is a negative personality trait that contradicts the candidate's *pleasant demeanor*.

13. b. Someone who is *stoic* would not complain about chores such as doing hours of homework. Choice **a**, *tainted*, means spoiled or contaminated, which does not make sense within the context of the sentence. Choice **c**, *angry*, means mad, and it would not be *surprising* if a child was angry about having to do hours of homework. Choice **d**, *self-defeating*, means ruining oneself, which does not make sense within the context of the sentence.

14. a. The root *belli-* means *warlike*, which is what *belligerent* means. Choice **b**, *flighty*, means unable to concentrate or fanciful. Choice **c**, *easily tired*, and choice **d**, *beautiful*, do not share the same meanings as *belligerent*.

15. c. The root *retro-* means *before* and *-spect* refers to *seeing*, so *retrospect* means *hindsight*, or viewing an event that occurred in the past. Choice **a**, *analytic*, means logical. Choice **b**, *careful*, means full of care. Choice **d**, *a magnifying instrument*, is a tool for making objects appear larger.

16. c. A *subsidy* is money given in support of a cause or industry. Choices **a**, **b**, and **d** do not share this meaning.

17. a. *Cryptic* is derived from the word crypt, which is an *underground vault*, and it refers to something that causes a sensation of mysteriousness. *A tomb* shares the same meaning as the noun crypt but not the adjective *cryptic*, so choice **d** is incorrect. Choice **b**, *evil*, means devoid of good. Choice **c**, *a spy code*, might be a mystery, but it does not mean *cryptic*.

18. b. The root word *aud-* refers to *sound*, so a sigh that is *audible* is capable of being heard. Choice **a**, *incredible*, means unbelievable, and it would not be unbelievable to heave a sigh of relief after a drowning man was rescued. Choice **c** is incorrect because a sigh would not be *worthy of praise*. Choice **d**, *able to be seen*, is incorrect because a sigh cannot be seen.

19. a. *Requisite* is derived from *require*, so it has the same meaning as *required*. Choice **b**, *safe*, means devoid of danger, which would not describe a check for food and water supplies, nor would choice **c**, *ample*, meaning plentiful, or choice **d**, *up-to-date*, meaning current.

20. d. The root word *viv-* means *life*, so *lively* is the best synonym for *vivacious*. Choice **a**, *grave*, means serious, and the word *contrasted* in the sentence implies that *vivacious* has the opposite meaning of *serious*. Choice **b**, *hostile*, means aggressive, which would not necessarily contrast seriousness. Choice **c**, *joyous*, means full of joy, not full of life.

21. a. The root *ver-* in *verify* means *truth*, and to *confirm* something means to check its truthfulness. Choice **b**, *total*, means sum. Choice **c**, *analyze*, means examine. Choice **d**, *measure*, means calculate.

22. b. Someone who is *loquacious* is *talkative*. Choice **a**, *intoxicated*, means under the influence of drugs or alcohol. Such a person might try to dominate a conversation, but this is not a certainty. Choice **c**, *silent*, is incorrect because one cannot dominate a conversation while being silent. Choice **d**, *greedy*, means selfish. Though dominating a conversation may be selfish, this choice does not make as much sense in the context of the sentence as choice **b**.

23. a. The words *rather than* in the sentence imply that the soap opera focused on the opposite of comfort or order, and *disorder* is the opposite of order. Choice **b**, *humor*, means comedy, which is not the opposite of *comfort*; neither is choice **c**, *activity*, or choice **d**, *sentiment*.

24. a. Something that changes would keep someone guessing, so *changing* is the best synonym for *fluctuating*. Choices **b**, *inexpensive*, **c**, *costly*, and **d**, *reasonable*, are absolutes that would not keep anyone guessing.

25. b. The root of *chronic*, *chron-*, refers to time, as does *constant*, which means occurring through time consistently. Choice **a**, *occasional*, is also related to time, but it means rarely. Rare lateness is not a situation requiring forgiving humor, so *occasional* does not make sense in the context of this sentence. Choice **c**, *unusual*, and choice **d**, *rare*, are synonyms of *occasional* and are incorrect for the same reason as choice **a**.

26. c. *Abeyance* means *suspension*. Choice **a**, *obedience*, means compliance or submission. Choice **b**, *reluctance*, means hesitation. Choice **d**, *relief*, means release.

27. a. The prefix *multi-* means many, and *assorted* means *many different kinds*. Choice **b**, *complex*, means complicated. Choice **c**, *impossible*, means not possible. Choice **d**, *bleak*, means depressing or unwelcoming.

28. d. *Plaintive* means *mournful* or sad. Music may have *plaintive* qualities, but *musical* and *plaintive* are not synonyms, so choice **a** is incorrect. Choice **b**, *uninteresting*, means boring. Choice **c**, *loud*, means noisy.

29. b. *Inveterate* shares the same meaning as *ingrained*, which means fixed or unchangeable. A more open-minded person might be frustrated by another's refusal to adapt to his or her beliefs, so choice **b** makes the most sense in the context of this sentence. Choice

a, *kindly*, makes less sense because it is less likely a person would be frustrated by another's kindliness. This is also true of choice **c**, *wise*, and choice **d**, *respectful*.

30. a. The words *deeply affected* in the sentence are a clue indicating that the prosecutor's closing statement was *effective*. Choice **b**, *polite*, means respectful. Choice **c**, *long*, and choice **d**, *mild*, do not indicate the kind of statement that would deeply affect a jury.

31. a. A situation requiring rescue would likely be *traumatic* for the person being rescued. Choice **b**, *mundane*, means ordinary. Choice **c**, *sensual*, means full of feeling. Choice **d**, *joyful*, means full of joy.

32. c. *Arcane* means *mysterious*. Choice **a**, *foreign*, means unfamiliar. Choice **b**, *outdated*, means no longer relevant. Choice **d**, *active*, means lively.

33. a. The root *per-* means ruin and the root *nic-* means death, so *pernicious* means having the quality of *destructiveness*. Choice **b**, *contagious*, means catching. Choice **c**, *mild*, means weak. Choice **d**, *fabricated*, means human-made.

34. b. *Stringent* means *rigorous*, which describes a set of rules well. It is not likely that a school's rules would be *creative* or artistic, so choice **a** is incorrect. Choice **c**, *liberal*, means free, and it is not likely that rules would be free. Choice **d**, *amorous*, means romantic, which does not make sense in the context of this sentence.

35. d. That the words *ineluctable* and *unavoidable* both contain prefixes meaning *not* is a clue that they share the same meaning. Choice **a**, *loose*, means slack. Choice **b**, *anticipated*, means expected. Choice **c**, *desirable*, means attractive or wanted.

10 ▶ PARAGRAPH COMPREHENSION REVIEW

CHAPTER SUMMARY

The Armed Services Vocational Aptitude Battery includes a reading comprehension section that tests your ability to understand what you read. The tips and exercises in this chapter will help you improve your comprehension of written passages, as well as of tables, charts, and graphs, so that you can increase your score in this area.

Memos, policies, procedures, reports—these are all things you will be expected to understand if you enlist in the armed services. In fact, understanding written materials is part of almost any job. That's why the ASVAB attempts to measure this skill in applicants.

The Paragraph Comprehension subtest of the ASVAB is in multiple-choice format, and asks questions based on brief passages, much like the standardized tests that are offered in schools. Almost all standardized test questions evaluate your reading skills. After all, you can't answer the question if you can't read it. Similarly, you can't study your training materials or learn new procedures once you are on the job if you can't read well. So, reading comprehension is vital not only for the test but also for the rest of your career.

Types of Reading Comprehension Questions

You have probably encountered reading comprehension questions before, where you have to read a passage, and then answer multiple-choice questions about it. This kind of question has advantages for you as a test taker: you don't have to know anything about the topic of the passage, because you are being tested only on the information the passage provides.

But the disadvantage is that you have to know where and how to find that information quickly in an unfamiliar text. This makes it easy to fall for one of the incorrect answer choices, especially since they are designed to mislead you.

The best way to succeed on this type of question is to be very familiar with the kinds of questions that are typically asked on the test. Questions most frequently ask you to:

- identify a specific **fact or detail** in the passage
- note the **main idea** of the passage
- make an **inference** based on the passage
- define a **vocabulary** word from the passage

To succeed on a reading comprehension test, you need to know exactly what each of these questions is asking. **Facts and details** are the specific pieces of information that support the passage's main idea. The **main idea** is the thought, opinion, or attitude that governs the whole passage. Generally speaking, facts and details are indisputable—things that don't need to be proven, like statistics (*18 million people*) or descriptions (*a green overcoat*). Let's say, for example, you read a sentence that says, *After the department's reorganization, workers were 50% more productive.* A sentence like this, which gives you the fact that 50% of workers were more productive, might support a main idea that says, *Every department should be reorganized.* Notice that this main idea is not something indisputable; it is an opinion. The writer thinks all departments should be reorganized, and because this is his opinion (and not everyone shares it), he needs to support his opinion with facts and details.

An **inference**, on the other hand, is a conclusion that can be drawn based on fact or evidence. For example, you can infer—based on the fact that workers became 50% more productive after the reorganization, which is a dramatic change—that the department had not been efficiently organized. The statement of fact, *After the department's reorganization, workers were 50% more productive,* also implies that the reorgani-

zation of the department was the reason workers became more productive. There may, of course, have been other reasons, but we can infer only one from this sentence.

As you might expect, **vocabulary** questions ask you to determine the meanings of particular words. Often, if you've read carefully, you can determine the meaning of such words from their context   that is, how the word is used in the sentence or paragraph.

Practice Passage 1: Using the Four Question Types

The following is a sample test passage, followed by four questions. Read the passage carefully, and then answer the questions based on your reading of the text. Then, refer to the previous list, and note under your answer which type of question has been asked. Correct answers appear immediately after the questions.

In the last decade, community policing has been frequently touted as the best way to reform urban law enforcement. The idea of putting more officers on foot patrol in high crime areas, where relations with police have frequently been strained, was initiated in Houston in 1983 under the leadership of then-Commissioner Lee Brown. He believed that officers should be accessible to the community at the street level. If officers were assigned to the same area over a period of time, those officers would eventually build a network of trust with neighborhood residents. That trust would mean merchants and residents in the community would let officers know about criminal activities in the area and support police intervention. Since then, many large cities have experimented with Community-Oriented Policing (COP), with mixed results. Some have found that police and citizens are grateful for the opportunity to work together. Others have found that unrealistic expectations by citizens and resistance from officers have combined to hinder the effectiveness of COP. It seems possible, therefore, that a good idea may need improvement before it can truly be considered a reform.

1. Community policing has been used in law enforcement since
   a. the late 1970s.
   b. the early 1980s.
   c. the Carter administration.
   d. Lee Brown was New York City Police Commissioner.
   Question type _____

2. The phrase *a network of trust* in this passage suggests that
   a. police officers can rely only on each other for support.
   b. community members rely on the police to protect them.
   c. police and community members rely on each other.
   d. community members trust only each other.
   Question type _____

3. The best title for this passage would be
   a. Community Policing: The Solution to the Drug Problem.
   b. Houston Sets the Pace in Community Policing.
   c. Communities and Cops: Partners for Peace.
   d. Community Policing: An Uncertain Future?
   Question type _____

4. The word *touted* in the first sentence of the passage most nearly means
   a. praised.
   b. denied.
   c. exposed.
   d. criticized.
   Question type _____

Answers and Explanations

Don't just look at the right answers and move on. The explanations are the most important part, so read them carefully. Use these explanations to help you understand how to tackle each kind of question the next time you come across it.

1. b. Question type: **fact or detail**. The passage identifies 1983 as the first large-scale use of community policing in Houston. Don't be misled by trying to figure out when Carter was president. Also, if you happen to know that Lee Brown was New York City's police commissioner, don't let that information lead you away from the information contained in the passage alone. Brown was commissioner in Houston when he initiated community policing.

2. c. Question type: **inference**. The *network of trust* referred to in this passage is between the community and the police, as you can see from the sentence where the phrase appears. The key phrase in the question is *in this passage.* You may think that police can rely only on each other, or one of the other answer choices may appear equally plausible to you. But, your choice of answers must be limited to the one suggested *in this passage.* Another tip for questions like this: Beware of absolutes! Be suspicious of any answer containing words like *only, always,* or *never.*

3. d. Question type: **main idea**. The title always expresses the main idea. In this passage, the main idea comes at the end. The sum of all the details in the passage suggests that community policing is not without its critics, and therefore, its future is uncertain. Another key phrase is *mixed results,* which means that some communities haven't had full success with community policing.

4. a. Question type: **vocabulary**. The word *touted* is linked in this passage with the phrase *the best way to reform*. Most people would think that a good way to reform something is praiseworthy. In addition, the next few sentences in the passage describe the benefits of community policing. Criticism of or a negative response to the subject doesn't come until later in the passage.

Detail and Main Idea Questions

Fact or detail questions and **main idea** questions are both asking you for information that's right there in the passage. All you have to do is find it.

Fact or Detail Questions

In detail or fact questions, you have to identify a specific item of information from the text. This is usually the simplest kind of question. You just have to be able to separate important information from less important information. However, the choices may often be very similar, so you must be careful not to get confused.

Be sure you read the passage and questions carefully. In fact, it is usually a good idea to read the questions first, *before* you even read the passage, so you will know what details to look out for.

Main Idea Questions

The main idea of a passage, like that of a paragraph or a book, is what it is *mostly* about. The main idea is like an umbrella that covers all the ideas and details in the passage, so it is usually something general, not specific. For example, in Practice Passage 1, question 3 asked you what title would be best for the passage, and the correct answer was "Community Policing: An Uncertain Future." This is the best answer because it's the only one that includes both the positive and negative sides of community policing, both of which are discussed in the passage.

Sometimes the main idea is stated clearly, often in the first or last sentence of the passage. The main idea is expressed in the *last* sentence of Practice Passage 1, for example. The sentence that expresses the main idea is often referred to as the **topic sentence**.

At other times, the main idea is not stated in a topic sentence but is *implied* in the overall passage, and you will need to determine the main idea by inference. Because there may be much information in the passage, the trick is to understand what all that information adds up to—the gist of what the author wants you to know. Often, some of the wrong answers on main idea questions are specific facts or details from the passage. A good way to test yourself is to ask, "Can this answer serve as a *net* to hold the whole passage together?" If not, chances are you have chosen a fact or detail, not a main idea.

Practice Passage 2: Detail and Main Idea Questions

Practice answering main idea and detail questions by working on the questions that follow this passage. Select the answers to the questions, and then check your answers against the key that appears immediately after the questions.

There are three different kinds of burns: first degree, second degree, and third degree. It is important for firefighters to be able to recognize each of these types of burns so that they can be sure burn victims are given proper medical treatment. The least serious burn is the first-degree burn, which causes the skin to turn red but does not cause blistering. A mild sunburn is a good example of a first-degree burn, and, like a mild sunburn, first-degree burns generally do not require medical treatment other than a gentle cooling of the burned skin with ice or cold tap water.

Second-degree burns, on the other hand, do cause blistering of the skin and should be treated immediately. These burns should be immersed in warm water and then wrapped in a sterile dressing or bandage. (Do not apply butter or grease to these burns; despite the old wives' tale, butter does *not* help burns heal and actually increases chances of infection.) If second-degree burns cover a large part of the body, then the victim should be taken to the hospital immediately for medical care.

Third-degree burns are those that char the skin and turn it black, or burn so deeply that the skin shows white. These burns usually result from direct contact with flames and have a great chance of becoming infected. All third-degree burns should receive immediate hospital care. They should not be immersed in water, and charred clothing should not be removed from the victim. If possible, a sterile dressing or bandage should be applied to burns before the victim is transported to the hospital.

1. Which of the following would be the best title for this passage?
   a. Dealing with Third-Degree Burns
   b. How to Recognize and Treat Different Burns
   c. Burn Categories
   d. Preventing Infection in Burns

2. Second-degree burns should be treated with
   a. butter.
   b. nothing.
   c. cold water.
   d. warm water.

3. First-degree burns turn the skin
   a. red.
   b. blue.
   c. black.
   d. white.

4. Which of the following best expresses the main idea of the passage?
   a. There are three different types of burns.
   b. Firefighters should always have cold compresses on hand.
   c. Different burns require different types of treatment.
   d. Butter is not good for healing burns.

Answers and Explanations

1. **b.** A question that asks you to choose a title for a passage is a main idea question. This main idea is expressed in the topic sentence: *It is important for firefighters to be able to recognize each of these types of burns so that they can be sure burn victims are given proper treatment.* Choice **b** expresses this idea and is the only title that encompasses all the ideas expressed in the passage. Choice **a** is too limited; it deals only with one of the kinds of burns discussed in the passage. Likewise, choices **c** and **d** are also too limited. Choice **c** covers types of burns but not their treatment, and choice **d** deals only with preventing infection, which is a secondary part of the discussion of treatment.

2. **d.** The answer to this fact question is clearly expressed in the sentence, *These burns should be immersed in warm water and then wrapped in a sterile dressing or bandage.* However, it's easy to choose a wrong answer here because all the choices are mentioned in the passage. You need to read carefully to be sure you match the right burn to the right treatment.

3. a. This is another fact or detail question. The passage says that a first-degree burn *causes the skin to turn red*. Again, it's important to read carefully because all the choices (except **b**, which can be eliminated immediately) are listed elsewhere in the passage.

4. c. Clearly this is a main idea question, and **c** is the only choice that encompasses the whole passage. Choices **b** and **d** are limited to *particular* burns or treatments, and choice **a** discusses only burns and not their treatment. In addition, the second sentence tells us that *it is important for firefighters to be able to recognize each of these types of burns so that they can be sure burn victims are given proper medical treatment.*

Inference and Vocabulary Questions

Questions that ask you about the meaning of vocabulary words in the passage, and those that ask what the passage *suggests* or *implies* (inference questions), are different from detail or main idea questions. In **vocabulary** and **inference** questions, you usually have to pull ideas from the passage, sometimes from more than one place.

Inference Questions

Inference questions can be the most difficult to answer, because they require you to draw meaning from the text when that meaning is implied rather than directly stated. Inferences are conclusions that we draw based on the clues the writer has given us. When you draw inferences, you have to look for such clues as word choice, tone, and specific details that suggest a certain conclusion, attitude, or point of view. You have to read between the lines in order to make a judgment about what an author was implying in the passage.

A good way to test whether you have drawn an acceptable inference is to ask, "What evidence do I have for this inference?" If you can't find any, you probably have the wrong answer. You need to be sure that your inference is logical, and that it is based on something suggested or implied in the passage itself—not on what you or others might think. You need to base your conclusions on evidence—facts, details, and other information—not on random hunches or guesses.

Vocabulary Questions

Questions designed to test vocabulary are really trying to measure how well you can figure out the meaning of an unfamiliar word from its context. *Context* refers to the words and ideas surrounding a vocabulary word. You should be able to substitute a nonsense word for the one being sought, and still make the right choice, because you could determine meaning strictly from the context of the sentence.

For example, you should be able to determine the meaning of the italicized nonsense word in the following sentence based on its context:

> The speaker noted that it gave him great *terivinix* to announce the winner of the Outstanding Leadership Award.
>
> In this sentence, *terivinix* most likely means
> **a.** pain.
> **b.** sympathy.
> **c.** pleasure.
> **d.** anxiety.

Clearly, the context of an award makes **c**, *pleasure,* the best choice. Awards don't usually bring pain, sympathy, or anxiety.

When confronted with an unfamiliar word, try substituting a nonsense word and see whether the context gives you the clue. If you are familiar with prefixes, suffixes, and word roots, you can also use this knowledge to help you determine the meaning of an unfamiliar word.

You should be careful not to guess at the answer to vocabulary questions based on how you may have seen the word used before, or what you *think* it means.

Many words have more than one possible meaning, depending on the context in which they are used, and a word you have seen used one way may mean something else in a test passage. Also, if you don't look at the context carefully, you may make the mistake of confusing the vocabulary word with a similar word. For example, the vocabulary word may be *taut* (meaning *tight*), but if you read too quickly or don't check the context, you might think the word is *tout* (meaning *publicize* or *praise*) or *taunt* (meaning *tease*). Always read carefully and be sure that what you think the word means fits into the context of the passage.

Practice Passage 3: Inference and Vocabulary Questions

The questions that follow this passage are strictly vocabulary and inference questions. Select the answers to the questions, and then check your answers against the key that appears immediately after the questions.

> Dealing with irritable patients is a great challenge for healthcare workers on every level. It is critical that you do not lose your patience when confronted by such a patient. When handling irate patients, be sure to remember that they are not angry at you; they are simply projecting their anger at something else *onto* you. Remember that if you respond to these patients as irritably as they act toward you, you will only increase their hostility, making it much more difficult to give them proper treatment. The best thing to do is to remain calm and ignore any imprecations patients may hurl your way. Such patients may be irrational and may not realize what they are saying. Often these patients will purposely try to anger you just to get a reaction. If you respond to this behavior with anger, they win by getting your attention, but you both lose because the patient is less likely to get proper care.

1. The word *irate* as it is used in the passage most nearly means
   a. irregular, odd.
   b. happy, cheerful.
   c. ill-tempered, angry.
   d. sloppy, lazy.

2. The passage suggests that healthcare workers
   a. easily lose control of their emotions.
   b. are better off not talking to their patients.
   c. must be careful in dealing with irate patients because the patients may sue the hospital.
   d. may provide inadequate treatment if they become angry at patients.

3. An *imprecation* is most likely
   a. an object.
   b. a curse.
   c. a joke.
   d. a medication.

4. Which of the following best expresses the writer's views about irate patients?
   a. Some irate patients just want attention.
   b. Irate patients are always miserable.
   c. Irate patients should be made to wait for treatment.
   d. Managing irate patients is the key to a successful career.

Answers and Explanations

1. **c.** This is a vocabulary question. *Irate* means *ill-tempered, angry.* It should be clear that choice **b**, *happy, cheerful*, is not the answer; dealing with happy patients is normally not *a great challenge.* Patients who are *irregular* (choice **a**) or *sloppy* (choice **d**) may be a challenge in their own ways, but they aren't likely to rouse a healthcare worker to anger. In addition, the passage explains that irate patients are not *angry at you*, and *irate* is used as a synonym for *irritable*, which describes the patients under discussion in the very first sentence.

2. d. This is an inference question, as the phrase *the passage suggests* might have told you. The idea that angry healthcare workers might give inadequate treatment is implied by the passage as a whole, which seems to be an attempt to prevent angry reactions to irate patients. Furthermore, the last sentence in particular makes this inference possible: *If you react to this behavior with anger . . . you both lose because the patient is less likely to get proper care.* Choice **c** is not correct, because while it may be true that some irate patients have sued the hospital in the past, there is no mention of suits anywhere in this passage. Likewise, choice **b** is incorrect; the passage does suggest ignoring patients' insults, but nowhere does it recommend not talking to patients—it simply recommends not talking angrily. And while it may be true that some healthcare workers may lose control of their emotions, the passage does not provide any facts or details to support choice **a**, that they *easily lose control.* Watch out for key words like *easily* that may distort the intent of the passage.

3. b. If you didn't know what an *imprecation* is, the context should reveal that it's something you can ignore, so neither choice **a**, an *object,* nor choice **d**, a *medication,* is a likely answer. Furthermore, choice **c** is not likely either, since an irate patient is not likely to be making jokes.

4. a. The writer seems to believe that some irate patients just want attention, as is suggested by the sentences, *Often these patients will purposely try to anger you just to get a reaction. If you react to this behavior with anger, they win by getting your attention.* It should be clear that choice **b** cannot be the answer, because it includes an absolute: *Irate patients are always miserable.* Perhaps *some* of the patients are *often* miserable, but an absolute like *always* is usually wrong. Besides, this passage refers to patients who may be irate in the hospital, but we have no indication of what these patients are like at other times. Choice **c** is also incorrect because the purpose of the passage is to ensure that patients receive *proper treatment* and that irate patients are not discriminated against because of their behavior. Thus, *irate patients should be made to wait for treatment* is not a logical answer. Finally, choice **d** cannot be correct because though it may be true, there is no discussion of career advancement in the passage.

Review: Putting It All Together

A good way to solidify what you have learned about reading comprehension questions is for *you* to write the questions. Here's a passage, followed by space for you to write your own questions. Write one question for each of the four types: **fact or detail**, **main idea**, **inference**, and **vocabulary**.

The "broken window" theory was originally developed to explain how minor acts of vandalism or disrespect can quickly escalate to crimes and attitudes that break down the entire social fabric of an area. It is a theory that can easily be applied to any situation in society. The theory contends that if a broken window in an abandoned building is not replaced quickly, soon all the windows will be broken. In other words, a small violation, if condoned, leads others to commit similar or greater violations. Thus, after all the windows have been broken, the building is likely to be looted, and perhaps even burned down. According to this theory, violations increase exponentially. Thus, if disrespect to a superior is tolerated, others will be tempted to be disrespectful as well. A management crisis could erupt literally overnight. For example, if one firefighter begins to disregard proper housewatch procedure by neglecting to keep up the housewatch administrative journal, and this firefighter is not reprimanded, others will follow suit by committing similar violations of procedure, thinking, "If he can get away with it, why can't I?" So, what starts out as a small thing, a violation that may seem not to warrant disciplinary action, may actually ruin the efficiency of the entire firehouse, putting the people the firehouse serves at risk.

1. Detail or fact question: _____

_____

  a.

  b.

  c.

  d.

2. Main idea question: _____

_____

  a.

  b.

  c.

  d.

3. Inference question: _____

_____

  a.

  b.

  c.

  d.

4. Vocabulary question: _____

_____

  a.

  b.

  c.

  d.

Possible Questions

Here is one question of each type based on the previous passage. Your questions may be very different, but these will give you an idea of the kinds of questions that could be asked.

1. Detail question: According to the passage, which of the following could happen "overnight"?
  a. The building will be burned down.
  b. The firehouse may become unmanageable.
  c. A management crisis might erupt.
  d. The windows will all be broken.

2. Main idea question: Which of the following best expresses the main idea of the passage?
  a. Even minor infractions warrant disciplinary action.
  b. Broken windows must be repaired immediately.
  c. People shouldn't be disrespectful to their superiors.
  d. Housewatch must be taken seriously.

3. Inference question: The passage suggests that
  a. the broken window theory is inadequate.
  b. managers need to know how to handle a crisis.
  c. firefighters are lazy.
  d. people will get away with as much as they can.

4. Vocabulary question: In this passage, *condoned* most nearly means
  a. punished.
  b. overlooked.
  c. condemned.
  d. applauded.

Answers
1. c.
2. a.
3. d.
4. b.

Additional Resources

Here are two other ways you can build the vocabulary and knowledge that will help you do well on reading comprehension questions:

- Practice asking the four sample question types about passages you read for information or pleasure.
- Use your library. Many public libraries have sections that contain materials for adult learners. In these sections you can find books with exercises in reading and study skills. It's a good idea to enlarge your base of information by reading related books and articles. Most libraries also have computer systems that allow you to access information quickly and easily. Library personnel will show you how to use the computers and other equipment.

IF ENGLISH ISN'T YOUR FIRST LANGUAGE

When non-native speakers of English have trouble with reading comprehension tests, it's often because they lack the cultural, linguistic, and historical frame of reference that native speakers have. People who have not lived in or been educated in the United States often don't have the background information that comes from growing up reading American newspapers, magazines, and textbooks.

A second problem for non-native English speakers is the difficulty in recognizing vocabulary and idioms (expressions like "chewing the fat") that assist comprehension. In order to read with good understanding, it's important to have an immediate grasp of as many words as possible in the text. Test takers need to be able to recognize vocabulary and idioms immediately, so that the ideas those words express are clear.

The Long View

Read newspapers, magazines, and other periodicals that deal with current events and matters of local, state, and national importance. Pay special attention to articles related to the career you want to pursue.

Be alert to new or unfamiliar vocabulary or terms that occur frequently in the popular press. Use a highlighter pen to mark new or unfamiliar words as you read. Keep a list of those words and their definitions. Review them for 15 minutes each day. Although at first you may find yourself looking up a lot of words, don't be frustrated—you'll look up fewer and fewer as your vocabulary expands.

During the Test

When you are taking the test, make a picture in your mind of the situation being described in the passage. Ask yourself, "What did the writer mostly want me to think about this subject?"

Locate and underline the topic sentence that carries the main idea of the passage. Remember that the topic sentence—if there is one—may not always be the first sentence. If there doesn't seem to be one, try to determine what idea summarizes the whole passage.

11

▶ READING PRACTICE

CHAPTER SUMMARY

This chapter provides more instruction on reading and gives you further opportunity for practice with Paragraph Comprehension questions.

Being able to correctly answer Paragraph Comprehension questions on the ASVAB requires much more than simply knowing what the words mean. This chapter will help you improve your reading ability, focusing on three of the most important things you have to do when reading:

- understanding the basic facts
- finding the main idea
- making inferences or drawing conclusions

Accomplishing these tasks starts with active reading.

Active Reading

Perhaps the most important thing you can do to build your reading skills is to become an *active reader*. Active readers generally do two things when they read:

1. They mark up the text.
2. They make specific observations about the text.

Marking Up the Text

Marking the text actively engages you with the words and ideas you are reading. Marking up the text includes three specific strategies:

- underlining key words and ideas
- circling and defining any unfamiliar words or phrases
- recording your reactions and questions in the margins

When you **underline key words and ideas**, you highlight the most important parts of the text you are reading. You also make it easier to summarize and remember the key points.

Circling unfamiliar vocabulary words is important, too, because a key word or phrase could change the meaning of an entire passage. As an active reader, make sure you look up unknown words immediately. If no dictionary is available, try to determine the meaning of the word as best you can from the surrounding sentences (the *context*).

Finally, **recording your reactions and questions in the margins** turns you from a passive receiver of information into an active learner. You will be much more likely to profit from the ideas and information you read about if you create a "conversation" with the writer in this way.

Of course, if this or any other book you read comes from the library, you should avoid marking in the book itself. If the book you are reading belongs to someone else, mark key points on a piece of paper instead.

Making Observations

Good readers know that writers use many different strategies to express their ideas. Even if you know very little about writing strategies, you can make useful observations about what you read that will help you better understand the author's ideas. You can notice, for example, the author's choice of words; the structure of sentences and paragraphs; any repetition of words or ideas; important details about people, places, and things; and so on.

This step—making observations—is essential, because our observations are what lead us to logical *inferences* about what we read. Inferences are conclusions based on reason, fact, or evidence. When we misunderstand what we read, it is often because we haven't looked closely enough at the text, and so we base our inferences on our own ideas, not on what's actually written in the text. We end up forcing our own ideas on the author rather than listening to what the author has to say and *then* forming our own ideas about it.

Finding the Facts

As a reader faced with a text, you must get the basic facts: the who, what, when, where, how, and why. What does this piece of writing tell you? What happens? To whom? When, where, how, and why? If you can answer these basic questions, you are on your way to really comprehending what you read.

Let's start with a definition. A fact is

- something that we know for certain to have happened.
- something that we know for certain to be true.
- something that we know for certain to exist.

Much of what you read is designed to provide you with facts. Reading comprehension questions often ask you about the facts in a passage you read. It is very important, therefore, for you to be able to read through these materials and understand the information they convey. What facts are you expected to know? What are you to learn or be aware of? What happened? What is true? What exists?

Fact-Finding Practice 1

Jump right in to the task of finding facts. The brief passage that follows is similar to something you might see in a newspaper. Read the passage carefully, and then answer the questions. Remember, careful reading is active reading, so mark up the text as you go. Underline key words and ideas; circle and define any unfamiliar words or phrases; record your reactions and questions in the margins.

On Tuesday, August 30, Mr. Blank, a prominent local citizen, arrived home from work to find his apartment had been robbed. The thieves somehow managed to slip past building security at 131 West Elm Street, with nearly all of Mr. Blank's belongings. In fact, the thieves left behind nothing but a stack of old *Home Decorator* magazines and a can of pork and beans.

The robbery was reported by Mr. Blank's neighbor, who found Mr. Blank unconscious in his doorway. Apparently, Mr. Blank was so shocked by the robbery that he fainted. His neighbor immediately called an ambulance and then the police. Mr. Blank is now staying with relatives and is offering a reward of $25,000 for any information leading to the arrest of the thieves.

1. What happened to Mr. Blank?

2. When did it happen?

3. Where did it happen?

4. How did Mr. Blank react?

5. Who called the police?

6. What was left in the apartment?

Remember, good reading is active reading. Did you mark up the passage? If so, it may have looked something like this:

standing out; widely & popularly known

when → *who* →

On Tuesday, August 30, Mr. Blank, a prominent local citizen, arrived home from work to find his apartment had been robbed. The thieves somehow managed to slip past building security at 131 West Elm Street with nearly all of Mr. Blank's belongings. In fact, the thieves left behind nothing but a stack of old *Home Decorator* magazines and a can of pork and beans. The robbery was reported by Mr. Blank's neighbor, who found Mr. Blank unconscious in his doorway. Apparently Mr. Blank was so shocked by the robbery that he fainted. His neighbor immediately called an ambulance and then the police. Mr. Blank is now staying with relatives and is offering a reward of $25,000 for any information leading to the arrest of the thieves.

What happened — robbery

where

how did they manage this?

interesting detail.

who else was involved

Wow!

lots of $!

You will notice that the answers to the questions have all been underlined, because these are the key words and ideas in this passage. But here are the answers in a more conventional form:

1. What happened to Mr. Blank? *His apartment was robbed.*

2. When did it happen? *sometime while Mr. Blank was at work on Tuesday, August 30*

3. Where did it happen? *131 West Elm Street*

4. How did Mr. Blank react? *He fainted.*

5. Who called the police? *Mr. Blank's neighbor*

6. What was left in the apartment? *some old* Home Decorator *magazines and a can of pork and beans*

Notice that these questions went beyond the basic who, what, when, and where to include some of the details, like what was left in the apartment. This is because details in reading comprehension can be very important clues that may help answer the remaining questions: who did it, how, and why.

Fact-Finding Practice 2

Here's another passage. Read it carefully, and answer the questions that follow.

To: All New Employees
From: Human Resources

In order for your first paycheck to be processed, we must have a number of documents completed and in our files. Once these documents are in our hands, you will be entered into our payroll system. These documents include: a completed company application; a W-4 form; an I-9 form; a Confidentiality Agreement, if applicable; an emergency contact sheet; and a copy of your resume. You should be sure all these documents are filled out within your first week of work. In addition, we will need the following documents from you for your file to be complete: two letters of recommendation from previous employers, high school and college transcripts, and an insurance coverage application. We request that you complete your file within your first month of employment.

7. What papers must new employees have on file? List them here:

   [ ]

8. In your list, circle the items that employees must have on file in order to get paid.

9. When should these circled items be completed?

10. When must the rest of the file be completed?

11. True or false: Everyone must sign a Confidentiality Agreement.

Before you look at the answers, look at this marked-up version to see how you might have highlighted the important information.

To: All New Employees
From: Human Resources

In order for your first paycheck to be processed, we must have a number of documents completed and in our files. Once these documents are in our hands, you will be entered into our payroll system. These documents include: [a completed company application; a W-4 form; an I-9 form; a Confidentiality Agreement, if applicable; an emergency contact sheet; and a copy of your resume.] You should be sure all of these documents are filled out <u>within your first week of work.</u> In addition, we will need the following documents from you for your file to be complete: [two letters of recommendation from previous employers, high school and college transcripts, and an insurance coverage application.] We request that you complete your file within your <u>first month of employment.</u>

Documents I need in order to get paid

Important deadline!

Official copy of student's educational records

Documents I need to complete file

Deadline for completing file

With a marked-up text like this, it's very easy to find the answers.

7. What papers must new employees have on file?

(Company application)
(W-4 form)
(I-9 form)
(Confidentiality Agreement (if applicable))
(Emergency contact sheet)
(Resume)
Two letters of recommendation
High school and college transcripts
Insurance coverage application

8. In the previous list, the items that employees must have on file in order to get paid are circled.

9. When should these circled items be completed? *within the employee's first week of work*

10. When must the rest of the file be completed? *within the employee's first month of work*

11. True or false: Everyone must sign a Confidentiality Agreement. *false; only those for whom it is "applicable"*

Fact-Finding Practice 3

Now, look at one more short passage. Again, read carefully and then answer the questions that follow.

Today's postal service is more efficient and reliable than ever before. Mail that used to take months to move by horse and by foot, now moves around the country in days or hours by truck, train, and plane. First-Class Mail usually moves from New York City to Los Angeles in three days or less. If your letter or package is urgent, the U.S. Postal Service offers Priority Mail and Express Mail services. Priority Mail is guaranteed to go anywhere in the United States in about two days. Express Mail will get your package there overnight.

12. Who or what is this passage about?

13. How was mail transported in the past?

14. How is mail transported now?

15. How long does First-Class Mail take?

16. How long does Priority Mail take?

17. How long does Express Mail take?

Once again, here's how you might have marked up this passage:

then → Today's postal service is more efficient and reliable than ever before. Mail that used to take <u>months to</u> move by <u>horse</u> and b<u>y foot,</u> *now* → now moves around the country in days or hours by <u>truck, train, and plane.</u> <u>First-Class Mail</u> usually moves from New York City to Los Angeles in three days or less. If your letter or package is urgent, the U.S. Postal Service offers <u>Priority Mail</u> and <u>Express Mail</u> services. Priority Mail is guaranteed to go anywhere in the United States in about two days. Express Mail will get your package there overnight.

What a long time!

3 services listed—
First class—3 days
Priority—2 days
Express—Overnight
Fastest

Are there other services?

You can see how marking up a text helps make it easier to understand the information a passage conveys.

12. Who or what is this passage about?
the U.S. Postal Service

13. How was mail transported in the past?
by horse and foot

14. How is mail transported now?
by truck, train, and plane

15. How long does First-Class Mail take?
three days or less

16. How long does Priority Mail take?
about two days

17. How long does Express Mail take?
overnight

Active reading is the first essential step to improving comprehension. Why? Because active reading forces you to really *see* what you are reading, to look closely at what's there. If you look carefully and ask the right questions (who, what, when, where, how, and why), you are on your way to really comprehending what you read.

Finding the Main Idea

When the previous section talked about establishing the facts—the who, what, when, where, and how—it omitted one very important question: Why? Now you are ready to tackle that question.

All writing is communication: a writer wants to convey his or her thoughts to an audience (the reader—you). Just as you have something to say when you pick up the phone to call someone, writers have something to say when they pick up a pen or pencil to write. The reader might ask, "Why did the author write this? What idea is he or she trying to convey?" What you are really asking is, "What is the writer's main idea?"

Finding the main idea is much like finding the *why*. It usually determines the other factors (the *who, what, when, where,* and *how*). Similarly, in writing, the main idea also determines the *who, what, when,* and *where* the author will write about, as well as *how* he or she will write.

Subject versus Main Idea

There's a difference between the *subject* of a piece of writing and its *main idea*. To see the difference, look again at the passage about the postal system.

Today's postal service is more efficient and reliable than ever before. Mail that used to take months to move by horse and by foot now moves around the country in days or hours by truck, train, and plane. First-Class Mail usually moves from New York City to Los Angeles in three days or less. If your letter or package is urgent, the U.S. Postal Service offers Priority Mail and Express Mail services. Priority Mail is guaranteed to go anywhere in the United States in about two days. Express Mail will get your package there overnight.

You will often see a question in the reading comprehension portion of a test that asks, in essence, "What is the main idea of this passage?"

For this passage, you might be tempted to answer: "The post office."

But you would be wrong.

This passage is *about* the post office, yes—but "the post office" is not the main idea of the passage. The post office is merely the *subject* of the passage (*who* or *what* the passage is about). The main idea must say something *about* this subject. The main idea of a text is usually an *assertion* about the subject. An assertion is a statement that requires *evidence* (proof) to be accepted as true.

The main idea of a passage is an assertion about its subject, but it is also something more: it is the idea that holds together or controls the passage. The other sentences and ideas in the passage will all relate to the main idea and serve as evidence that the assertion is true. You might think of the main idea as a net that is cast over the other sentences. The main idea must be general enough to hold all these ideas together.

Thus, the main idea a passage is:

- an assertion about the subject
- the general idea that controls or holds together the paragraph or passage

Look at the postal service paragraph once more. You know what the subject is: the post office. Now, see whether you can determine the main idea. Read the passage again and look for the idea that makes an assertion about the postal service *and* holds together or controls the whole paragraph. Then answer the following question.

18. Which of the following sentences best summarizes the main idea of the passage?
   a. Express Mail is a good way to send urgent mail.
   b. Mail service today is more effective and dependable.
   c. First-Class Mail usually takes three days or less.
   d. Priority Mail is a quick alternative to First-Class Mail.

Because choice **a** is specific—it tells us *only* about Express Mail—it cannot be the main idea. It does not encompass the rest of the sentences in the paragraph—it doesn't cover Priority Mail or First-Class Mail. Choices **c** and **d** are also very specific. They tell us only about First-Class Mail and Priority Mail, so they, too, cannot be the main idea.

But choice **b**—*Mail service today is more effective and dependable*—is general enough to encompass the whole passage. And the rest of the sentences *support* the idea that this sentence asserts: each sentence offers proof that the postal service today is indeed more efficient and reliable. Thus, the writer's motive is to tell us about the efficiency and reliability of today's postal service.

Topic Sentences

You will notice that in the paragraph about the postal service, the main idea is expressed clearly in the first sentence: *Today's postal service is more efficient and reliable than ever before.* A sentence such as this one, that clearly expresses the main idea of a paragraph or passage, is often called a **topic sentence**.

In many cases, like the postal service paragraph, you will find the topic sentence at the beginning of the paragraph. You will also frequently find it at the end. Less often, but on occasion, the topic sentence may be found in the middle of the passage. Whatever the case may be, the topic sentence—like *Today's postal service is more efficient and reliable than ever before*—is an assertion, and it needs proof. The proof is found in the facts and ideas that make up the rest of the passage. (Not all passages provide a clear topic sentence that states the main idea. Such passages come up later in this chapter.)

Remember that a topic sentence is a clear statement of the main idea of a passage; it must be general enough to encompass all the ideas in that passage, and it usually makes an assertion about the subject of that passage. Knowing all that, you can answer the following question even without reading a passage.

Topic Sentence Practice 1

19. Which of the following sentences is general enough to be a topic sentence?
   a. Java is a computer language.
   b. There are many different computer languages.
   c. An old computer language is BASIC.
   d. Most PCs run Microsoft programs.

The answer is choice **b**, *There are many different computer languages.* Choices **a**, **c**, and **d** are all specific examples of what is said in **b**, so they are not general enough to be topic sentences.

Topic Sentence Practice 2

Now, look at the following paragraph. Underline the sentence that expresses the main idea, and notice how the other sentences work to support that main idea.

> Erik always played cops and robbers when he was a boy; now, he's a police officer. Preeti always played school as a little girl; today, she is a high school math teacher. Kara always played store; today, she owns a chain of retail clothing shops. Long before they are faced with the question, "What do you want to be when you grow up?" some lucky people know exactly what they want to do with their lives.

Which sentence did you underline? You should have underlined the *last* sentence: *Long before they are faced with that question, "What do you want to be when you grow up?" some lucky people know exactly what they want to do with their lives.* This sentence is a good topic sentence; it expresses the idea that holds together the whole paragraph. The first three sentences—about Erik, Preeti, and Kara—are *specific examples* of these lucky people. Notice that this time the topic sentence is found at the *end* of the paragraph.

Topic Sentence Practice 3

Among the eight sentences below are *two* topic sentences. The other sentences are supporting sentences. Circle the two topic sentences. Then, write the numbers of the supporting sentences that go with each topic sentence.

1. Furthermore, government employees receive terrific heathcare coverage.
2. Some police officer duties, like writing reports, have no risk at all.
3. For example, government employees have more paid holidays than employees of private companies.
4. Not all police duties are dangerous.
5. Others, like traffic duty, put police officers at very little risk.
6. Government employees enjoy numerous benefits.
7. Still other duties, like investigating accidents, leave officers free of danger.
8. In addition, government employees are well compensated for overtime hours.

Sentences **4** and **6** are the two topic sentences because both make an assertion about a general subject. The supporting sentences for topic sentence **4**, *Not all police duties are dangerous*, are sentences **2**, **5**, and **7**. The supporting sentences for topic sentence **6**, *Government employees enjoy numerous benefits*, are the remaining sentences: **1**, **3**, and **8**.

Here's how they look as paragraphs:

Not all police duties are dangerous. Some duties, like writing reports, have no risk at all. Others, like traffic duty, offer very little risk. Still other duties, like investigating accidents, leave officers free of danger.

Government employees enjoy numerous benefits. For example, they have more paid holidays than employees of private companies. In addition, they are well compensated for overtime hours. Furthermore, they receive terrific healthcare coverage.

You might have noticed the supporting sentences in the first paragraph about police duties begin with the following words: *some, others,* and *still other.* These words are often used to introduce examples. The second paragraph uses different words, but they have the same function: *for example, in addition*, and *furthermore*. If a sentence begins with such a word or phrase, that is a good indication it is *not* a topic sentence—because it is providing a specific example.

Here are some words and phrases often used to introduce specific examples:

for example	in particular
for instance	some
in addition	others
furthermore	

If you are having trouble finding the main idea of a paragraph, you might try eliminating the sentences that you know contain supporting evidence.

Now, you can answer the last of the questions—the *why*. What's the main idea the author wants to convey? By finding the sentence that makes an assertion about the subject of the paragraph and that encompasses the other sentences in the paragraph, you can uncover the author's motive.

Drawing Conclusions

Writers know that they can get an idea across to their readers without directly saying it. Instead of providing a topic sentence that expresses their main idea, many times they simply omit that sentence, and instead provide a series of clues, through structure and language, to get their ideas across.

Finding an **implied main idea** is much like finding a stated main idea. Remember, a main idea is an assertion about the subject that controls or holds together all the ideas in the passage. If the writer provides a topic sentence that states the main idea, finding the main idea is something of a process of elimination: you eliminate the sentences that aren't general enough to encompass the whole passage. But what do you do when there is no topic sentence?

You use your observations to make an **inference**—a conclusion about the main idea or point of the passage.

Finding an implied main idea requires you to use your observations to make an inference that, like a topic sentence, encompasses the whole passage. It might take a little work, but you can make observations that will enable you to find main ideas even when they are not explicitly stated.

Inference Practice 1

For the first example of finding an implied main idea, let's return to our friend, Mr. Blank. If you remember, earlier in this chapter, his apartment was robbed. Now, look at a statement from the building manager in response to news of the robbery:

> We have never had a robbery in our building before Mr. Blank's unfortunate incident. After all, our neighborhood is one of the safest in the area, and police patrol the streets regularly. In addition, I have personally seen to it that all the building's windows and doors are locked and secure, and the superintendent maintains such security as well.

Now, there is no topic sentence in this paragraph, but you should be able to determine the manager's main idea from the facts he provides and from his tone. What is he suggesting?

20. Which of the following best summarizes the manager's main idea?
  a. The police are thorough when they patrol the neighborhood.
  b. It is unlikely that another robbery would occur in the building.
  c. The superintendent relies on the police to maintain the building's security.
  d. Mr. Blank is at fault for allowing his apartment to be robbed.

The correct answer is **b**, *It is highly unlikely that another robbery would occur in the building.* How can you tell that this is the main idea? It's the only one of the choices that is general enough to serve as a net for the paragraph: choice **a** is only a detail in the passage; choice **c** is not true, according to the information in the passage; and choice **d** isn't an inference that is supported by the details in the passage.

Inference Practice 2

Now, examine the following statement from Mr. Blank's neighbor, who was also interviewed after the robbery:

> I live right next door to Mr. Blank, and I heard a little scuffle outside my apartment door about the time of the robbery. I didn't think to check it out, and now, of course, I wish I had. I thought it was just Mr. Blank doing something in the hallway. Later, I went out to take my dog Millie for a walk and saw that the stairwell window was open. It was such a hot day, I didn't think much of that either, at least at first. But on a closer look, I saw some torn clothing on the windowsill, and some dirty footprints leading from Mr. Blank's apartment.

21. What is Mr. Blank's neighbor suggesting?
   a. Mr. Blank's neighbor heard a scuffle outside her door.
   b. The robbers probably escaped out the stairwell window.
   c. The stairwell window was left open.
   d. Mr. Blank's neighbor saw torn clothing on the windowsill.

   Which of these four statements do the sentences in the neighbor's statement support? Try the process of elimination. Do all the sentences support choice **a**? If not, cross out choice **a**. Do all the sentences support choice **b**? Choices **c** or **d**?

   The correct answer is **b**, *The robbers probably escaped out the stairwell window.* How can you tell? This is the only idea that all the statements support. You know that Mr. Blank's neighbor heard a scuffle outside her door; you also know the stairwell window was open and that Mr. Blank's neighbor saw torn clothing on the windowsill. Thus, the neighbor's statement contains **a**, **c**, and **d**, but none of these can be the main idea because the neighbor discusses all three things in combination. This combination makes it likely that the robbers escaped out the stairwell window.

Inference Practice 3

Now, look at a paragraph in which the *language* the writer uses is what enables you to determine meaning. Read the following paragraph carefully and see whether you can determine the implied main idea of the paragraph.

   My team captain, Will, is an exceptional leader with a heart of gold. He arrives 30 minutes before every practice so that he can check in with as many teammates as possible. He politely asks people about themselves and genuinely takes note about what they have to say. When I'm troubled, he'll notice and talk to me about it. Just having those warm eyes concentrate on

me and only me practically takes away any troubles I had.

   Before you decide on the implied main idea, list your observations. What did you notice about the language in this paragraph? An example is provided to get you started.

Observations

   Example:
   I noticed that Will's heart is described as being "gold."

22. Which of the following best expresses the implied message of the passage?
   a. Having Will as a team captain is a pleasure.
   b. Will has a warm personality.
   c. Will is an effective team captain.
   d. Having Will as a team captain is like having a best friend.

   The correct answer is **d**, *having Will as a team captain is like having a best friend.* There are many clues in the language of this paragraph that lead you to this inference. First, you probably noticed that Will has *a heart of gold.* This comparison (called a *metaphor*) suggests that Will is a caring person, with the utmost compassion and understanding for others.

   Second, the writer tells us that Will *genuinely takes note* of what his teammates have to say. *Genuinely takes note* are key word choices. The writer could have said that Will *hears* what they have to say or even *listens to* what they have to say, but neither convey his sincere care for others as the keywords *genuinely takes note* do. Furthermore, Will is described as having *warm eyes,* which also suggests a compassionate person, one who looks at others from a considerate point of view, rather than a cold, callous point of view. Thus, although choices **a**, **b**, and **c** may be true, choice **d** is the only idea that all the sentences in the paragraph support.

Of course, this person's description of Will is very subjective, as it uses the first-person point of view. As an active reader, you should wonder whether everyone sees Will this way, or if this teammate is unable to be objective about Will.

Many writers use implication to convey meaning rather than directly stating their ideas. Finding the implied main idea requires a little detective work, but it is not as difficult as you may have thought.

Tips for Continuing to Improve Your Reading

Reading is like exercise: If you don't keep doing it, you will get out of shape. Like muscles that grow stronger and bigger with each repetition, your reading skills will grow stronger with each text that you read.

The following are some ways you can continue to strengthen your reading comprehension skills:

- **Read!** Read anything—books, newspapers, magazines, novels, blogs. The more you read, the better. Set yourself a reading goal: it might be one book a month, two books while you are on vacation, or a half hour of reading every night before bed.

- **Spend some time in bookstores and libraries.** There are bound to be books and authors out there that appeal to some of your interests. Don't be afraid to ask a salesperson or librarian to help you. Describe your interests and your preferences in style, and he or she can help you find books you will enjoy reading.

- **Take a course at a local college.** Most courses (other than mathematics and computer science) require a significant amount of reading, so they are a great way to sharpen your reading comprehension skills while you work toward a degree or greater understanding of a certain subject. In addition, if you are in a class, you will have a teacher who can guide you to make sure you are correctly comprehending what you read.

12 ▶ PRACTICE ASVAB CORE TEST 2

CHAPTER SUMMARY
Here's another sample ASVAB core test for your practice. After working through the review and practice material in the previous chapters, take this test to see how much your score has improved.

This practice test will be a good measure of how much you've learned from working through the lessons in this book, especially if you took the first practice test in Chapter 5. Like that test, this one includes four out of the nine subtests that make up the ASVAB. These four subtests count toward your Armed Forces Qualifying Test (AFQT) score, which will determine whether you will be allowed to enlist in the military.

For this test, simulate the actual test-taking experience as closely as you can. Find a quiet place to work where you won't be disturbed. Use the answer sheet provided and use a timer or stopwatch to time each section. The times are marked at the beginning of each section.

After the exam, review the answer explanations to understand each question you missed. To find out more about your score, review Chapter 3.

Part 1: Arithmetic Reasoning

1. ⓐ ⓑ ⓒ ⓓ	11. ⓐ ⓑ ⓒ ⓓ	21. ⓐ ⓑ ⓒ ⓓ
2. ⓐ ⓑ ⓒ ⓓ	12. ⓐ ⓑ ⓒ ⓓ	22. ⓐ ⓑ ⓒ ⓓ
3. ⓐ ⓑ ⓒ ⓓ	13. ⓐ ⓑ ⓒ ⓓ	23. ⓐ ⓑ ⓒ ⓓ
4. ⓐ ⓑ ⓒ ⓓ	14. ⓐ ⓑ ⓒ ⓓ	24. ⓐ ⓑ ⓒ ⓓ
5. ⓐ ⓑ ⓒ ⓓ	15. ⓐ ⓑ ⓒ ⓓ	25. ⓐ ⓑ ⓒ ⓓ
6. ⓐ ⓑ ⓒ ⓓ	16. ⓐ ⓑ ⓒ ⓓ	26. ⓐ ⓑ ⓒ ⓓ
7. ⓐ ⓑ ⓒ ⓓ	17. ⓐ ⓑ ⓒ ⓓ	27. ⓐ ⓑ ⓒ ⓓ
8. ⓐ ⓑ ⓒ ⓓ	18. ⓐ ⓑ ⓒ ⓓ	28. ⓐ ⓑ ⓒ ⓓ
9. ⓐ ⓑ ⓒ ⓓ	19. ⓐ ⓑ ⓒ ⓓ	29. ⓐ ⓑ ⓒ ⓓ
10. ⓐ ⓑ ⓒ ⓓ	20. ⓐ ⓑ ⓒ ⓓ	30. ⓐ ⓑ ⓒ ⓓ

Part 2: Word Knowledge

1. ⓐ ⓑ ⓒ ⓓ	13. ⓐ ⓑ ⓒ ⓓ	25. ⓐ ⓑ ⓒ ⓓ
2. ⓐ ⓑ ⓒ ⓓ	14. ⓐ ⓑ ⓒ ⓓ	26. ⓐ ⓑ ⓒ ⓓ
3. ⓐ ⓑ ⓒ ⓓ	15. ⓐ ⓑ ⓒ ⓓ	27. ⓐ ⓑ ⓒ ⓓ
4. ⓐ ⓑ ⓒ ⓓ	16. ⓐ ⓑ ⓒ ⓓ	28. ⓐ ⓑ ⓒ ⓓ
5. ⓐ ⓑ ⓒ ⓓ	17. ⓐ ⓑ ⓒ ⓓ	29. ⓐ ⓑ ⓒ ⓓ
6. ⓐ ⓑ ⓒ ⓓ	18. ⓐ ⓑ ⓒ ⓓ	30. ⓐ ⓑ ⓒ ⓓ
7. ⓐ ⓑ ⓒ ⓓ	19. ⓐ ⓑ ⓒ ⓓ	31. ⓐ ⓑ ⓒ ⓓ
8. ⓐ ⓑ ⓒ ⓓ	20. ⓐ ⓑ ⓒ ⓓ	32. ⓐ ⓑ ⓒ ⓓ
9. ⓐ ⓑ ⓒ ⓓ	21. ⓐ ⓑ ⓒ ⓓ	33. ⓐ ⓑ ⓒ ⓓ
10. ⓐ ⓑ ⓒ ⓓ	22. ⓐ ⓑ ⓒ ⓓ	34. ⓐ ⓑ ⓒ ⓓ
11. ⓐ ⓑ ⓒ ⓓ	23. ⓐ ⓑ ⓒ ⓓ	35. ⓐ ⓑ ⓒ ⓓ
12. ⓐ ⓑ ⓒ ⓓ	24. ⓐ ⓑ ⓒ ⓓ	

Part 3: Paragraph Comprehension

1. ⓐ ⓑ ⓒ ⓓ	6. ⓐ ⓑ ⓒ ⓓ	11. ⓐ ⓑ ⓒ ⓓ
2. ⓐ ⓑ ⓒ ⓓ	7. ⓐ ⓑ ⓒ ⓓ	12. ⓐ ⓑ ⓒ ⓓ
3. ⓐ ⓑ ⓒ ⓓ	8. ⓐ ⓑ ⓒ ⓓ	13. ⓐ ⓑ ⓒ ⓓ
4. ⓐ ⓑ ⓒ ⓓ	9. ⓐ ⓑ ⓒ ⓓ	14. ⓐ ⓑ ⓒ ⓓ
5. ⓐ ⓑ ⓒ ⓓ	10. ⓐ ⓑ ⓒ ⓓ	15. ⓐ ⓑ ⓒ ⓓ

Part 4: Mathematics Knowledge

1. ⓐ ⓑ ⓒ ⓓ	10. ⓐ ⓑ ⓒ ⓓ	19. ⓐ ⓑ ⓒ ⓓ
2. ⓐ ⓑ ⓒ ⓓ	11. ⓐ ⓑ ⓒ ⓓ	20. ⓐ ⓑ ⓒ ⓓ
3. ⓐ ⓑ ⓒ ⓓ	12. ⓐ ⓑ ⓒ ⓓ	21. ⓐ ⓑ ⓒ ⓓ
4. ⓐ ⓑ ⓒ ⓓ	13. ⓐ ⓑ ⓒ ⓓ	22. ⓐ ⓑ ⓒ ⓓ
5. ⓐ ⓑ ⓒ ⓓ	14. ⓐ ⓑ ⓒ ⓓ	23. ⓐ ⓑ ⓒ ⓓ
6. ⓐ ⓑ ⓒ ⓓ	15. ⓐ ⓑ ⓒ ⓓ	24. ⓐ ⓑ ⓒ ⓓ
7. ⓐ ⓑ ⓒ ⓓ	16. ⓐ ⓑ ⓒ ⓓ	25. ⓐ ⓑ ⓒ ⓓ
8. ⓐ ⓑ ⓒ ⓓ	17. ⓐ ⓑ ⓒ ⓓ	
9. ⓐ ⓑ ⓒ ⓓ	18. ⓐ ⓑ ⓒ ⓓ	

Part 1: Arithmetic Reasoning

Time: 36 minutes

1. What is the estimated product when 157 and 817 are rounded to the nearest hundred and multiplied?
   - **a.** 160,000
   - **b.** 180,000
   - **c.** 16,000
   - **d.** 80,000

2. A large coffee pot holds 120 cups. It is about two-thirds full. About how many cups are in the pot?
   - **a.** 40 cups
   - **b.** 80 cups
   - **c.** 60 cups
   - **d.** 90 cups

3. Mr. Tupper is purchasing gifts for his family. He stops to consider what else he has to buy. A quick mental inventory of his shopping bag so far reveals the following:

1 cashmere sweater, valued at	$260
3 diamond bracelets, each valued at	$365
1 computer game, valued at	$78
1 cameo brooch, valued at	$130

   Later, having coffee in the Food Court, he suddenly remembers that he has purchased only two diamond bracelets, not three, and that the cashmere sweater was on sale for $245. What is the total value of the gifts Mr. Tupper has purchased so far?
   - **a.** $818
   - **b.** $1,183
   - **c.** $1,198
   - **d.** $1,563

This is a list of ingredients needed to make 16 brownies. Use this list to answer questions 4 and 5.

Deluxe Brownies
$\frac{2}{3}$ cup butter
5 squares (1 ounce each) unsweetened chocolate
$1\frac{1}{2}$ cups sugar
2 teaspoons vanilla
2 eggs
1 cup flour

4. How much sugar is needed to make 8 brownies?
   - **a.** $\frac{3}{4}$ cup
   - **b.** 3 cups
   - **c.** $\frac{1}{3}$ cup
   - **d.** $1\frac{1}{2}$ cups

5. What is the greatest number of brownies that can be made if the baker has only one cup of butter?
   - **a.** 12
   - **b.** 16
   - **c.** 24
   - **d.** 32

6. An outdoor swimming pool at the Shulkind residence can be filled with water from the garden hose at a rate of $3\frac{1}{2}$ inches per hour. If the Shulkinds want to fill the empty pool with 49 inches of water, how many hours will it take to get to this level?
   - **a.** 3.5 hours
   - **b.** 171.5 hours
   - **c.** 14 hours
   - **d.** 16.3 hours

7. The state of Connecticut will pay two-fifths of the cost of a new school building. If the city of New Haven is building a school that will cost a total of $15,500,000, what will the state pay?
   a. $3,100,000
   b. $7,750,000
   c. $6,200,000
   d. $9,300,000

8. Body mass index (BMI) is equal to $\frac{\text{weight in kilograms}}{(\text{height in meters})^2}$. A man who weighs 64.8 kilograms has a BMI of 20. How tall is he?
   a. 1.8 meters
   b. 0.9 meters
   c. 1.62 meters
   d. 3.24 meters

9. Maya is using written instructions to create an airplane made out of thin balsa wood. Her instructions are drawn to scale so that every $\frac{1}{8}$ inch in the drawing represents $1\frac{1}{2}$ inches of balsa wood. How tall will the tail of the airplane be if it is $2\frac{3}{4}$ inches tall in the drawing?
   a. $14\frac{2}{3}$ inches
   b. 22 inches
   c. 33 inches
   d. 44 inches

10. Newly hired nurses have to buy duty shoes at the full price of $84.50, but nurses who have served at least a year get a 15% discount. Nurses who have served at least three years get an additional 10% off the discounted price. How much does a nurse who has served at least three years have to pay for shoes?
   a. $63.38
   b. $64.65
   c. $71.83
   d. $76.05

11. Katie has a drawer of unmarked spare keys for the dorm that she manages. If the drawer contains 9 keys to the front door, 4 keys to the laundry room, and 3 keys to the storage closet, what is the probability that when she grabs a key at random, it will be a key to either the front door or the storage closet?
   a. 75%
   b. 56.25%
   c. 43.75%
   d. 25%

12. The basal metabolic rate (BMR) is the rate at which our body uses calories. The BMR for a man in his twenties is about 1,700 calories per day. If 204 of those calories should come from protein, about what percent of this man's diet should be protein?
   a. 1.2%
   b. 8.3%
   c. 12%
   d. 88%

13. The condition known as Down syndrome occurs in about one in 1,500 children when the mothers are in their twenties. About what percent of all children born to mothers in their twenties are likely to have Down syndrome?
   a. 0.0067%
   b. 0.67%
   c. 6.7%
   d. 0.067%

14. If a population of yeast cells grows from 10 to 320 in a period of five hours, what is the rate of growth?
   a. It doubles its numbers every hour.
   b. It triples its numbers every hour.
   c. It doubles its numbers every two hours.
   d. It triples its numbers every two hours.

15. How much water must be added to 1 liter of a 5% saline solution to get a 2% saline solution?
  a. 1 L
  b. 1.5 L
  c. 2 L
  d. 2.5 L

16. Susan and Bill are training for a marathon together. They were given instructions to run for 52 minutes on Friday, and increase their run time by 10% every Friday. If their first Friday run is 52 minutes, approximately how many minutes will their third Friday run last?
  a. 60 minutes
  b. 63 minutes
  c. 67 minutes
  d. 70 minutes

17. All the rooms in a building are rectangular, with 8-foot ceilings. One room is 9 feet wide by 11 feet long. What is the combined area of the four walls, including doors and windows?
  a. 99 square feet
  b. 160 square feet
  c. 320 square feet
  d. 72 square feet

18. What is the volume of a pyramid that has a rectangular base of 10 inches by 12 inches and a height of 10 inches? ($V = \frac{1}{3}lwh$)
  a. 40 cubic inches
  b. 120 cubic inches
  c. 400 cubic inches
  d. 1,200 cubic inches

19. A child has a temperature of 40°C. What is the child's temperature in degrees Fahrenheit? ($F = \frac{9}{5}C + 32$)
  a. 95°F
  b. 102°F
  c. 104°F
  d. 113°F

20. If jogging for one mile uses 150 calories and brisk walking for one mile uses 100 calories, a jogger has to go how many times as far as a walker to use the same number of calories?
  a. $\frac{1}{2}$
  b. $\frac{2}{3}$
  c. $\frac{3}{2}$
  d. 2

21. A dosage of a certain medication is 12 cc per 100 pounds. What is the dosage for a patient who weighs 175 pounds?
  a. 15 cc
  b. 18 cc
  c. 21 cc
  d. 24 cc

22. A hiker walks 40 miles on the first day of a five-day trip. On each day after that, he can walk only half as far as he did the day before. On average, how far does he walk each day?
  a. 10 miles
  b. 15.5 miles
  c. 19.375 miles
  d. 24 miles

23. Mr. Thaler is driving from Los Angeles to San Francisco. If he drives 3 hours in traffic at an average speed of 32 miles per hour, and then 4.5 hours on the freeway, at an average speed of 72 miles per hour, what was his overall average speed on his trip to San Francisco?
  a. 52 miles per hour
  b. 52.5 miles per hour
  c. 56 miles per hour
  d. 60 miles per hour

24. A family's gas and electricity bill averages $80 a month for seven months of the year and $20 a month the rest of the year. If the family's bills were averaged over the entire year, what would the monthly bill be?
   a. $45
   b. $50
   c. $55
   d. $60

25. Jason is six times as old as Kate. In two years, Jason will be twice as old as Kate is then. How old is Jason now?
   a. 6 months old
   b. 3 years old
   c. 6 years old
   d. 9 years old

26. During her first three months at college, a student's food costs are $103.30, $71.60, and $84.00. She spends $18.00 each month on coffee. What is her average total monthly food and drink costs?
   a. $86.30
   b. $92.30
   c. $98.30
   d. $104.30

27. A Boeing 747 airplane burns approximately 1 gallon of fuel for every second flown. If the flight from New York to Beijing is 13.5 hours, approximately how many gallons of fuel will be used during this trip?
   a. 19,440 gallons
   b. 810 gallons
   c. 48,600 gallons
   d. cannot be determined with the information given

28. Land in a development is selling for $60,000 per acre. If Jack purchases $1\frac{3}{4}$ acres, how much will he pay?
   a. $45,000
   b. $135,000
   c. $105,000
   d. $120,000

29. For every dollar Kyra saves, her employer contributes a dime to her savings, with a maximum employer contribution of $10 per month. If Kyra saves $60 in January, $130 in March, and $70 in April, how much will she have in savings at the end of that time?
   a. $270
   b. $283
   c. $286
   d. $290

30. Jackie is paid $822.40 twice a month. If she saves $150.00 per paycheck and pays $84.71 on her student loan each month, how much does she have left to spend each month?
   a. $1,175.38
   b. $1,260.09
   c. $1,410.09
   d. $1,560.09

Part 2: Word Knowledge

Time: 11 minutes

Select the choice that best matches the underlined word.

1. According to the code of conduct, "Every officer will be <u>accountable</u> for his or her decisions."
   a. applauded
   b. compensated
   c. responsible
   d. approached

2. <u>Scrutinize</u> most nearly means
   a. vanish.
   b. dissect.
   c. neglect.
   d. weaken.

3. <u>Enumerate</u> most nearly means
   a. pronounce.
   b. count.
   c. explain.
   d. plead.

4. <u>Emulate</u> most nearly means
   a. imitate.
   b. authorize.
   c. fascinate.
   d. punish.

5. The residents of that area were considered to be <u>compliant</u> in regard to the seat belt law.
   a. skeptical
   b. obedient
   c. forgetful
   d. appreciative

6. Following the disturbance, town officials felt the need to <u>augment</u> the laws pertaining to mass demonstrations.
   a. repeal
   b. evaluate
   c. expand
   d. criticize

7. <u>Aversion</u> most nearly means
   a. harmony.
   b. greed.
   c. weariness.
   d. dislike.

8. <u>Validate</u> most nearly means
   a. confirm.
   b. retrieve.
   c. communicate.
   d. appoint.

9. <u>Antagonist</u> most nearly means
   a. comrade.
   b. opponent.
   c. master.
   d. perfectionist.

10. <u>Perseverance</u> most nearly means
   a. unhappiness.
   b. fame.
   c. persistence.
   d. humility.

11. As soon as the details of the affair were released to the media, the newspaper was <u>inundated</u> with calls from a curious public.
   a. provided
   b. bothered
   c. rewarded
   d. flooded

12. <u>Homogeneous</u> most nearly means
   a. alike.
   b. plain.
   c. native.
   d. dissimilar.

13. <u>Ominous</u> most nearly means
   a. ordinary.
   b. gracious.
   c. quarrelsome.
   d. threatening.

14. When people heard that timid Bob had taken up skydiving, they were <u>incredulous</u>.
   a. fearful
   b. outraged
   c. disbelieving
   d. inconsolable

15. <u>Recluse</u> most nearly means
   a. prophet.
   b. fool.
   c. intellectual.
   d. hermit.

16. The company recruited her because she was <u>proficient</u> in the use of computers.
   a. incompetent
   b. careful
   c. efficient
   d. skilled

17. <u>Defray</u> most nearly means
   a. pay.
   b. defend.
   c. cheat.
   d. disobey.

18. <u>Placid</u> most nearly means
   a. flabby.
   b. peaceful.
   c. wise.
   d. obedient.

19. The city council has given <u>tentative</u> approval to the idea of banning smoking from all public buildings.
   a. provisional
   b. ambiguous
   c. confused
   d. unnecessary

20. <u>Vast</u> most nearly means
   a. attentive.
   b. immense.
   c. steady.
   d. slight.

21. <u>Animosity</u> most nearly means
   a. natural.
   b. climax.
   c. hostility.
   d. untold.

22. <u>Adage</u> most nearly means
   a. saying.
   b. language.
   c. elderly.
   d. superior.

23. Otto's <u>prosperous</u> store was busy seven days a week.
   a. lavish
   b. successful
   c. memorable
   d. competitive

24. The novel included <u>figurative</u> language such as metaphors.
   a. theoretical
   b. symbolic
   c. complex
   d. truthful

25. Jimin wanted to keep his father's school ring for <u>posterity</u>.
   a. proof of the past
   b. memorabilia
   c. future generations
   d. investment

26. <u>Subliminal</u> most nearly means
  a. concealed.
  b. identifiable.
  c. original.
  d. mysterious.

27. <u>Resonant</u> most nearly means
  a. echoing.
  b. harsh.
  c. delicate.
  d. illegible.

28. <u>Expedient</u> most nearly means
  a. cumbersome.
  b. inappropriate.
  c. quick.
  d. slow.

29. The helicopter is used for patients with <u>exigent</u> medical conditions.
  a. urgent
  b. commonplace
  c. underdeveloped
  d. extreme

30. The corner store sold <u>sundry</u> items.
  a. precious
  b. meager
  c. exotic
  d. assorted

31. After the contest ended, Lisala offered her competitors <u>fulsome</u> praise.
  a. excessive
  b. irritating
  c. pleasing
  d. inspiring

32. <u>Tumultuous</u> most nearly means
  a. dedicated.
  b. respectful.
  c. quiet.
  d. disorderly.

33. <u>Exorbitant</u> most nearly means
  a. valuable.
  b. overpriced.
  c. wild.
  d. unbelievable.

34. Her <u>blatant</u> expression revealed her feelings.
  a. secretive
  b. fabricated
  c. transparent
  d. loud

35. <u>Empirical</u> most nearly means
  a. ancient.
  b. practical.
  c. false.
  d. unwieldy.

Part 3: Paragraph Comprehension

Time: 13 minutes

Read each passage and answer the questions that follow.

The supervisors have received numerous complaints over the past several weeks about buses on several routes running hot. Drivers are reminded that each route has several checkpoints at which drivers should check the time. If the bus is ahead of schedule, drivers should delay at the checkpoint until it is the proper time to leave.

1. According to the passage, when a bus is *running hot*, it means
  a. the engine is overheating.
  b. the bus is running ahead of schedule.
  c. the air conditioning is not working.
  d. there is no more room for passengers.

2. According to the passage,
  a. every bus stop is also a checkpoint.
  b. it is important to keep customer complaints to a minimum.
  c. drivers tend to rush their routes so they can leave work early.
  d. each bus route has several points at which drivers should check the time.

Drivers are responsible for refueling their trucks at the end of each shift. All other routine maintenance is performed by maintenance department personnel, who are also responsible for maintaining service records. If a driver believes a truck is in need of mechanical repair, he or she should fill out the pink Repair Requisition form and turn it in to the shift supervisor.

3. If a truck is due to have the oil changed, it will be done by
  a. maintenance department personnel.
  b. truck drivers.
  c. shift supervisors.
  d. outside contractors.

4. The passage suggests that trucks
  a. are refueled when they have less than half a tank of gas.
  b. have the oil changed every 1,000 miles.
  c. are refueled at the end of every shift.
  d. are in frequent need of repair.

Hazardous waste is defined as any waste designated by the U.S. Environmental Protection Agency as hazardous. If a sanitation worker is unsure if a particular item is hazardous, he or she should not handle the item but should instead notify the supervisor for directions.

5. Hazardous waste is
  a. anything too dangerous for workers to handle.
  b. picked up by special trucks.
  c. defined by the U.S. Environmental Protection Agency.
  d. not allowed with regular residential garbage.

6. A sanitation worker comes upon a container of cleaning solvent along with the regular garbage in front of a residence. The container does not list the contents of the cleaner. He should
  a. assume the solvent is safe and deposit it in the sanitation truck.
  b. leave a note for the residents, asking them to list the contents.
  c. contact the supervisor for directions.
  d. leave the container on the curb.

Many people hesitate to adopt a retired racing greyhound because they worry that it will be nervous and will need a large space to run. This is a false impression. Greyhounds have naturally sweet, mild dispositions and are sprinters rather than distance runners; they are sufficiently exercised with a few laps around a fenced-in backyard every day. Greyhounds do not make good watchdogs, but they are very good with children, get along well with other dogs (and usually cats as well), and are very affectionate and loyal.

7. According to the passage, adopting a greyhound is a good idea for people who
a. do not have children.
b. live in apartment buildings.
c. do not usually like dogs.
d. already have another dog or a cat.

8. One drawback of adopting a greyhound is that they
a. are not good watchdogs.
b. are very old when they retire from racing.
c. are very competitive.
d. need lots of room to run.

One easy way to plan healthy menus is to shop only in the outer aisles of the grocery store. In most supermarkets, fresh fruit and vegetables, dairy, fresh meat, and frozen foods are in the outer aisles. Grains, like pasta, rice, bread, and cereal, are located on the next aisles, the first inner rows. The inside aisles are where you'll find chips and snacks, cookies and pastries, soda pop and drink mixes—foods that nutritionists say should be eaten rarely, if at all. A side benefit of shopping this way is that grocery shopping takes less time.

9. A good title for this article would be
a. Why You Should Shop in a Health Food Store.
b. How to Complete Your Grocery Shopping in Less Time.
c. How to Shop for Healthy Food.
d. How to Cook Healthy Food.

10. According to the passage, the best way to shop in the grocery store is to
a. make a list and stick to it.
b. stay in the outside aisles.
c. look for the best prices.
d. check the newspaper ads each week.

Graduating from veterinary school is not the last step in the process of becoming a veterinarian. There are two final exams every veterinarian must pass before being allowed to practice: the difficult national veterinary medical board exam, as well as the state board exam for the state or states in which they ultimately want to practice. Some veterinarians feel the state-specific exam is unnecessary, however, and argue that passing the national veterinary medical board exam should be enough because medical knowledge does not differ from state to state. However, not everyone agrees with that sentiment. They believe that the state board exam is a necessity because there will always be area-specific issues of which veterinarians must be aware.

11. According to the passage, in order to practice, a veterinarian must
a. pass only the national veterinary medical board exam.
b. complete three years of residency in veterinary medicine.
c. be knowledgeable about medical issues in all states.
d. pass both a national and a state exam.

12. This passage is probably taken from a(n)
a. memo entitled, "State Veterinarian Exams Deemed Unimportant."
b. pet owner's training manual.
c. article entitled, "Pros and Cons of Veterinarian Requirements."
d. novel in which the protagonist is a veterinarian.

13. According to the passage, state exams are important because they
  a. require veterinarians to be knowledgeable about regional issues.
  b. give veterinarians needed practice in test taking.
  c. are similar to the requirements made of medical doctors.
  d. demand veterinarians have a high level of medical knowledge.

In the summer, the northern hemisphere is slanted toward the sun, making the days longer and warmer than in winter. The first day of summer is called the *summer solstice* and is also the longest day of the year. However, June 21 marks the beginning of winter in the southern hemisphere, when that hemisphere is tilted away from the sun.

14. According to the passage, when it is summer in the northern hemisphere, in the southern hemisphere it is
  a. spring.
  b. summer.
  c. autumn.
  d. winter.

15. It can be inferred from the passage that, in the southern hemisphere, June 21 is the
  a. autumnal equinox.
  b. winter solstice.
  c. vernal equinox.
  d. summer solstice.

Part 4:
Mathematics Knowledge

Time: 24 minutes

1. Which of these lines are parallel?

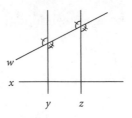

  a. w and x
  b. x and y
  c. x and z
  d. y and z

2. $5\frac{2}{3} - 2\frac{5}{7} =$
  a. $8\frac{8}{21}$
  b. $3\frac{3}{4}$
  c. $2\frac{20}{21}$
  d. $3\frac{1}{21}$

3. 35% of what number is equal to 14?
  a. 4
  b. 4.9
  c. 40
  d. 400

4. $\frac{1}{4}$ is equal to
  a. 0.15.
  b. 0.25.
  c. 0.20.
  d. 0.75.

5. If $8n + 25 = 65$, then n is
  a. 5.
  b. 11.25.
  c. 40.
  d. 90.

6. What is the reciprocal of $3\frac{7}{8}$?
- **a.** $\frac{31}{8}$
- **b.** $\frac{8}{31}$
- **c.** $\frac{8}{21}$
- **d.** $-\frac{31}{8}$

7. Which of these sets of angles would make an isosceles triangle?
- **a.** 80º, 80º, 100º
- **b.** 90º, 40º, 50º
- **c.** 50º, 50º, 50º
- **d.** 70º, 55º, 55º

8. What is another way to write $3\sqrt{12}$?
- **a.** $12\sqrt{3}$
- **b.** $6\sqrt{3}$
- **c.** $2\sqrt{10}$
- **d.** 18

9. What is another way to write 3^4?
- **a.** 12
- **b.** 64
- **c.** 27
- **d.** 81

10. What is the decimal form of $-1\frac{1}{3}$ rounded to the nearest hundredth?
- **a.** 1.33
- **b.** −1.33
- **c.** 3.67
- **d.** −3.67

11. $2\frac{4}{5}$ is equal to which of the following?
- **a.** 2.45%
- **b.** 2.8%
- **c.** 2.8
- **d.** 2.45

12. Triangles *RST* and *MNO* are similar. What is the length of line segment *MO*?

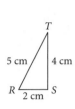
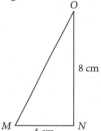

- **a.** 10 cm
- **b.** 20 cm
- **c.** 32 cm
- **d.** 40 cm

13. Put the following fractions in order of least to greatest: $\frac{5}{6}, \frac{2}{7}, \frac{17}{20}, \frac{1}{3}$.
- **a.** $\frac{2}{7}, \frac{1}{3}, \frac{5}{6}, \frac{17}{20}$
- **b.** $\frac{2}{7}, \frac{1}{3}, \frac{17}{20}, \frac{5}{6}$
- **c.** $\frac{1}{3}, \frac{2}{7}, \frac{17}{20}, \frac{5}{6}$
- **d.** $\frac{1}{3}, \frac{5}{6}, \frac{2}{7}, \frac{17}{20}$

14. $0.40 =$
- **a.** $\frac{1}{4}$
- **b.** $\frac{1}{5}$
- **c.** $\frac{2}{5}$
- **d.** $\frac{3}{4}$

15. Which of the following expressions correctly demonstrates "three less than twice a number"?
- **a.** $(x + 2) - 3$
- **b.** $3 - 2x$
- **c.** $3 < x^2$
- **d.** $2x - 3$

16. Lines *a*, *b*, and *c* intersect at point *O*. Which of these pairs are NOT adjacent angles?

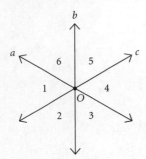

  a. ∠1 and ∠6
  b. ∠1 and ∠4
  c. ∠4 and ∠5
  d. ∠2 and ∠3

17. 2.25 =
  a. $2\frac{1}{4}$
  b. $2\frac{1}{5}$
  c. $\frac{2}{5}$
  d. $1\frac{3}{4}$

18. 6^3 is equal to
  a. 36.
  b. 1,296.
  c. 18.
  d. 216.

19. $10 + 40 \div 10 \times 2 =$
  a. 18
  b. 10
  c. 12
  d. $\frac{50}{20}$

20. 0.125 =
  a. $\frac{1}{25}$
  b. $\frac{1}{8}$
  c. $\frac{2}{5}$
  d. $\frac{1}{5}$

21. One side of a square bandage is 4 inches long. What is the perimeter of the bandage?
  a. 4 inches
  b. 8 inches
  c. 12 inches
  d. 16 inches

22. 33 is 12% of which of the following?
  a. 37.5
  b. 3.96
  c. 275
  d. 2,750

23. What is the area of a circle whose circumference is 12π?
  a. 144π
  b. 24π
  c. 36π
  d. $36\pi^2$

24. 17^2 is equal to
  a. 34.
  b. 68.
  c. 131,072.
  d. 289.

25. If the following two triangles are similar, with ∠*A* equal to ∠*D*, what is the perimeter of △*DEF*?

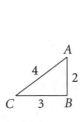
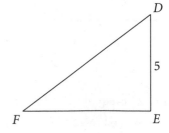

  a. 18
  b. 19
  c. 22.5
  d. 29.5

Answers

Part 1: Arithmetic Reasoning

1. This is a decimals problem.
   a. 157 is rounded to 200; 817 is rounded to 800; (200)(800) = 160,000. Choice **b** is incorrect because you incorrectly rounded 817 up to 900. Choice **c** is incorrect because you are missing a factor of 10. Choice **d** is incorrect because you incorrectly rounded 157 down to 100.

2. This is a fractions problem.
   b. Multiply 120 by $\frac{2}{3}$. Thus, $\frac{120}{1} \times \frac{2}{3} = \frac{240}{3} = 80$; 120 is written as a fraction with a denominator of 1. The fraction $\frac{240}{1}$ is simplified by dividing 240 by 3 to get 80 cups. Choice **a** is incorrect because this is the number of cups that has been used from a full pot, not the number that remain. Choice **c** is incorrect because this is half the pot, not $\frac{2}{3}$ of it. Choice **d** is incorrect because this is $\frac{3}{4}$ of the pot, not $\frac{2}{3}$ of it.

3. This is a decimals problem.
   b. Add the corrected value of the sweater ($245) to the value of the two, not three, bracelets ($730), plus the other two items ($78 and $130). Choice **a** is incorrect because you only accounted for 1 bracelet, not 2. Choice **c** is incorrect because you didn't use the sale price for the sweater. Choice **d** is incorrect because you didn't use the sale price of the sweater, and you counted 3, not 2, bracelets.

4. This is a fractions problem.
   a. The recipe is for 16 brownies. Half of that, 8, would reduce the ingredients by half. Half of $1\frac{1}{2}$ cups of sugar is $\frac{3}{4}$ cup. Choice **b** is incorrect because this would be the amount for 32 brownies (double batch), not 8 (half a batch). Choice **c** is incorrect because you computed $\frac{1}{2} \div \frac{3}{2}$ instead of multiplying these fractions. Choice **d** is incorrect because this is the amount needed to make 16 brownies, not 8.

5. This is a fractions problem.
   c. The recipe for 16 brownies calls for $\frac{2}{3}$ cup butter. An additional $\frac{1}{3}$ cup would make 8 more brownies, for a total of 24 brownies. Choices **a and b** are incorrect because it takes only $\frac{2}{3}$ cup of butter to make 16 brownies and you have more butter than this. Choice **d** is incorrect because this would require $2(\frac{2}{3}$ cup$) = \frac{4}{3}$ cups $= 1\frac{1}{3}$ cups of butter, but you have only 1 cup.

6. This is a decimals problem.
   c. Since the Shulkinds want 49 inches of water and they can get only $3\frac{1}{2}$ inches of water per hour, you must divide 49 inches by $3\frac{1}{2}$ inches to see how many hours that will take. $\frac{49}{1} \div 3\frac{1}{2} = \frac{49}{1} \div \frac{7}{2} = \frac{49}{1} \times \frac{2}{7}$. Reduce diagonally to get $\frac{7}{1} \times \frac{2}{1} = 14$. So, 14 hours is the answer. Choice **a** is incorrect because 3.5 is the number of inches per hour, not the number of hours to fill the pool. Choice **b** is incorrect because you multiplied $\frac{49}{1}$ by $\frac{7}{2}$ instead of its reciprocal. Choice **d** is incorrect because you divided 49 by 3, not $3\frac{1}{2}$.

7. This is a fractions problem.

    c. Multiply \$15,500,000 by $\frac{2}{5}$: $\frac{\$15,500,000}{1} \times \frac{2}{5} =$ \$6,200,000. Choice **a** is incorrect because this is $\frac{1}{5}$, not $\frac{2}{5}$, of the amount. Choice **b** is incorrect because this is half, not $\frac{2}{5}$, of the amount. Choice **d** is incorrect because this is the amount that the state will NOT pay; that is, it is the remaining $\frac{3}{5}$.

8. This is a decimals problem.

    a. Substituting known quantities into the formula yields $20 = \frac{64.8}{x^2}$. Next, you must multiply through by x^2 to get $20x^2 = 64.8$. Now divide through by 20 to get $x^2 = \frac{64.8}{20} = 3.24$. Now take the square root of both sides to get x equals 1.8. Choice **b** is incorrect because this is half of the correct answer. Choice **c** is incorrect because you didn't compute the square root correctly; you multiplied by $\frac{1}{2}$ instead. Choice **d** is incorrect because you didn't take the square root.

9. This is a fractions problem.

    c. You must first divide $2\frac{3}{4}$ inches by $\frac{1}{8}$ inches to see how many $\frac{1}{8}$-inch segments are in $2\frac{3}{4}$. $2\frac{3}{4} \div \frac{1}{8} = \frac{11}{4} \div \frac{1}{8} = \times \frac{11}{4} \times \frac{8}{1} = \frac{11}{1} \times \frac{2}{1} = 22$. There are 22 **eighth**-inch segments in $2\frac{3}{4}$ inches. Since each segment represents $1\frac{1}{2}$ inches, multiply $1\frac{1}{2}$ by 22 to see how many inches tall the tail will be. $\frac{3}{2} \times 22 = 33$ inches. Choice **a** is incorrect because you divided 22 by $\frac{3}{2}$ instead of multiplying the two together. Choice **b** is incorrect because this is the number of $\frac{1}{8}$-inch segments in $2\frac{3}{4}$ inches, but you didn't convert this to the actual length it represents. Choice **d** is incorrect because you multiplied the fractions incorrectly.

10. This is a percents problem.

    b. You can't just take 25% off the original price, because the 10% discount after three years of service is taken off the price that has already been reduced by 15%. Solve the problem in two steps: After the 15% discount the price is \$71.83. Ninety percent of that—subtracting 10%—is \$64.65. Choice **a** is incorrect because you mistakenly added the percentages together as if they applied to the same original whole. Choice **c** is incorrect because you applied only the 15% discount; you need to take an additional 10% off the price. Choice **d** is incorrect because you applied only the 10% discount.

11. This is a fractions problem.

    a. There are 16 keys in total $(9 + 4 + 3 = 16)$. Since 12 of those keys are to the front door or the storage closet, the probability of grabbing one of those keys at random is $\frac{12}{16} = \frac{3}{4} = 75\%$. Choice **b** is incorrect because this is the probability of grabbing the key to the front door; you didn't account for the key to the storage closet. Choice **c** is incorrect because this is the probability of grabbing the key to the storage closet or the laundry room. Choice **d** is incorrect because this is the probability of grabbing the key to the laundry room.

12. This is a percents problem.

    c. The problem is solved by dividing 204 by 1,700. The answer, 0.12, is then converted to a percentage. Choice **a** is incorrect because you didn't convert 0.12 to a percent correctly; move the decimal point 2 places to the right. Choice **b** is incorrect because you divided 1,700 by 204 and affixed a % sign to the end of the resulting decimal. This division was performed in the wrong order. Choice **d** is incorrect because this is the percent of the diet that should NOT be protein.

13. This is a percents problem.

    d. The simplest way to solve this problem is to divide 1 by 1,500, which is 0.0006667, and then count off two decimal places to arrive at the percentage, which is 0.06667%. Since the question asks *about what percentage,* the nearest value is 0.067%. Choice **a** is incorrect because you moved the decimal point only 1 place to the right instead of 2 to convert to a decimal. Choice **b** is incorrect because you moved the decimal point 3 places to the right instead of 2. Choice **c** is incorrect because you moved the decimal point 4 places to the right instead of 2.

14. This is an algebra problem.

    a. You can use trial and error to arrive at a solution to this problem. After the first hour, the number would be 20, after the second hour 40, after the third hour 80, after the fourth hour 160, and after the fifth hour 320. The other answer choices do not have the same outcome. Choice **b** is incorrect because the population during the first 5 one-hour periods is 10 to 30 to 90 to 270 to 810 to 2,430; this is not the given 320. Choice **c** is incorrect because the population during the first 4 hours, in two-hour periods, is 10 to 20 to 40. Then, the population in the fifth hour will not reach 320. Choice **d** is incorrect because the population during the first 4 hours, in two-hour periods, is 10 to 30 to 90. Then, by the fifth hour, the population will not reach 320.

15. This is a percents problem.

    b. Use the equation $0.05(1) = 0.02(x)$, where x is the total amount of water in the resulting 2% solution. Solving for x, you get 2.5. Subtracting the 1 liter of water already present in the 5% solution, you will find that 1.5 liters need to be added. Choice **a** is incorrect because this would not quite yield a 2% solution; its concentration is a little larger. Choice **c** is incorrect because this would not quite yield a 2% solution; its concentration is a little smaller. Choice **d** is incorrect because you didn't subtract the 1 liter already present.

16. This is a decimals problem.

    b. The second week's run will increase by 10% of 52: $10\% \times 52 = 0.10 \times 52 = 5.2$ minutes (this will be the increase in minutes); $52 + 5.2 = 57.2$ minutes. This will be how long their *second* Friday run will last. Then the third Friday run will increase by another 10%: $10\% \times 57.2 = 0.10 \times 57.2 = 5.72$ minutes (this will be the increase in minutes); $57.2 + 5.72 = 62.93$ minutes. So their run on their third Friday will last for approximately 63 minutes. Choice **a** is incorrect because you added only 5% for one of the two increases; both should be 10% increases. Choice **c** is incorrect because you added 10 minutes for the second increase, not 10% of the time. Choice **d** is incorrect because you added one too many 10% increases.

17. This is a geometry problem.

    c. Each 9-foot wall has an area of 9(8) or 72 square feet. There are two such walls, so those two walls combined have an area of 144 square feet. Each 11-foot wall has an area of 11(8) or 88 square feet, and again there are two such walls: 88(2) = 176. Finally, add 144 and 176 to get 320 square feet. Choice **a** is incorrect because this is the area of the floor, not the combined areas of the walls. Choice **b** is incorrect because you didn't account for two walls of each set of dimensions. Choice **d** is incorrect because this is the area of only one wall of the four.

18. This is a geometry problem.

    c. Using the formula, $V = \frac{1}{3}(10)(12)(10)$, choice **a** is incorrect because this is off by a multiple of 10. Choice **b** is incorrect because you are missing a multiple of 10 and you didn't multiply by $\frac{1}{3}$. Choice **d** is incorrect because you didn't multiply by $\frac{1}{3}$.

19. This is a fractions problem.

    c. Substituting 40 for C in the equation yields $F = (\frac{9}{5})(40) + 32 = 72 + 32 = 104$. Choice **a** is incorrect because this would be correct for 35°C, not 40°C. Choice **b** is incorrect because of an arithmetic error. Choice **d** is incorrect because this would be correct for 45°C, not 40°C.

20. This is a fractions problem.

    b. $150(x) = (100)(1)$, where x is the part of a mile a jogger has to go to burn the calories a walker burns in 1 mile. If you divide both sides of this equation by 150, you get $x = \frac{100}{150}$. Cancel 50 from both the numerator and denominator to get $\frac{2}{3}$. This means that a jogger has to jog only $\frac{2}{3}$ of a mile to burn the same number of calories a walker burns in a mile of brisk walking. Choice **a** is incorrect because you divided the difference of 50 by 100, which is the percent difference in calories burned in one hour. Choice **c** is incorrect because you divided in the wrong order. Choice **d** is incorrect because of an arithmetic error.

21. This is a fractions problem.

    c. The ratio is $\frac{12 \text{ cc}}{100 \text{ pounds}} = \frac{x}{175 \text{ pounds}}$, where x is the number of cc's per 175 pounds. Multiply both sides by 175 to get $(175)(\frac{12}{100})$ equals x, so x equals 21. Choice **a** is incorrect because this corresponds to about an 8.6 cc dosage per 100 pounds, not 12 cc. Choice **b** is incorrect because this corresponds to about a 10.29 cc dosage per 100 pounds, not 12 cc. Choice **d** is incorrect because this corresponds to about a 13.71 cc dosage per 100 pounds, not 12 cc.

22. This is an averages problem.

   b. On the first day, the hiker walks 40 miles. On the second day, he walks 20 miles. On the third day, he walks 10 miles. On the fourth day, he walks 5 miles. On the fifth day, he walks 2.5 miles. The sum of the miles walked, then, is 77.5 miles. The average over 5 days is 77.5 divided by 5, or 15.5 miles per day. Choice **a** is incorrect because this would imply that the hiker hiked a total of 50 miles in 5 days when, in fact, he had already hiked 60 miles in the first 2 days. Choice **c** is incorrect because you divided the total distance by 4 days, not 5. Choice **d** is incorrect because this would imply that the hiker hiked 120 miles in 5 days, which is too high.

23. This is an averages problem.

   c. This is a weighted average problem. To find the average speed, use the formula: average speed (in miles per hour) = $\frac{\text{total miles driven}}{\text{total hours driven}}$:
   3 hr × 32 mph = 96 miles driven at slow speeds.
   4.5 hr × 72 mph = 324 miles driven at highway speeds.
   The total distance driven is 420 miles in 7.5 hours. $\frac{420 \text{ miles}}{7.5 \text{ hours}}$ = 56 miles per hour. Choice **a** is incorrect because you computed $\frac{32 + 72}{2}$ = 52, but this doesn't account for having traveled at these two rates for different durations of time. Choice **b** is incorrect because you divided the total distance traveled by 8 hours, not 7.5. Choice **d** is incorrect because you divided the total distance traveled by 7 hours, not 7.5.

24. This is an averages problem.

   c. $80 per month times 7 months is $560. $20 per month times the remaining 5 months is $100. $560 plus $100 equals $660 for the entire year. $660 divided by 12 months is $55. Choice **a** is incorrect because you applied the $80 per month rate for 5 months, not 7. Choice **b** is incorrect because you computed $\frac{20 + 80}{2}$ = 50, but this doesn't account for the fact that the amounts were applicable for different numbers of months. Choice **d** is incorrect because you applied the $80 per month rate for 8 months, not 7.

25. This is an algebra problem.

   b. $J = 6K$; $J + 2 = 2(K + 2)$, so $6K + 2 = 2K + 4$, which means K equals $\frac{1}{2}$—half a year, or 6 months. J equals $6K$, or 3. Choice **a** is incorrect because this is Kate's age now. Choice **c** is incorrect because this is double his true age. Choice **d** is incorrect because you have the wrong value of K; it is $\frac{1}{2}$, not $\frac{3}{2}$.

26. This is an averages problem.

   d. Add each monthly food cost plus $54 for total coffee costs to get $312.90 for three months. Dividing by 3 gives an average of $104.30. Choice **a** is incorrect because this is the average food cost; it doesn't account for coffee costs. Choice **b** is incorrect because you averaged food costs, then divided a single coffee cost by 3, and added it to the average food cost. Choice **c** is incorrect because you averaged food costs and added $\frac{2}{3}$ of a single month's coffee cost to it; you should have added the average of the coffee costs.

27. This is a decimals problem.

    c. Change 13.5 hours into minutes by multiplying by 60: $13.5 \times 60 = 810$ minutes. Then change 810 minutes into seconds by multiplying by 60 again: $810 \times 60 = 48,600$ seconds. 48,600 seconds between the two cities means 48,600 gallons used. Choice **a** is incorrect because you multiplied (13.5)(60)(24); you should have 60 in place of 24. Choice **b** is incorrect because this assumes you burn 1 gallon per *minute*, not per *second*. Choice **d** is incorrect because the answer can be determined—convert 13.5 to seconds.

28. This is a fractions problem.

    c. Multiply the cost per acre by the number of acres; $\$60,000 \times 1\frac{3}{4}$. Choice **a** is incorrect because you treated the mixed number $1\frac{3}{4}$ as if it were $1 \times \frac{3}{4}$. Choice **b** is incorrect because this is the cost for $2\frac{1}{4}$ acres. Choice **d** is incorrect because this is the cost for 2 acres.

29. This is a decimals problem.

    b. Kyra saves $\$60 + \$130 + \$70 = \$260$. In January, her employer contributes $6 and in April, $7. In March, her employer contributes only $10, the maximum amount. The total in savings is $\$260 + \$6 + \$7 + \$10 = \$283$. Choice **a** is incorrect because you neglected to include employer contributions for January and April. Choice **c** is incorrect because it assumes that the employer contributed $13 in March, but its maximum contribution is $10. Choice **d** is incorrect because it assumes that each of the three employer contributions was $10.

30. This is a decimals problem.

    b. Jackie is paid and saves twice a month, while she pays her student loan only once a month. Her monthly salary is $1,644.80. Subtract $300 in savings and $84.71 for the student loan to get $1,260.09. Choice **a** is incorrect because you subtracted the loan amount twice instead of once. Choice **c** is incorrect because you subtracted only one savings deposit of $150 when it should have been accounted for twice. Choice **d** is incorrect because you didn't subtract the savings of $300.

Part 2: Word Knowledge

1. **c.** To be held *accountable* is to be held *responsible*. It is not likely that an officer would be *applauded* (choice **a**), or *compensated* or paid (choice **b**), for every decision he or she makes, so choices **a** and **b** do not make much sense. Choice **d**, *approached*, does not make much sense in the context of the sentence either.

2. **b.** To *scrutinize* is to examine in detail or *dissect*. Choice **a**, *vanish*, means disappear. Choice **c**, *neglect*, means ignore. Choice **d**, *weaken*, means make less strong.

3. **b.** To *enumerate* contains the same root word as number, so you can conclude that it means *count*. Choice **a**, *pronounce*, means articulate. Choice **c**, *explain*, means describe or inform. Choice **d**, *plead*, means beg.

4. **a.** To *emulate* a person is to strive to equal that person or to *imitate* that person. Choice **b**, *authorize*, means allow. Choice **c**, *fascinate*, means interest. Choice **d**, *punish*, means discipline.

5. b. When one is *compliant*, one is *obedient*, which is a reasonable response to a seat belt law. Being *skeptical*, or suspicious, is not a reasonable response, so choice **a** is incorrect. Choices **c**, *forgetful*, and **d**, *appreciative*, do not make as much sense in the context of the sentence as choice **b** does.

6. c. To *augment* something is to add to or *expand* it, and a disturbance is a likely reason to expand mass demonstration laws. Choice **a**, *repeal*, means cancel, which is almost the opposite of *augment*. Choice **b**, *evaluate*, means analyze. Choice **d** does not make sense in the context of the sentence because it is unlikely that town officials would *criticize*, or find fault with, their own laws.

7. d. To have an *aversion* to something is to have a feeling of *dislike* for it. Choice **a**, *harmony*, means togetherness. Choice **b**, *greed*, means self-indulgent desire. Choice **c**, *weariness*, means tiredness.

8. a. To *validate* something is to *confirm* the authenticity of it. Choice **b**, *retrieve*, means take back, which is indicated by its prefix *re-*, meaning again or back. Choice **c**, *communicate*, means speak with, which is indicated by its prefix *co-*, meaning together. Choice **d**, *appoint*, means select.

9. b. To have an *antagonist* is to have an *opponent*, or one who opposes you, which is indicated by its prefix *ant-*, meaning against. The prefix *co-* means together, and a *comrade* is a friend, so choice **a** is incorrect. Choice **c**, *master*, is a teacher or ruler. Choice **d**, *perfectionist*, is someone obsessed with perfection.

10. c. To have *perseverance* is to have *persistence*. The prefix *un-* means not, so choice **a**, *unhappiness*, means the opposite of happiness, or sadness. Choice **b**, *fame*, means celebrity. Choice **d**, *humility*, means humbleness.

11. d. To be *inundated* is to be overwhelmed or *flooded*, and a curious public would likely *flood* a newspaper with questions about an article about a scandalous affair. Although a flood of calls might be *bothersome*, choice **b** does not make as much sense in the context of the sentence as choice **d** does. To *provide* (choice **a**) or *reward* (choice **c**) calls does not make sense.

12. a. *Homogeneous* means of the same or a similar kind, *alike*. Choice **d**, *dissimilar*, means the opposite of *alike*, which can be concluded from its prefix *dis-*, meaning not. Choice **b**, *plain*, means simple. Choice **c**, *native*, means local or resident.

13. d. *Ominous* means foreshadowing evil, *threatening*. Choice **a**, *ordinary*, means common. Choice **b**, *gracious*, means polite. Choice **c**, *quarrelsome*, means argumentative.

14. c. When one is *incredulous*, one is skeptical or *disbelieving*, which is a reasonable response to a timid person deciding to do something as daring and dangerous as skydiving. Choice **a**, *fearful*, though it might be reasonable to be *fearful* for someone who has decided to do something dangerous, would make the detail about Bob being *timid* unnecessary. Choice **b**, *outraged*, means extremely angry. Choice **d**, *inconsolable*, means extremely upset or grief stricken.

15. d. A *recluse* is a person who lives withdrawn from the world, a *hermit*, which is indicated by its prefix *re-*, meaning back. Choice **a**, *prophet*, means spiritual forecaster. Choice **b**, *fool*, means clown or ridiculous person. Choice **c**, *intellectual*, means deep thinker.

16. d. When one is *proficient* at something, one is expert or *skilled* at it, and a company would likely want to hire someone who is *proficient* at the task he or she is required to do. Choice **a**, *incompetent*, means without skill, and a company most likely would not hire a person it knew to be *incompetent*. Choice **c**, *efficient*, means adequate, and it is more likely a company would hire someone because he or she is skilled rather than merely *efficient*. Choice **b**, *careful*, does not make as much sense as choice **d** in the context of the sentence.

17. a. To *defray* is to provide for the payment of something, to *pay*. Choice **b**, *defend*, may look like *defray*, but it means protect. Choice **c**, *cheat*, means trick or deceive. Choice **d**, *disobey*, means defy.

18. b. *Placid* means serenely free of disturbance; calm, *peaceful*. Choice **a**, *flabby*, means fat. Choice **c**, *wise*, means intelligent. Choice **d**, *obedient*, means respectful or compliant.

19. a. When something is *tentative*, it is of an experimental or *provisional* nature. Choice **b**, *ambiguous*, means vague, and it does not make sense that a city council would give vague approval of a ban. It does not make sense that it would give *confused* (choice **c**) or *unnecessary* (choice **d**) approval either.

20. b. Something that is *vast* is huge or *immense*. Choice **a**, *attentive*, means helpful. Choice **c**, *steady*, means constant. Choice **d**, *slight*, means little.

21. c. *Animosity* is ill will or *hostility*. Choice **a**, *natural*, means normal or unadorned. Choice **b**, *climax*, means end or top. Choice **d**, *untold*, means not spoken, which is indicated by its prefix *un-*, meaning not.

22. a. An *adage* is a motto or wise *saying*. Choice **b**, *language*, means speech. Choice **c**, *elderly*, means old. Choice **d**, *superior*, means better.

23. b. Something that is *prosperous* is thriving or *successful*, and it is likely that a store that needs to stay open all week long to accommodate public demand would be *successful*. Choice **a**, *lavish*, means rich or fancy. Choice **c**, *memorable*, means unforgettable. Choice **d**, *competitive*, means aggressive. None of these choices make as much sense in the context of the sentence as choice **b** does.

24. b. *Figurative* language is not literal but metaphorical or symbolic. Choice **a**, *theoretical*, means possible. Choice **c**, *complex*, means complicated, which does not describe all metaphors well. Choice **d**, *truthful*, means full of truth.

25. c. *Posterity* refers to descendants or *future generations*, and a school ring that belonged to one's father is something one might reasonably pass on to *future generations*. Choice **a**, *proof of the past*, does not make as much sense in the context of the sentence. Choice **b**, *memorabilia*, is a memento or souvenir, and though a class ring might be a piece of *memorabilia*, one would not keep something for *memorabilia*. One would not keep something for *investment*; he or she would keep it as an *investment*, so choice **d** does not make sense in the context of the sentence.

26. a. The prefix *sub-* means under, and something that is *subliminal* is hidden or *concealed*. Choice **b**, *identifiable*, has almost the opposite meaning of *subliminal*; the word means something easily noticeable. Choice **c**, *original*, means first or unique. Choice **d**, *mysterious*, means secretive or strange.

27. a. A *resonant* sound is one that is *echoing*. Choice **b**, *harsh*, means loud or irritating. Choice **c**, *delicate*, means light, weak, or fine. Choice **d**, *illegible*, means impossible to read, which is indicated by its prefix, *il-*, meaning not.

28. c. Something that is *expedient* is advantageous and *quick*. Choice **a**, *cumbersome*, means awkward. Choice **b**, *inappropriate*, means not appropriate, which is indicated by the prefix, *in-*, meaning not. Choice **d**, *slow*, has the opposite meaning of *expedient*.

29. a. A helicopter would logically be needed to transport a patient in an *urgent* emergency situation, so something that is *exigent* is *urgent*. Choice **b**, *commonplace*, means average or everyday, which is indicated by its root word, *common*. Choice **c**, *underdeveloped*, means less than developed. Choice **d**, *extreme*, means tremendous or severe and does not fit the context of the sentence as well as *urgent* does.

30. d. Most corner stores sell various household and grocery items, so *sundry* items are miscellaneous or assorted. Choice **a**, *precious*, means rare and valuable, and choice **c**, *exotic*, means foreign or unusual; it is unlikely a common corner store would sell such items. Choice **b**, *meager*, means skimpy or miserable, which does not really describe the kinds of items sold in a corner store.

31. a. Something that is *fulsome* is overgenerous or *excessive*, which is indicated by its root word *ful-*, meaning full. Although choice **c**, *pleasing*, and choice **d**, *inspiring*, may fit the context of the sentence, neither of these words suggest *excessiveness*. Choice **b**, *irritating*, means annoying.

32. d. *Tumultuous* is turbulent, chaotic, or *disorderly*. Choice **c**, *quiet*, means the opposite of *tumultuous*. Choice **a**, *dedicated*, means loyal. Choice **b**, *respectful*, means full of respect.

33. b. Something that is *exorbitant* is ridiculously expensive or *overpriced*. Choice **a**, *valuable*, means precious or full of value. Choice **c**, *wild*, means untamed. Choice **d**, *unbelievable*, means not believable.

34. c. Something that is *blatant* is unconcealed or *transparent*. Choice **a**, *secretive*, means mysterious. Choice **b**, *fabricated*, means human made. Choice **d**, *loud*, means noisy.

35. b. *Empirical* is observed or *practical*. Choice **a**, *ancient*, means extremely old or prehistoric. Choice **c**, *false*, means fake. Choice **d**, *unwieldy*, means bulky or awkward.

Part 3: Paragraph Comprehension

1. b. This is an inference question, because the answer is not stated explicitly in the passage. The passage explains the procedure for bus drivers to follow when their bus gets ahead of schedule, so one can infer that *running hot* means running ahead of schedule. Read on its own, "running hot" may seem to indicate literal hotness or overheating, but the way it is used in the context of the passage contradicts this inference, so choices **a** and **c** are incorrect. The passage never deals with overcrowding on buses, so choice **d** is incorrect.

2. d. This is a facts and details question, and the answer is stated explicitly in the second sentence: *Drivers are reminded that each route has several checkpoints at which drivers should check the time.* The passage never states that *every bus stop is also a checkpoint*, so choice **a** is incorrect. While it is logical to assume that it is important to keep customer complaints to a minimum, this is not stated explicitly in the passage, so choice **b** is incorrect. The passage never suggests why drivers might rush their routes, so choice **c** is incorrect.

3. a. This is an inference question, because the answer is not stated explicitly in the passage. The second sentence states that routine maintenance, which would likely include oil changes, is performed by the maintenance department. The first sentence of the passage states that drivers are only responsible for refueling their trucks, so choice **b** is incorrect. The only thing the passage states about shift supervisors is that they take Repair Requisition forms, so choice **c** is not a logical conclusion. Choice **d** is incorrect because outside contractors are never mentioned in the passage.

4. c. This is a facts and details question, because the answer is explicitly stated in the opening sentence: *Drivers are responsible for refueling their trucks at the end of each shift.* There is no evidence in the passage to support choices **a**, **b**, and **d**.

5. c. This is a facts and details question, because the answer is explicitly stated in the opening sentence: *Hazardous waste is defined as any waste designated by the U.S. Environmental Protection Agency as hazardous.* Although one might logically infer that hazardous waste is dangerous for *unqualified* workers to handle, workers who are qualified may handle it, so choice **a** is incorrect. Choice **b** is incorrect because there is no mention of special trucks in the passage. Although it is likely that hazardous waste is *not allowed with regular residential garbage*, this does not define hazardous waste, so choice **d** is incorrect.

6. c. This is an inference question, because it requires the reader to make an educated assumption based on information in the passage. The passage states that the worker should call his or her supervisor for directions if he or she is unsure if any item is safe. If one does not know what the solvent contains, it could be dangerous to assume it is safe, so choice **a** is incorrect. Choices **b** and **d** are contradicted by the second sentence of the passage: *If a sanitation worker is unsure if a particular item is hazardous, he or she should not handle the item but should instead notify the supervisor for directions.*

7. d. This is an inference question, and the answer is suggested in the final sentence of the passage: *Greyhounds do not make good watchdogs, but they are very good with children, get along well with other dogs (and usually cats as well). . . .* The passage does not mention choice **b** or choice **c**. Choice **a** is clearly wrong; the passage states the opposite.

8. a. This is a facts and details question; the answer is stated explicitly in the final sentence of the passage: *Greyhounds do not make good watchdogs. . . .* Choices **b** and **c** are not mentioned in the passage, and choice **d** is directly contradicted in the third sentence of the passage.

9. c. This is a main idea question, because the title should capture the passage's main idea well, which "How to Shop for Healthy Food" accomplishes well. The passage only discusses standard grocery stores, not specialty health food stores, so choice **a** is not an appropriate title. Although the passage does mention that following its suggestions may result in a shorter shopping trip, this is just a detail and not the main idea of the passage, so choice **b** is incorrect. Choice **d** is incorrect because the passage only discusses shopping for healthy food, not cooking it.

10. b. This is a facts and details question, and the answer is stated explicitly in the opening sentence of the passage: *One easy way to plan healthy menus is to shop only in the outer aisles of the grocery store.* Choices **a**, **c**, and **d** are not mentioned in the passage at all.

11. d. This is a facts and details question; the first sentence of the passage states explicitly that veterinarians must pass both the national veterinary medical board exam and a state board exam in order to practice. Choice **a** is incorrect because the second sentence of the passage states that veterinarians must pass *two* final exams. The passage never discusses residency requirements, so choice **b** is incorrect. Choice **c** is contradicted by the final sentence of the passage.

12. c. This is a main idea question. The passage contains two different opinions about the state exam veterinarians must pass: why it is important and why it is unimportant, and the title "Pros and Cons of Veterinarian Requirements" sums up this main idea well. Although the passage states that some veterinarians believe the state exam is unimportant, this is just a minor detail, so choice **a** is incorrect. Future veterinarians are the target audience of this passage, not pet owners, so choice **b** is incorrect. This is a factual passage, not a work of fiction, so choice **d** is wrong.

13. a. This is a facts and details question. The third sentence mentions that state exams are important because they require veterinarians to be knowledgeable about regional issues. Choices **b**, **c**, and **d** are not mentioned in the passage at all.

14. d. This is a facts and details question, because the passage states explicitly that the first day of summer in the northern hemisphere is the first day of winter in the southern hemisphere. This fact contradicts choices **a**, **b**, and **c**.

15. b. This is an inference question, as is evident from the word *inferred*. The first day of summer is summer solstice; therefore, the first day of winter must be the winter solstice. This contradicts choices **a**, **c**, and **d**.

Part 4: Mathematics Knowledge

1. This is a geometry problem.
   d. The only parallel lines are y and z. Choice **a** is incorrect because these lines will eventually intersect further to the left, so they cannot be parallel. Choice **b** is incorrect because these lines intersect, so they cannot be parallel. Choice **c** is incorrect because these lines intersect, so they cannot be parallel.

2. This is a fractions problem.
   c. Change both mixed numbers to improper fractions before finding common denominators: $\frac{17}{3} - \frac{19}{7}$. Then, use 21 as your common denominator when subtracting: $\frac{119}{21} - \frac{57}{21} = \frac{62}{21} = 2\frac{20}{21}$. Choice **a** is incorrect because you added instead of subtracting. Choice **b** is incorrect because you subtracted the fraction parts by subtracting top and bottom numbers separately—you didn't get a least common denominator. Choice **d** is incorrect because you didn't subtract correctly.

3. This is a percents problem.
   c. Divide 14 by 0.35 to find the number, which is 40. Choice **a** is incorrect because you didn't convert 35% to a decimal correctly; 35% = 0.35, not 3.5. Choice **b** is incorrect because this is 35% of 14. Choice **d** is incorrect because 3.5%, not 35%, of this number is 14.

4. This is a decimals problem.
   b. Divide 1 by 4 in order to convert the fraction into a decimal. $1 \div 4 = 0.25$. Choice **a** is incorrect because this is equivalent to $\frac{15}{100} = \frac{3}{20}$, not $\frac{1}{4}$. Choice **c** is incorrect because this is equivalent to $\frac{20}{100} = \frac{1}{5}$, not $\frac{1}{4}$. Choice **d** is incorrect because this is equivalent to $\frac{75}{100} = \frac{3}{4}$, not $\frac{1}{4}$.

5. This is an algebra problem.
   a. The problem is solved by first determining that $8n$ equals 40 and then dividing 40 by 8. Choice **b** is incorrect because you added 25 to both sides of the equation instead of subtracting it. Choice **c** is incorrect because this is equal to $8n$, not n. Choice **d** is incorrect because this would be the right-side if you mistakenly added 25 to both sides of the equation instead of subtracting it.

6. This is a fractions problem.
   b. Convert the mixed number $3\frac{7}{8}$ to the improper fraction $\frac{31}{8}$ and then invert. Choice **a** is incorrect because this is equivalent to the given fraction, not its reciprocal. Choice **c** is incorrect because the denominator is incorrect. Choice **d** is incorrect because this is the additive inverse of $3\frac{7}{8}$ (that is, the number you add to $3\frac{7}{8}$ to get 0).

7. This is a geometry problem.
   d. An isosceles triangle has two equal angles and one different angle, and its angles must add up to to 180°. Choices **a and c** are incorrect because the angles don't add up to 180°. Choice **b** is incorrect because you need two angles with the same measure for an isosceles triangle.

8. This is an algebra problem.
   b. The square root of 12 is the same as $\sqrt{4 \times 3}$, which is the same as $\sqrt{4} \times \sqrt{3}$. The square root of 4 is 2. So $3 \times \sqrt{12}$ is the same as $3 \times 2 \times \sqrt{3}$. Choice **a** is incorrect because you pulled the 4 out of the $\sqrt{4}$, not 2. Choice **c** is incorrect because this is equivalent to $\sqrt{40}$. Choice **d** is incorrect because $\sqrt{12}$ is not equal to 6.

9. This is an algebra problem.

    d. $(3)(3)(3)(3) = 81$. Choice **a** is incorrect because you multiplied the base times the exponent. Choice **b** is incorrect because this is 4^3, not 3^4. Choice **c** is incorrect because this is 3^3, not 3^4.

10. This is a decimals problem.

    b. $-1\frac{1}{3}$ is a mixed fraction and is equal to the whole number plus the fraction; $-1\frac{1}{3} = -(1 + \frac{1}{3})$. Convert $\frac{1}{3}$ into a decimal by dividing 1 by 3; $1 \div 3 = 0.33\overline{3}$; round this portion of the answer to the nearest hundredth (two decimal places), to get 0.33; $-(1 + 0.33) = -1.33$. Choice **a** is incorrect because you forgot the negative sign. Choice **c** is incorrect because this is approximately $3\frac{2}{3}$, not $-1\frac{2}{3}$. Choice **d** is incorrect because this is approximately $-3\frac{2}{3}$, not $-1\frac{2}{3}$.

11. This is a percents problem.

    c. $2\frac{4}{5} = \frac{14}{15} = 2.8$. Choice **a** is incorrect because 2.45% = 0.0245, which is less than $2\frac{4}{5}$; so, they cannot be equal. Choice **b** is incorrect because 2.8% = 0.028, which is less than $2\frac{4}{5}$, so they cannot be equal. Choice **d** is incorrect because you are not interpreting the fractional part correctly.

12. This is a geometry problem.

    a. The dimensions of ΔMNO are double those of ΔRST. Line segment RT is 5 cm; therefore line segment MO is 10 cm. Choice **b** is incorrect because the correct scale factor is 2 to 1, not 4 to 1. Choice **c** is incorrect because you multiplied the length of corresponding sides, which is an incorrect usage of the scale factor linking the two triangles. Choice **d** is incorrect because you forgot to divide by 4 when solving the proportion for the missing side using $\frac{8}{4} = \frac{x}{5}$.

13. This is a fractions problem.

    a. To compare two fractions, raise them up to a common denominator and then compare their numerators. For example, $\frac{2}{7} = \frac{6}{21}$ and $\frac{1}{3} = \frac{7}{21}$, so $\frac{1}{3}$ is greater than $\frac{2}{7}$. Choice **b** is incorrect because $\frac{17}{20}$ is not less than $\frac{5}{6}$. Choice **c** is incorrect because $\frac{1}{3}$ is not less than $\frac{2}{7}$. Choice **d** is incorrect because $\frac{5}{6}$ is not less than $\frac{2}{7}$.

14. This is a decimals problem.

    c. To convert a decimal into a fraction, first note the number of place positions to the right of the decimal point. In 0.4, the 4 is in the tenths place, which is one place to the right of the decimal point. Therefore, the fraction would be $\frac{4}{10}$. Now, the fraction needs to be reduced to its lowest terms. The number 2 is the greatest common factor of 4 and 10, so divide the numerator and denominator by 2. The final fraction is $\frac{2}{5}$. Choice **a** is incorrect because $\frac{1}{4} = 0.25$, not 0.40. Choice **b** is incorrect because $\frac{1}{5} = 0.20$, not 0.40. Choice **d** is incorrect because $\frac{3}{4} = 0.75$, not 0.40.

15. This is an algebra problem.

    d. *Less than* means subtraction, but you must switch the order of the numbers being subtracted. *Twice* means multiplied by two. *A number* is represented by the variable x. Choice **a** is incorrect because $2 + x$ is not twice a number. Choice **b** is incorrect because this is twice a number less than 3, which is the opposite order to what is given. Choice **c** is incorrect because x^2 is not twice a number.

16. This is a geometry problem.

    b. Angles 1 and 4 are the only ones not adjacent to each other. Choices **a**, **c**, and **d** are incorrect because these angles are next to each other, hence are adjacent.

17. This is a decimals problem.

 a. The number 2.25 involves a whole number, which is the 2 to the left of the decimal. This means that the answer will be a mixed number—a whole number plus a fraction. Convert the 0.25 into a fraction; $\frac{25 \div 25}{100 \div 25} = \frac{1}{4}$; adding the whole number, 2, to this fraction gives the answer $2\frac{1}{4}$. Choice **b** is incorrect because $2\frac{1}{5} = 2.20$, not 2.25. Choice **c** is incorrect because $2\frac{2}{5} = 2.40$, not 2.25. Choice **d** is incorrect because $1\frac{3}{4} = 1.75$, not 2.25.

18. This is an algebra problem.

 d. 6^3 is equal to $(6)(6)(6) = 216$. Choice **a** is incorrect because this is 6^2. Choice **b** is incorrect because this is 6^4. Choice **c** is incorrect because you multiplied base times exponent.

19. This is an algebra problem.

 a. The correct order of operations for this calculation is $10 + [(40 \div 10) \times 2]$. Choice **b** is incorrect because you applied the operations in the order in which they arose left to right; you should have performed multiplication and division from left to right FIRST. Choice **c** is incorrect because you multiplied $(10)(2)$ before computing $(40 \div 10)$, which is wrong because the division occurred first, going left to right. Choice **d** is incorrect because you proceeded as $(10 + 40) \div (10 \times 2)$.

20. This is a decimals problem.

 b. In the decimal 0.125, the 125 is three places to the right of the decimal point; 125 is the greatest common factor of 125 and 1,000. The fraction is $\frac{125 \div 125}{1,000 \div 25} = \frac{1}{8}$. Choice **a** is incorrect because $\frac{1}{25} = 0.04$, not 0.125. Choice **c** is incorrect because $\frac{2}{5} = 0.40$, not 0.125. Choice **d** is incorrect because $\frac{1}{5} = 0.20$, not 0.125.

21. This is a geometry problem.

 d. The perimeter is the total length of all sides. In a square, all four sides are of equal length, so the perimeter is $(4)(4) = 16$. Choice **a** is incorrect because this is only the length of one of the four sides, not the perimeter. Choice **b** is incorrect because this is only the length of two of the four sides, not the perimeter. Choice **c** is incorrect because this is only the length of three of the four sides, not the perimeter.

22. This is a percents problem.

 c. Divide 33 by 0.12 (12%) to get 275. Choice **a** is incorrect because you divided 33 by 0.88 instead of 0.12. Choice **b** is incorrect because you computed 12% of 33. Choice **d** is incorrect because this is a multiple of 10 too large.

23. This is a geometry problem.

 c. If the circumference ($C = 2\pi r$) is 12π, then the radius must be 6. Find the area by using the formula $A = \pi r^2$; $A = \pi 6^2 = 36\pi$. Choice **a** is incorrect because you used 12 as the radius, but this is the diameter; you should have used $r = 6$. Choice **b** is incorrect because you multiplied the circumference by 2, which does not give the area. Choice **d** is incorrect because you should not have squared π.

24. This is an algebra problem.

 d. 17^2 is equivalent to 17 times 17, which is 289. Choice **a** is incorrect because you multiplied the base times the exponent. Choice **b** is incorrect because this is $17(4)$, not 17^2. Choice **c** is incorrect because this is 2^{17}, not 17^2.

25. This is a geometry problem.

    c. $\overline{DE}$ is 2.5 times greater than $\overline{AB}$; therefore, $\overline{EF}$ is 7.5 and $\overline{DF}$ is 10. Add the three sides together to arrive at the perimeter. Choice **a** is incorrect because you added 3 to each side of $\triangle ABC$ to get lengths of the corresponding sides of $\triangle DEF$. This is not how you use scale factor. Choice **b** is incorrect because you used the wrong scale factor of 2 instead of 2.5. Choice **d** is incorrect because you used the wrong scale factor of 3.5 instead of 2.5.

SCORING

Write your raw score (the number you got right) for each test in the blanks below. Then, turn to Chapter 3 to find out how to convert these raw scores into the scores the armed services use.

1. Arithmetic
Reasoning: _____ right out of 30
2. Word Knowledge: _____ right out of 35
3. Paragraph
Comprehension: _____ right out of 15
4. Mathematics
Knowledge: _____ right out of 25

Here are the steps you should take, depending on your AFQT score on this practice test:

- **If your AFQT is below 29,** you need more help in reading and/or math. You should spend plenty of time reviewing the lessons and practice questions found in this book.
- **If your AFQT is 29–31,** be sure to focus on your weakest subjects in the review lessons and practice questions that are found in this book.
- **If your AFQT is above 31,** review the areas that give you trouble, and then take the third practice test in Chapter 13 to make sure you are able to get a passing score again.

13 ▶ PRACTICE ASVAB CORE TEST 3

CHAPTER SUMMARY
This is the third of three practice battery tests based on the ASVAB core. Take this test for more practice and additional improvement over your score on the first two tests.

Like the previous practice exams, this test contains four of the subtests that make up the ASVAB. These four subtests count toward your Armed Forces Qualifying Test (AFQT) score, which will determine whether you will be allowed to enlist in the military.

For this exam, simulate the actual test-taking experience as closely as you can. Work in a quiet place where you won't be interrupted. If you own this book, tear out the answer sheet on page 191 and use your #2 pencils to fill in the circles. Set a timer or stopwatch, and give yourself the appropriate amount of time marked at the beginning of each subtest.

After the exam, use the answer explanations to review the questions you may have missed. Then, use the scoring section at the end of the test and Chapter 3 to see how you did.

Part 1: Arithmetic Reasoning

1.	ⓐ	ⓑ	ⓒ	ⓓ
2.	ⓐ	ⓑ	ⓒ	ⓓ
3.	ⓐ	ⓑ	ⓒ	ⓓ
4.	ⓐ	ⓑ	ⓒ	ⓓ
5.	ⓐ	ⓑ	ⓒ	ⓓ
6.	ⓐ	ⓑ	ⓒ	ⓓ
7.	ⓐ	ⓑ	ⓒ	ⓓ
8.	ⓐ	ⓑ	ⓒ	ⓓ
9.	ⓐ	ⓑ	ⓒ	ⓓ
10.	ⓐ	ⓑ	ⓒ	ⓓ

11.	ⓐ	ⓑ	ⓒ	ⓓ
12.	ⓐ	ⓑ	ⓒ	ⓓ
13.	ⓐ	ⓑ	ⓒ	ⓓ
14.	ⓐ	ⓑ	ⓒ	ⓓ
15.	ⓐ	ⓑ	ⓒ	ⓓ
16.	ⓐ	ⓑ	ⓒ	ⓓ
17.	ⓐ	ⓑ	ⓒ	ⓓ
18.	ⓐ	ⓑ	ⓒ	ⓓ
19.	ⓐ	ⓑ	ⓒ	ⓓ
20.	ⓐ	ⓑ	ⓒ	ⓓ

21.	ⓐ	ⓑ	ⓒ	ⓓ
22.	ⓐ	ⓑ	ⓒ	ⓓ
23.	ⓐ	ⓑ	ⓒ	ⓓ
24.	ⓐ	ⓑ	ⓒ	ⓓ
25.	ⓐ	ⓑ	ⓒ	ⓓ
26.	ⓐ	ⓑ	ⓒ	ⓓ
27.	ⓐ	ⓑ	ⓒ	ⓓ
28.	ⓐ	ⓑ	ⓒ	ⓓ
29.	ⓐ	ⓑ	ⓒ	ⓓ
30.	ⓐ	ⓑ	ⓒ	ⓓ

Part 2: Word Knowledge

1.	ⓐ	ⓑ	ⓒ	ⓓ
2.	ⓐ	ⓑ	ⓒ	ⓓ
3.	ⓐ	ⓑ	ⓒ	ⓓ
4.	ⓐ	ⓑ	ⓒ	ⓓ
5.	ⓐ	ⓑ	ⓒ	ⓓ
6.	ⓐ	ⓑ	ⓒ	ⓓ
7.	ⓐ	ⓑ	ⓒ	ⓓ
8.	ⓐ	ⓑ	ⓒ	ⓓ
9.	ⓐ	ⓑ	ⓒ	ⓓ
10.	ⓐ	ⓑ	ⓒ	ⓓ
11.	ⓐ	ⓑ	ⓒ	ⓓ
12.	ⓐ	ⓑ	ⓒ	ⓓ

13.	ⓐ	ⓑ	ⓒ	ⓓ
14.	ⓐ	ⓑ	ⓒ	ⓓ
15.	ⓐ	ⓑ	ⓒ	ⓓ
16.	ⓐ	ⓑ	ⓒ	ⓓ
17.	ⓐ	ⓑ	ⓒ	ⓓ
18.	ⓐ	ⓑ	ⓒ	ⓓ
19.	ⓐ	ⓑ	ⓒ	ⓓ
20.	ⓐ	ⓑ	ⓒ	ⓓ
21.	ⓐ	ⓑ	ⓒ	ⓓ
22.	ⓐ	ⓑ	ⓒ	ⓓ
23.	ⓐ	ⓑ	ⓒ	ⓓ
24.	ⓐ	ⓑ	ⓒ	ⓓ

25.	ⓐ	ⓑ	ⓒ	ⓓ
26.	ⓐ	ⓑ	ⓒ	ⓓ
27.	ⓐ	ⓑ	ⓒ	ⓓ
28.	ⓐ	ⓑ	ⓒ	ⓓ
29.	ⓐ	ⓑ	ⓒ	ⓓ
30.	ⓐ	ⓑ	ⓒ	ⓓ
31.	ⓐ	ⓑ	ⓒ	ⓓ
32.	ⓐ	ⓑ	ⓒ	ⓓ
33.	ⓐ	ⓑ	ⓒ	ⓓ
34.	ⓐ	ⓑ	ⓒ	ⓓ
35.	ⓐ	ⓑ	ⓒ	ⓓ

Part 3: Paragraph Comprehension

1.	ⓐ	ⓑ	ⓒ	ⓓ
2.	ⓐ	ⓑ	ⓒ	ⓓ
3.	ⓐ	ⓑ	ⓒ	ⓓ
4.	ⓐ	ⓑ	ⓒ	ⓓ
5.	ⓐ	ⓑ	ⓒ	ⓓ

6.	ⓐ	ⓑ	ⓒ	ⓓ
7.	ⓐ	ⓑ	ⓒ	ⓓ
8.	ⓐ	ⓑ	ⓒ	ⓓ
9.	ⓐ	ⓑ	ⓒ	ⓓ
10.	ⓐ	ⓑ	ⓒ	ⓓ

11.	ⓐ	ⓑ	ⓒ	ⓓ
12.	ⓐ	ⓑ	ⓒ	ⓓ
13.	ⓐ	ⓑ	ⓒ	ⓓ
14.	ⓐ	ⓑ	ⓒ	ⓓ
15.	ⓐ	ⓑ	ⓒ	ⓓ

Part 4: Mathematics Knowledge

1.	ⓐ	ⓑ	ⓒ	ⓓ
2.	ⓐ	ⓑ	ⓒ	ⓓ
3.	ⓐ	ⓑ	ⓒ	ⓓ
4.	ⓐ	ⓑ	ⓒ	ⓓ
5.	ⓐ	ⓑ	ⓒ	ⓓ
6.	ⓐ	ⓑ	ⓒ	ⓓ
7.	ⓐ	ⓑ	ⓒ	ⓓ
8.	ⓐ	ⓑ	ⓒ	ⓓ
9.	ⓐ	ⓑ	ⓒ	ⓓ

10.	ⓐ	ⓑ	ⓒ	ⓓ
11.	ⓐ	ⓑ	ⓒ	ⓓ
12.	ⓐ	ⓑ	ⓒ	ⓓ
13.	ⓐ	ⓑ	ⓒ	ⓓ
14.	ⓐ	ⓑ	ⓒ	ⓓ
15.	ⓐ	ⓑ	ⓒ	ⓓ
16.	ⓐ	ⓑ	ⓒ	ⓓ
17.	ⓐ	ⓑ	ⓒ	ⓓ
18.	ⓐ	ⓑ	ⓒ	ⓓ

19.	ⓐ	ⓑ	ⓒ	ⓓ
20.	ⓐ	ⓑ	ⓒ	ⓓ
21.	ⓐ	ⓑ	ⓒ	ⓓ
22.	ⓐ	ⓑ	ⓒ	ⓓ
23.	ⓐ	ⓑ	ⓒ	ⓓ
24.	ⓐ	ⓑ	ⓒ	ⓓ
25.	ⓐ	ⓑ	ⓒ	ⓓ

Part 1: Arithmetic Reasoning

Time: 36 minutes

1. Mr. Blake has inherited some musical instruments from his father. They are:

1 violin valued at	$3,500
2 violin bows, each valued at	$850
2 music stands, each valued at	$85
1 cello valued at	$2,300

   In addition, Mr. Blake's father has left him a watch, valued at $250, and some old sheet music valued at $85 total. What is the value of Mr. Blake's inheritance?
   a. $6,735
   b. $7,070
   c. $7,670
   d. $8,005

2. An Olympic athlete has the following weekday-training schedule:

DAY	TRAINING TIME
Monday	3 hours and 30 minutes
Tuesday	2 hours and 15 minutes
Wednesday	1 hour and 45 minutes
Thursday	4 hours and 30 minutes
Friday	3 hours

   What is the average amount of time per weekday that she trains?
   a. 2 hours and 45 minutes
   b. 3 hours
   c. 3 hours and 15 minutes
   d. 3 hours and 45 minutes

3. If a particular woman's resting heartbeat is 72 beats per minute and she is at rest for 6.5 hours, about how many times will her heart beat during that period of time?
   a. 11,232
   b. 28,080
   c. 468
   d. 43,200

4. A patient's hospice stay costs $\frac{1}{4}$ as much as his visit to the emergency room. His home nursing costs twice as much as his hospice stay. If his total healthcare bill was $140,000, how much did his home nursing cost?
   a. $10,000
   b. $20,000
   c. $40,000
   d. $80,000

5. Chuck is making a patio using $1\frac{1}{2}$ foot cement squares. The patio will be 10 cement squares by 10 cement squares. If the cement squares are placed right next to each other without any space in between, what will the dimensions of the patio be?
   a. 10 feet by 10 feet
   b. 20 feet by 20 feet
   c. $12\frac{1}{2}$ feet by $12\frac{1}{2}$ feet
   d. 15 feet by 15 feet

6. At a certain school, half the students are female and one-twelfth of the students are from outside the state. What proportion of the students would you expect to be females from outside the state?
   a. $\frac{1}{12}$
   b. $\frac{1}{24}$
   c. $\frac{1}{6}$
   d. $\frac{1}{3}$

7. Izzy is going to buy a tent that originally cost $220.00, and is now 30% off. What is the sale price of the tent?

  a. $314.29

  b. $154.00

  c. $165.00

  d. $66.00

8. Based on the following information, estimate the weight of a person who is 5′5″ tall.

HEIGHT	WEIGHT
5′	110 pounds
6′	170 pounds

  a. 125

  b. 130

  c. 135

  d. 140

9. During exercise, a person's heart rate should be between 60% and 90% of the difference between 220 and the person's age. According to this guideline, what should a 30-year-old person's maximum heart rate be during exercise?

  a. 114

  b. 142.5

  c. 171

  d. 225

10. The local firefighters are doing a "fill the boot" fundraiser. Their goal is to raise $3,500. After three hours, they have raised $2,275. Which statement below is accurate?

  a. They have raised 35% of their goal.

  b. They have $\frac{7}{20}$ of their goal left to raise.

  c. They have raised less than $\frac{1}{2}$ of their goal.

  d. They have raised more than $\frac{3}{4}$ of their goal.

11. A shoe company decides to sell a pair of sneakers for $78.00. If this pair of sneakers cost the shoe company $6.00 to manufacture, what is the percentage increase they are using to determine their selling price?

  a. 12%

  b. 72%

  c. 120%

  d. 1,200%

12. In half of migraine sufferers, a certain drug reduces the number of migraines by 50%. What percentage of all migraines can be eliminated by this drug?

  a. 25%

  b. 50%

  c. 75%

  d. 100%

13. Joey, Aaron, Barbara, and Stu have been collecting pennies and putting them in identical containers. Joey's container is $\frac{3}{4}$ full, Aaron's is $\frac{3}{5}$ full, Barbara's is $\frac{2}{3}$ full, and Stu's is $\frac{2}{5}$ full. Whose container has the most pennies?

  a. Joey

  b. Aaron

  c. Barbara

  d. Stu

14. Rosa kept track of how many hours she spent reading during the month of August. The first week she read for $4\frac{1}{2}$ hours, the second week for $3\frac{3}{4}$ hours, the third week for $8\frac{1}{2}$ hours, and the fourth week for $1\frac{1}{3}$ hours. How many hours altogether did she spend reading in the month of August?

  a. $17\frac{47}{60}$

  b. 16

  c. $16\frac{1}{8}$

  d. $18\frac{1}{12}$

15. A study shows that 600,000 people die of heart disease in the U.S. every year, one-fifth more than scientists previously estimated. How many such deaths did the scientists previously estimate?
 a. 120,000
 b. 300,000
 c. 500,000
 d. 720,000

16. A gram of fat contains nine calories. An 1,800-calorie diet allows no more than 20% calories from fat. How many grams of fat are allowed in that diet?
 a. 40 g
 b. 90 g
 c. 160 g
 d. 360 g

17. If a vehicle is traveling through a desert at an average speed of 90 kilometers an hour, how many meters will it have traveled after 5 hours and 30 minutes of driving at this speed?
 a. 48,000 meters
 b. 480,000 meters
 c. 49,500 meters
 d. 495,000 meters

18. After three days, a group of hikers discovers that they have used $\frac{2}{5}$ of their supplies. At this rate, how many more days can they go forward before they have to turn around? Keep in mind they must make their supplies last for the whole trip, going forward and returning.
 a. 0.75 days
 b. 3.75 days
 c. 4.5 days
 d. 7.5 days

19. A rations supply truck can carry three tons. A breakfast ration weighs 12 ounces, and the other two daily meals weigh 18 ounces each. On a ten-day trip, how many troops can be supplied by one truck?
 a. 133
 b. 160
 c. 200
 d. 320

20. A clerk can process 26 forms per hour. If 5,600 forms must be processed in an eight-hour day, how many clerks must you hire for that day?
 a. 24 clerks
 b. 25 clerks
 c. 26 clerks
 d. 27 clerks

21. On the same latitude, Company E travels east at 35 miles per hour and Company F travels west at 15 miles per hour. If the two companies start out 2,100 miles apart, how long will it take them to meet?
 a. 42 hours
 b. 60 hours
 c. 105 hours
 d. 140 hours

22. Laura has the following regular test scores in her economics class: 78, 94, 64, 81, 83. On her final exam, she scored a 90. When determining students' final averages, the professor drops the lowest regular test score, and then counts the average of the remaining regular tests as 50% of the final average. The final exam counts as the other 50% of the total average. What will Laura's final average be?
 a. 86
 b. 84
 c. 85
 d. 87

23. Mike types three times as fast as Nick types. Together they type 24 pages per hour. If Nick learns to type as fast as Mike, how much will they be able to type per hour?

a. 30 pages
b. 36 pages
c. 40 pages
d. 48 pages

24. If you take recyclables to whichever recycler will pay the most, what is the greatest amount of money you could get for 2,200 pounds of aluminum, 1,400 pounds of cardboard, 3,100 pounds of glass, and 900 pounds of plastic?

	ALUMI-NUM	CARD-BOARD	GLASS	PLASTIC
Recycler X	6 cents/pound	3 cents/pound	8 cents/pound	2 cents/pound
Recycler Y	7 cents/pound	4 cents/pound	7 cents/pound	3 cents/pound

a. $440
b. $409
c. $454
d. $485

25. Water is coming into a tank three times as fast as it is going out. After one hour, the tank contains 11,400 gallons of water. How fast is the water coming in?

a. $\frac{3,800 \text{ gallons}}{\text{hour}}$
b. $\frac{5,700 \text{ gallons}}{\text{hour}}$
c. $\frac{11,400 \text{ gallons}}{\text{hour}}$
d. $\frac{17,100 \text{ gallons}}{\text{hour}}$

26. A standard 18-wheel tractor-trailer is permitted to carry a load of up to 80,000 pounds. A smaller 6-wheel trailer is able to carry a load of up to 30,000 pounds. If the government needs to transport 350,000 pounds of supplies from Camp Pendleton to Fort Campbell, what is the most efficient use of vehicles for this move?

a. five 18-wheelers
b. twelve 6-wheelers
c. four 18-wheelers and one 6-wheeler
d. three 18-wheelers and four 6-wheelers

27. A uniform requires four square yards of cloth. To produce uniforms for 84,720 troops, how much cloth is required?

a. 330,880 square yards
b. 336,880 square yards
c. 338,880 square yards
d. 340,880 square yards

28. A dormitory now houses 30 students and allows 42 square feet of space per student. If five more students are put into this dormitory, how much less space will each student have?

a. 7 square feet
b. 6 square feet
c. 12 square feet
d. 8 square feet

29. Ron is half as old as Sam, who is three times as old as Ted. The sum of their ages is 55. How old is Ron?

a. 5
b. 10
c. 15
d. 30

30. To lower a fever of 105°F, ice packs are applied for one minute and then removed for five minutes before being applied again. Each application lowers the fever by half a degree. How long will it take to lower the fever to 99°F?
  a. one hour
  b. one hour and 12 minutes
  c. one hour and 18 minutes
  d. one hour and 30 minutes

Part 2: Word Knowledge

Time: 11 minutes

Select the choice that best matches the underlined word.

1. Erroneous most nearly means
  a. digressive.
  b. confused.
  c. impenetrable.
  d. faulty.

2. Grotesque most nearly means
  a. extreme.
  b. frenzied.
  c. hideous.
  d. typical.

3. The Adamsville Kennel Club's ancient computer system was outmoded.
  a. worthless
  b. unusable
  c. obsolete
  d. unnecessary

4. Garbled most nearly means
  a. lucid.
  b. unintelligible.
  c. devoured.
  d. outrageous.

5. Rigorous most nearly means
  a. demanding.
  b. tolerable.
  c. lenient.
  d. disorderly.

6. Flagrant most nearly means
  a. secret.
  b. careless.
  c. noble.
  d. glaring.

7. Oration most nearly means
  a. nuisance.
  b. independence.
  c. address.
  d. length.

8. Although the police might be able to help Mr. Chen recover his stolen property, he obstinately refuses to file a complaint.
  a. repeatedly
  b. reluctantly
  c. foolishly
  d. stubbornly

9. The student's glib remarks irritated the teacher.
  a. casual
  b. insincere
  c. brief
  d. horrific

10. Composure most nearly means
  a. agitation.
  b. poise.
  c. liveliness.
  d. stimulation.

11. <u>Eccentric</u> most nearly means
   a. normal.
   b. frugal.
   c. peculiar.
   d. selective.

12. <u>Commendable</u> most nearly means
   a. admirable.
   b. accountable.
   c. irresponsible.
   d. noticeable.

13. <u>Oblivious</u> most nearly means
   a. visible.
   b. sinister.
   c. aware.
   d. ignorant.

14. <u>Philanthropy</u> most nearly means
   a. selfishness.
   b. fascination.
   c. disrespect.
   d. generosity.

15. Most members of the conservative community thought the neighbor's bright pink Corvette was <u>ostentatious</u>.
   a. hilarious
   b. pretentious
   c. tasteful
   d. expensive

16. <u>Passive</u> most nearly means
   a. resigned.
   b. emotional.
   c. lively.
   d. woeful.

17. <u>Proximity</u> most nearly means
   a. distance.
   b. agreement.
   c. nearness.
   d. intelligence.

18. <u>Negligible</u> most nearly means
   a. insignificant.
   b. delicate.
   c. meaningful.
   d. illegible.

19. <u>Rational</u> most nearly means
   a. deliberate.
   b. invalid.
   c. prompt.
   d. sound.

20. <u>Vigilant</u> most nearly means
   a. nonchalant.
   b. alert.
   c. righteous.
   d. strenuous.

21. <u>Novel</u> most nearly means
   a. future.
   b. basic.
   c. former.
   d. new.

22. <u>Procure</u> most nearly means
   a. discover.
   b. acquire.
   c. drop.
   d. add.

23. The salary will be <u>commensurate</u> with the candidate's experience.
   a. forthcoming
   b. determined
   c. proportionate
   d. found

24. Franny was happy about the news, but her husband had the <u>converse</u> reaction.
   a. upsetting
   b. opposite
   c. worst
   d. extreme

25. The abstract painting was emotionally <u>evocative</u>.
a. difficult
b. designed
c. suggestive
d. pure

26. <u>Harbinger</u> most nearly means
a. follower.
b. convert.
c. harbor.
d. forerunner.

27. <u>Amulet</u> most nearly means
a. charm.
b. anklet.
c. potion.
d. emergency.

28. <u>Pundit</u> most nearly means
a. expert.
b. politician.
c. kicker.
d. evil-doer.

29. The <u>queue</u> for movie tickets went around the block.
a. quick
b. price
c. line
d. popularity

30. When his friends arrived an hour late, Jose's <u>countenance</u> showed that he was less than pleased.
a. goals
b. opinion
c. abilities
d. expression

31. Amy increased the size of the <u>aperture</u> in order to let more light in.
a. opening
b. apparatus
c. camera
d. brightness

32. <u>Surrogate</u> most nearly means
a. replacement.
b. copy.
c. original.
d. survivor.

33. <u>Paradigm</u> most nearly means
a. flying.
b. law.
c. timely.
d. example.

34. The <u>mélange</u> of musical acts made the festival unique.
a. clatter
b. mix
c. creation
d. profit

35. <u>Bravado</u> most nearly means
a. boldness.
b. cowardice.
c. scorn.
d. anti-establishment.

Part 3: Paragraph Comprehension

Time: 13 minutes

Read each passage and answer the questions that follow.

Police officers must read suspects their Miranda rights upon taking them into custody. When suspects who are merely being questioned incriminate themselves, they might later seek to have the case dismissed on the grounds that they were not apprised of their Miranda rights when arrested. Therefore, officers must take care not to give suspects grounds for later claiming they believed themselves to be in custody.

1. What is the main idea of the passage?
  a. Officers must remember to read suspects their Miranda rights.
  b. Suspects sometimes mistakenly believe they are in custody when in fact they are only being questioned.
  c. Officers who are merely questioning a suspect must not give the suspect the impression that he or she is in custody.
  d. Miranda rights needn't be read to all suspects before questioning.

2. When must police officers read Miranda rights to a suspect?
  a. while questioning the suspect
  b. while placing the suspect under arrest
  c. before taking the suspect to the police station
  d. before releasing the suspect

Dilly's Deli provides a dining experience like no other! Recently relocated to the old market area, Dilly's is especially popular for lunch. At the counter, you can place your order for one of Dilly's three daily lunch specials or one of several sandwiches, all at reasonable prices. Once you get your food, choose a seat at one of the four charming, communal tables. By the time you are ready to carry your paper plate to the trash bin, you have experienced some of the best food and most charming company our city has to offer.

3. According to the passage, if you eat lunch at Dilly's Deli, you should expect to
  a. be surrounded by antiques.
  b. place your order with the waiter who comes to your table.
  c. carry your own food to your table.
  d. be asked out on a date by someone charming.

4. The main purpose of the passage is to
  a. profile the owner of Dilly's Deli.
  b. describe the kind of food served at Dilly's Deli.
  c. encourage people to eat at Dilly's Deli.
  d. explain the historical significance of the Dilly's Deli building.

There are two types of diabetes: insulin-dependent and non-insulin-dependent. Between 90% and 95% of the estimated 13 to 14 million people in the United States with diabetes have non-insulin-dependent, or Type II, diabetes. Its symptoms often develop gradually and are hard to identify at first; therefore, nearly half of all people with diabetes do not know they have it. This can be particularly dangerous, because untreated diabetes can cause damage to the heart, blood vessels, eyes, kidneys, and nerves. While the causes, short-term effects, and treatments of Type I and Type II diabetes differ, both types can cause the same long-term health problems.

5. According to the passage, which of the following may be the most dangerous aspect of Type II diabetes?

   a. Insulin shots are needed daily for treatment of Type II diabetes.

   b. In Type II diabetes, the pancreas does not produce insulin.

   c. Type II diabetes interferes with digestion.

   d. Persons with Type II diabetes may not know they have it, and will therefore not seek treatment.

6. Which of the following are the same for Type I and Type II diabetes?

   a. treatments

   b. long-term health risks

   c. short-term effects

   d. causes

Because crimes against adolescents are likely to be committed by offenders of the same age (as well as the same sex and race), preventing violence among and against adolescents is a twofold challenge. New violence prevention programs in urban middle schools help reduce the crime rate by teaching both victims and perpetrators the skills of conflict resolution and how to apply reason to disputes. Also, they help to correct the attitude that respect may be achieved through violence and retaliation.

7. What is the main idea of the passage?

   a. Middle school violence prevention programs are designed to help lower the rate of crimes against adolescents.

   b. Adolescents are more likely to commit crimes than older people and must therefore be taught nonviolence in order to protect society.

   c. Middle school students appreciate the conflict resolution skills they acquire in violence prevention programs.

   d. Violence against adolescents is increasing.

8. According to the passage, why is preventing violence against adolescents a *twofold challenge*?

   a. because adolescents are as likely to be victims of violent crime as members of other age groups

   b. because adolescents must be prevented from both perpetrating and being victimized by violent crime

   c. because adolescents must change both their violent behavior and their attitudes toward violence

   d. because adolescents are vulnerable, yet reluctant to listen to adult advice

The camera shutter serves as a light valve. Opening and closing within a certain time frame, it helps determine how much light will be exposed onto the film. The numbers on the shutter speed dial indicate fractions of a second. With the shutter speed, you can freeze motion by using a fast shutter speed. The camera must be held steady while taking a picture, as movement will blur the photograph. The slower the shutter speed, the more likely it is that you will have a problem with handheld shots. With an SLR camera, one can generally hand-hold the camera at $\frac{1}{30}$ second or faster.

9. According to the passage, a fast shutter speed

   a. freezes motion.

   b. allows you to hold the camera at $\frac{1}{30}$ second or faster.

   c. serves as a light valve.

   d. makes handheld shots difficult.

10. According to the passage, the shutter works in conjunction with

   a. time.

   b. space.

   c. dials.

   d. demand.

11. Which of the following will result in a blurry picture?

 a. an SLR camera

 b. a lot of light exposed onto the film

 c. a $\frac{1}{60}$-second shutter speed

 d. a slow shutter speed

Some people argue that retribution is the purpose of punishing a person convicted of a crime, and that therefore the punishment must in some direct way fit the crime. Another view, the deterrence theory, promotes punishment in order to discourage commission of future crimes. In this view, punishment need not relate directly to the crime committed. However, punishment must necessarily be uniform and consistently applied, in order for the members of the public to understand how they would be punished if they committed a crime.

12. The passage suggests that a person who believes that the death penalty results in fewer murders most likely also believes in

 a. the deterrence theory.

 b. the retribution theory.

 c. giving judges considerable discretion in imposing sentences.

 d. the integrity of the criminal justice system.

13. A person who believes in the deterrence theory would probably also support

 a. non-unanimous jury verdicts.

 b. early release of prisoners because of prison overcrowding.

 c. a broad definition of the insanity defense.

 d. allowing television broadcasts of court proceedings.

The city ordinance reads, "Sanitation workers will not collect garbage in containers weighing more than 50 pounds." Workers are expected to use their best judgment in determining when a container weighs more than 50 pounds. If a container is too heavy, workers should attach one of the preprinted warning messages (which are carried in all trucks) to the container, informing the household that the container weighs more than 50 pounds and cannot be collected.

14. According to the passage, in order to determine whether a container is too heavy, sanitation workers should

 a. carry a scale in their truck to weigh containers.

 b. practice lifting 50 pounds at home to know what it feels like.

 c. assume any container they can lift weighs less than 50 pounds.

 d. use their best guess as to whether a container weighs more than 50 pounds.

15. According to the passage, if a sanitation worker believes that a container weighs more than 50 pounds, he or she should

 a. attach a preprinted warning to the container and leave it where it is.

 b. write a note to the household, informing them of the weight limit.

 c. collect it anyway, as the household probably did not know about the weight limit.

 d. notify a special collections truck.

Part 4: Mathematics Knowledge

Time: 24 minutes

1. $-\frac{5}{3}-\frac{1}{3}=$

 a. $\frac{4}{3}$

 b. $-\frac{4}{3}$

 c. 2

 d. −2

2. The volume of an object is measured in
   a. inches.
   b. square units.
   c. cubic units.
   d. quadrants.

3. When calculating the area of a figure, you are finding
   a. the distance around the object.
   b. the length of a side.
   c. the amount of space that the object covers.
   d. the number of sides it has.

4. $12(84 - 5) - (3 \times 54) =$
   a. 51,030
   b. 841
   c. 796
   d. 786

5. Which of the following numbers is the smallest?
   a. $\frac{6}{10}$
   b. $\frac{8}{15}$
   c. $\frac{33}{60}$
   d. $\frac{11}{20}$

6. Which of the following is equivalent to $42,549.23 \times 10^{-2}$?
   a. 425.4923×10
   b. $4,254,923 \times 10$
   c. 4.254923×10^4
   d. 4.254923×10^2

7. When measuring the area of a football field, you would most likely use
   a. square inches.
   b. square millimeters.
   c. square miles.
   d. square yards.

8. On the following number line, point L is to be located halfway between points M and N. What number will correspond to point L?

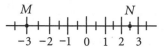

   a. $-\frac{1}{4}$
   b. $-\frac{1}{2}$
   c. $-1\frac{1}{4}$
   d. 0

9. Which of the following statements is true?
   a. Parallel lines intersect at right angles.
   b. Parallel lines never intersect.
   c. Perpendicular lines never intersect.
   d. Intersecting lines have two points in common.

10. A practice diving tank is 16 feet long, 12 feet wide, and 14 feet deep. It is currently filled up to the 3-foot mark, and must get filled to the 12-foot line in order for a class to practice their first dive. How many cubic feet of water must be added to the pool in order to fill it so that the water is 12 feet deep?
   a. 192 cubic feet
   b. 1,728 cubic feet
   c. 2,304 cubic feet
   d. 2,112 cubic feet

11. What is the next number in the following series?
   3 16 6 12 12 8 _____
   a. 4
   b. 15
   c. 20
   d. 24

12. Which number sentence is true?
   a. $4.3 < 0.43$
   b. $0.43 < 0.043$
   c. $0.043 > 0.0043$
   d. $0.0043 > 0.043$

13. What is the area of the triangle?

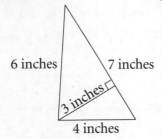

6 inches 7 inches

3 inches

4 inches

    a. 24 inches

    b. 12 inches

    c. 21 inches

    d. 10.5 inches

14. If $\frac{x}{2} + \frac{x}{6} = 4$, what is x?

    a. 24

    b. $\frac{1}{6}$

    c. 16

    d. 6

15. Choose the answer to the following problem:

$10^5 \div 10^2 =$

    a. $10^{\frac{5}{2}}$

    b. 10^3

    c. 10^7

    d. 10^{10}

16. $3.16 \div 0.079 =$

    a. 0.025

    b. 2.5

    c. 4.0

    d. 40

17. $\frac{21}{8}$ is equal to

    a. 21.8

    b. 2.58

    c. 2.6

    d. 2.625

18. What is the area of the following figure?

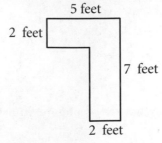

5 feet

2 feet

7 feet

2 feet

    a. 16 square feet

    b. 20 square feet

    c. 24 square feet

    d. 35 square feet

19. What is $7\frac{1}{5}$% of 465, rounded to the nearest tenth?

    a. 32.55

    b. 33

    c. 33.5

    d. 34

20. What kind of polygon is the following figure?

    a. heptagon

    b. octagon

    c. hexagon

    d. pentagon

21. Which of the following is equivalent to $3k^2 + 4k$?

    a. $7k^2$

    b. $7k^3$

    c. $3 \times k \times k + k \times k \times k \times k$

    d. $3 \times k \times k + k + k + k + k$

22. For which of the following values of x is this number sentence true: $25 - x < 10$?
   a. 16
   b. 15
   c. 14
   d. 13

23. If $4.60 is decreased by 15%, what is the resulting number?
   a. $3.91
   b. $0.69
   c. $4.45
   d. $5.29

24. What is the decimal form of $\frac{5}{6}$? (Round to the nearest hundredth.)
   a. 0.65
   b. 0.88
   c. 0.83
   d. 0.17

25. What is the volume of liquid remaining in this cylinder?

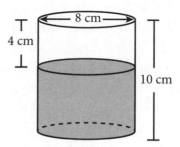

   a. 64π cm^3
   b. 80π cm^3
   c. 96π cm^3
   d. 160π cm^3

Part 1: Arithmetic Reasoning

1. This is a decimals problem.

   d. Don't forget that there are two bows and two music stands, and remember to add the value of the watch and the sheet music. Choice **a** is incorrect because you didn't add the value of the watch or sheet music, and you didn't account for the fact that there are 2 violin bows and 2 music stands. Choice **b** is incorrect because you didn't account for the fact that there are 2 violin bows and 2 music stands. Choice **c** is incorrect because you didn't add the value of the watch or sheet music.

2. This is an averages problem.

   b. Convert all the training times to minutes. The total number of minutes she trains is 900. Divided by 5, the average number of minutes trained per weekday is 180, which is 3 hours. Choice **a** is incorrect because you calculated the total minutes as 825 when it should be 900. Choice **c** is incorrect because you calculated the total minutes as 975 when it should be 900. Choice **d** is incorrect because you divided total minutes by 4, not 5.

3. This is a decimals problem.

   b. This is a two-step multiplication problem. To find out how many heartbeats there would be in one hour, you must multiply 72 by 60 (minutes) and then multiply this result, 4,320, by 6.5 hours. Choice **a** is incorrect because you multiplied 6.5 hours times 24 to convert to minutes; you should have multiplied by 60. Choice **c** is incorrect because you didn't convert hours to minutes first. Choice **d** is incorrect because this is the number of heartbeats in 10 hours, not 6.5 hours.

4. This is an algebra problem.

   c. Let E = emergency room cost; H = hospice cost, which is $(\frac{1}{4})E$; N = home nursing cost, which is $2H$, or $2(\frac{1}{4})E$. The total bill is $E + H + N$, which is $E + (\frac{1}{4})E + (\frac{2}{4})E$, = 140,000. Add the left side of the equation to get $\frac{7}{4}E$ = 140,000. To solve for E, multiply both sides of the equation by $(\frac{4}{7})$; $E = 140,000(\frac{4}{7})$, or 80,000; $H = (\frac{1}{4})E$, or 20,000, and $N = 2H$, or 40,000. Choice **a** is incorrect because this is half the cost of the hospice stay. Choice **b** is incorrect because this is the amount for the patient's hospice stay. Choice **d** is incorrect because this is the amount for the patient's emergency room visit.

5. This is a fractions problem.

   d. Multiply $1\frac{1}{2}$ by 10. Change $1\frac{1}{2}$ to an improper fraction $(\frac{3}{2})$ and make 10 into a fraction by placing it over 1 $(\frac{10}{1})$; $\frac{3}{2} \times \frac{10}{1} = \frac{30}{2} = 15$ feet. Each side is 15 feet long, so the dimensions are 15 feet by 15 feet. Choice **a** is incorrect because this would require the dimensions of each square to be 1 foot, not $1\frac{1}{2}$ feet. Choice **b** is incorrect because this would require the dimensions of each square to be 2 feet, not $1\frac{1}{2}$ feet. Choice **c** is incorrect because you didn't compute $1\frac{1}{2} \times 10$ correctly.

6. This is a fractions problem.

   b. If half the students are female, then you would expect half of the out-of-state students to be female. One half of $\frac{1}{12}$ is $\frac{1}{24}$. Choice **a** is incorrect because you didn't account for the fact that only $\frac{1}{2}$ the students are female. Choice **c** is incorrect because you multiplied $\frac{1}{12}$ by 2, not $\frac{1}{2}$. Choice **d** is incorrect because you multiplied $\frac{1}{12}$ by 4, not $\frac{1}{2}$.

7. This is a percents problem.

  b. To find the discount, take 30% of $220: $0.30 \times \$220 = \$66$. Subtract that from the original price: $\$220 - \$66 = \$154$. Choice **a** is incorrect because this assumes that $222 is the sale price, having been marked down 30% from a larger, original price. Choice **c** is incorrect because this assumes the sale is 25% off, not 30% off. Choice **d** is incorrect because this is the amount of the discount, not the sale price.

8. This is a fractions problem.

  c. A foot in height makes a difference of 60 pounds, or 5 pounds per inch of height over 5′. A person who is 5′5″ is (5)(5 pounds), or 25 pounds, heavier than the person who is 5′, so add 25 pounds to 110 pounds to get 135 pounds. Choice **a** is incorrect because this would be the weight for a height of 5′3″. Choice **b** is incorrect because this would be the weight for a height of 5′4″. Choice **d** is incorrect because this would be the weight for a height of 5′6″.

9. This is a percents problem.

  c. The difference between 220 and this person's age is 190. The maximum heart rate is 90% of this: $(0.9)(190) = 171$. Choice **a** is incorrect because this is the minimum heart rate. Choice **b** is incorrect because this is the average of the minimum and maximum heart rates. Choice **d** is incorrect because you added 220 and 30 when you should have subtracted them.

10. This is a fractions problem.

  b. The part of their goal that they have raised is $2,275 and the whole goal is $3,500. The fraction for this is $\frac{2,275}{3,500}$. The numerator and denominator can both be divided by 175 to get a simplified fraction of $\frac{13}{20}$. They have completed $\frac{13}{20}$ of their goal, which means that they have $\frac{7}{20}$ left to go $(\frac{20}{20} - \frac{13}{20} = \frac{7}{20})$. Choice **a** is incorrect because 35% of $3,500 is $1,225, which they have far surpassed. Choice **c** is incorrect because the fraction of their goal that was raised is $\frac{2,275}{3,500} = 0.65$, which is larger than $\frac{1}{2}$. Choice **d** is incorrect because the fraction of their goal that was raised is $\frac{2,275}{3,500} = 0.65$, which is less than $\frac{3}{4}$.

11. This is a percents problem.

  d. Percentage increase = $\frac{\text{amount of change}}{\text{original amount}}$; $\frac{78-6}{6} = \frac{72}{6} = 12 = 1,200\%$. Choice **a** is incorrect because you didn't convert the fraction, which ends up being 12, to an equivalent percent; you should have multiplied by 100. Choice **b** is incorrect because this is the net profit, not the percent increase. Choice **c** is incorrect because this is one multiple of 10 too small; you made an error when converting to a percent.

12. This is a percents problem.

  a. The drug is 50% effective for 50% of migraine sufferers, so it eliminates $(0.50) \times (0.50)$, or 0.25 of all migraines. Choice **b** is incorrect because you didn't account for one of the 50%s. Choice **c** is incorrect because you added $\frac{1}{2}$ of 50% to 50%; this overinflates the desired percentage. Choice **d** is incorrect because you added successive percentages when you should have multiplied them.

13. This is a fractions problem.

    a. Compare $\frac{3}{4}, \frac{3}{5}, \frac{2}{3}, \frac{2}{5}$ by finding a common denominator. The common denominator for 3, 4, and 5 is 60. Multiply the numerator and denominator of a fraction by the same number so that the denominator becomes 60. The fractions then become $\frac{45}{60}, \frac{36}{60}, \frac{40}{60}, \frac{24}{60}$. The fraction with the largest numerator is the largest fraction; $\frac{45}{60}$ is the largest fraction. It is equivalent to Joey's fraction of $\frac{3}{4}$. Choice **b** is incorrect because Joey has more pennies. Choice **c** is incorrect because Joey has more pennies. Choice **d** is incorrect because Stu actually has the least number of pennies.

14. This is a fractions problem.

    d. Add the number of hours together using a common denominator of 60: $4\frac{30}{60} + 3\frac{45}{60} + 8\frac{30}{60} + 1\frac{20}{60} = 16\frac{125}{60}$, which is simplified to $18\frac{1}{12}$ hours. Choice **a** is incorrect because you converted to the denominator of 60 incorrectly. Choice **b** is incorrect because you added only the whole parts; you didn't account for any of the fractional parts. Choice **c** is incorrect because the whole parts sum to 16 and each of the four fractional parts exceeds $\frac{1}{8}$, so this number is too small to be the actual sum.

15. This is a fractions problem.

    c. Let E = the estimate. *One-fifth more than the estimate* means $\frac{6}{5}$ or 120% of E, so 600,000 = $(1.20)(E)$. Dividing both sides by 1.2 leaves $E = 500,000$. Choice **a** is incorrect because this is $\frac{1}{5}$ of 600,000. Choice **b** is incorrect because this is $\frac{1}{2}$ of 600,000. Choice **c** is incorrect because you multiplied 600,000 by $\frac{6}{5}$, not $\frac{5}{6}$, when solving for the original number predicted by scientists.

16. This is a percents problem.

    a. 20% of 1,800, or $(0.2)(1,800) = 360$ calories allowed from fat. Since there are nine calories in each gram of fat, divide 360 by 9 to find that 40 grams of fat are allowed. Choice **b** is incorrect because you divided 1,800 by 20, which is not the correct manner in which to calculate a percent. Choice **c** is incorrect because you mistakenly used 80% instead of 20% in the computation. Choice **d** is incorrect because you didn't divide by 9 to get the number of grams of fat.

17. This is a decimals problem.

    d. *Distance = rate × time.* Kilometers traveled $= 90 \times 5.5$, so the vehicle traveled 495 kilometers. Since there are 1,000 meters in 1 kilometer, the vehicle traveled 495,000 meters. Choice **a** is incorrect because you didn't use 1 kilometer = 1,000 meters; you are off by a factor of 10. You also incorrectly translated 5 hours 30 minutes as $5\frac{1}{3}$ hours. Choice **b** is incorrect because you incorrectly translated 5 hours 30 minutes as $5\frac{1}{3}$ hours. Choice **c** is incorrect because you didn't use 1 kilometer = 1,000 meters; you are off by a factor of 10.

18. This is a fractions problem.

   a. First, find out how long the entire hike can be, based on the rate at which the hikers are using their supplies. If 1 = all supplies and x = entire hike, then $\frac{\frac{2}{5}}{3} = \frac{1}{x}$. Cross multiply to get $\frac{2x}{5} = 3$, so that $x = \frac{3 \cdot 5}{2} = \frac{15}{2}$, or $7\frac{1}{2}$ days for the length of the entire hike, going and returning. This means that the hikers could go forward for 3.75 days altogether before they would have to turn around in order to have enough supplies to get back. They have already hiked for three days, which allows 0.75 days to go forward before having to turn around. Choice **b** is incorrect because this is the total time for the outgoing half of the trip, not the amount of time left after 3 days. Choice **c** is incorrect because you have added 0.75 to the time for $\frac{1}{2}$ the trip. Choice **d** is incorrect because this is the total time for the round trip.

19. This is a decimals problem.

   c. Three tons is 6,000 pounds; 6,000 pounds multiplied by 16 ounces per pound is 96,000 ounces. The total weight of each daily ration is 48 ounces. Ninety-six thousand divided by 48 is 2,000 troops supplied. Two thousand divided by 10 days is 200 troops supplied. Choice **a** is incorrect because you used 4,000 pounds for 3 tons instead of 6,000 pounds. Choice **b** is incorrect because you counted two 12-ounce meals instead of one. Choice **d** is incorrect because you counted only one 18-ounce meal.

20. This is a decimals problem.

   d. Twenty-six forms multiplied by 8 hours is 208 forms per day per clerk. Divide 5,600 by 208 to get approximately 26.9, which means you have to hire 27 clerks for the day. Choice **a** is incorrect because only 4,992 forms could be completed with 24 clerks. Choice **b** is incorrect because only 5,200 forms could be completed with this many clerks. Choice **c** is incorrect because you rounded down instead of up.

21. This is a decimals problem.

   a. The companies' combined rate of travel is 50 miles per hour. 2,100 miles divided by 50 miles per hour is 42 hours. Choice **b** is incorrect because you are not accounting for the fact that Company F is traveling toward Company E at the same time. Choice **c** is incorrect because you incorrectly subtracted rates to get 20, and then divided 2,100 by that. Choice **d** is incorrect because you are not accounting for Company E moving toward Company F at the same time.

22. This is an averages problem.

   d. After dropping her 64, Laura's regular test average is $\frac{78 + 94 + 81 + 83}{4} = 84$. Since that counts equally with her final exam score of 90, Laura's final average is determined by averaging 84 and 90, which is 87. Choice **a** is incorrect because this is found assuming that the regular test average counts twice and the final exam counts once in the final average. Choice **b** is incorrect because this is the regular test average. Choice **c** is incorrect because you didn't drop the lowest exam score when computing the regular test average.

23. This is an averages problem.

b. $M = 3N$; $3N + N = 24$, so $N = 6$. Since $M = 3N$, $M = 18$. If Nick catches up to Mike's typing speed, then both M and N will equal 18, and then the combined rate will be 36 pages per hour. Choice **a** is incorrect because this is too low; it assumes their typing speed is 15 pages per hour when Nick catches Mike. Choice **c** is incorrect because this is too high; it assumes their typing speed is 20 pages per hour when Nick catches Mike. Choice **d** is incorrect because you mistakenly assumed Mike types 24 pages per hour.

24. This is a decimals problem.

d. $2,200(0.07) = \$154$; $\$154 + 1,400(0.04) = \$210$; $\$210 + 3,100(0.08) = \$458$; $\$458 + \$900(0.03) = \$485$. Choice **a** is incorrect because this is what you would get if you used Recycler X for all four types of recycling. This is not optimal on 3 of the 4 types. Choice **b** is incorrect because this is the minimum amount of money you can get. Choice **c** is incorrect because this is what you would get if you always use Recycler Y, whether it is optimal or not.

25. This is an algebra problem.

d. $3w =$ water coming in; $w =$ water going out; $3w - w = 11,400$, which means that w is 5,700 and $3w$ is 17,100. Choice **a** is incorrect because you incorrectly divided the amount in the tank by 3. Choice **b** is incorrect because this is the rate at which the water is going out. Choice **c** is incorrect because since water is leaving the tank, at this rate coming in, the tank would never contain 11,400 gallons.

26. This is a decimals problem.

c. Four 18-wheelers can carry $4 \times 80,000 = 320,000$ pounds and one 6-wheeler can carry another 30,000 pounds, which adds up to 350,000 pounds. Choice **a** is incorrect because this would yield 400,000 pounds, which is 50,000 in excess of what is needed. Choice **b** is incorrect because this would yield 360,000 pounds, which is 10,000 in excess of what is needed. Choice **d** is incorrect because this would also yield 360,000 pounds, which is 10,000 in excess of what is needed.

27. This is a decimals problem.

c. 84,720 troops multiplied by 4 square yards of cloth is 338,880 square yards of cloth required. Choice **a** is incorrect because the thousands digit is off. Choice **b** is incorrect because you didn't carry the 2 from the multiplication of the hundreds digits. Choice **d** is incorrect because the thousands digit is off.

28. This is a decimals problem.

b. 30 students multiplied by 42 square feet of space is 1,260 square feet of space; 1,260 square feet divided by 35 students is 36 square feet, so each student will have 6 less square feet of space. Choice **a** is incorrect because you mistakenly used 6 more students instead of adding 5 more. Choice **c** is incorrect because you subtracted the number of students from number of square feet. Choice **d** is incorrect because of an arithmetic error.

29. This is an algebra problem.

c. Let T = Ted's age; S = Sam's age = $3T$; R = Ron's age = $\frac{S}{2}$, or $\frac{3T}{2}$. The sum of the ages is 55, which means $T + 3T + \frac{3T}{2} = 55$. Find the common denominator (2) to add the left side of the equation; $T = 10$. If Ted is 10, then Sam is 30, and Ron is $\frac{3T}{2}$, which is 15 years old. Choice **a** is incorrect because you forgot to multiply half of Ted's age by 3. Choice **b** is incorrect because this is Ted's age. Choice **d** is incorrect because this is Sam's age.

30. This is a decimals problem.

b. The difference between 105 and 99 is 6 degrees. The temperature is lowered by half a degree every six minutes, or 1 degree every 12 minutes; 6 degrees multiplied by 12 minutes per degree is 72 minutes, or 1 hour and 12 minutes. Choice **a** is incorrect because you computed the difference between temperatures incorrectly. Choice **c** is incorrect because this temperature is lowered by 1 degree every 12 minutes, not every 13 minutes. Choice **d** is incorrect because this temperature is lowered by 1 degree every 12 minutes, not every 15 minutes.

Part 2: Word Knowledge

1. d. Something that is *erroneous* is wrong or *faulty*. Choice **a**, *digressive*, means off topic or meandering. Choice **b**, *confused*, means unclear. Choice **c**, *impenetrable*, means not penetrable, which is indicated by the prefix *in-*, meaning not.

2. c. Something that is *grotesque* is distorted, misshapen, or *hideous*. Choice **a**, *extreme*, means excessive or tremendous. Choice **b**, *frenzied*, means uncontrollable or crazed. Choice **d**, *typical*, means normal or common.

3. c. To be *outmoded* is to be out-of-date or *obsolete*, which are all words that might describe an *ancient* computer system. Choice **a**, *worthless*, means without worth, which is indicated by the suffix, *-less*, meaning without. Choice **b**, *unusable*, means not usable, which is indicated by the prefix *-un*, meaning not. Choice **d**, *unnecessary*, means not necessary.

4. b. A statement that is *garbled* is scrambled and confusing, or *unintelligible*. Choice **a**, *lucid*, means clear, which is the opposite of *garbled*. Choice **c**, *devoured*, means eaten. Choice **d**, *outrageous*, means bizarre, excessive, or ridiculous.

5. a. Something that is *rigorous* is strict or *demanding*. Choice **b**, *tolerable*, means bearable or reasonable. Choice **c**, *lenient*, means easy. Choice **d**, *disorderly*, means not orderly, which is indicated by its prefix *dis-*, meaning not.

6. d. A thing that is *flagrant* is conspicuous or *glaring*. Choice **a**, *secret*, means the opposite of *flagrant*. Choice **b**, *careless*, means without care. Choice **c**, *noble*, means dignified.

7. c. An *oration* is a formal speech or an *address*. Choice **a**, *nuisance*, means annoyance. Choice **b**, *independence*, means freedom. Choice **d**, *length*, is how long something is.

8. d. When something is done *obstinately*, it is done *stubbornly*, and this is indicated by Mr. Chen's refusal to do something. Although some may argue such a refusal is also foolish, or silly, *foolishly* is not a synonym of *obstinately*, so choice **c** is incorrect. Choices **a**, *repeatedly*, and **b**, *reluctantly*, are not synonyms of *obstinately* either.

9. b. A *glib* remark is a quick and *insincere* one, and such a remark might irritate a teacher. Choice **d**, *horrific*, is too extreme to merely irritate a teacher. Choice **a**, *casual*, means informal. Choice **c**, *brief*, means short. Neither choice **a** nor choice **c** is as likely to irritate a teacher as choice **b**.

10. b. When someone has *composure*, that person has self-possession or *poise*. Choice **a**, *agitation*, means anxiety, which is almost the opposite of *composure*. Choice **c**, *liveliness*, means animation. Choice **d**, *stimulation*, means excitement.

11. c. To be *eccentric* is to be unconventional or *peculiar*. Choice **a**, *normal*, means the opposite of *eccentric*. Choice **b**, *frugal*, means careful with money. Choice **d**, *selective*, means choosy.

12. a. If something is *commendable* it is praiseworthy or *admirable*. Choice **b**, *accountable*, means answerable. Choice **c**, *irresponsible*, means not responsible, which is indicated by the prefix *ir-*, meaning not. Choice **d**, *noticeable*, means able to be noticed, which is indicated by the suffix *-able*.

13. d. To be *oblivious* of something is to be unaware or *ignorant* of it. Choice **c**, *aware*, means the opposite of oblivious. Choice **a**, *visible*, means able to be seen. Choice **b**, *sinister*, means wicked.

14. d. An act of *philanthropy* is an act of charity or *generosity*. Choice **a**, *selfishness*, means the opposite of *philanthropy*. Choice **b**, *fascination*, means extreme interest. Choice **c**, *disrespect*, means without respect.

15. b. To be *ostentatious* is to be showy or *pretentious*, which are qualities that might be judged by a conservative community. Although a Corvette is probably *expensive*, choice **d** ignores an important detail: bright pink. Choice **a**, *hilarious*, means very funny and is not a synonym of *ostentatious*. Choice **c**, *tasteful*, means the opposite of *ostentatious*.

16. a. To be *passive* is to be compliant and accepting, or *resigned*. Choice **b**, *emotional*, means full of emotion. Choice **c**, *lively*, means energetic and full of life. Choice **d**, *woeful*, means sad or full of woe.

17. c. When something is in *proximity* to something else, it is close to or in *nearness* to it. Choice **a**, *distance*, means the opposite of *proximity*. Choice **b**, *agreement*, means harmony. Choice **d**, *intelligence*, means smartness.

18. a. To be *negligible* is to be unimportant or *insignificant*. Choice **b**, *delicate*, means fine or weak. Choice **c**, *meaningful*, means significant or full of meaning. Choice **d**, *illegible*, means impossible to read or not legible.

19. d. A *rational* judgment is a logical or *sound* one. Choice **a**, *deliberate*, means on purpose or thoughtful. Choice **b**, *invalid*, means not valid. Choice **c**, *prompt*, means on time.

20. b. To be *vigilant* is to be watchful or *alert*. Choice **a**, *nonchalant*, means uncaring. Choice **c**, *righteous*, means good or virtuous. Choice **d**, *strenuous*, means demanding or exhausting.

21. d. *Novel* is something that has never been done or is *new*. Choice **a**, *future*, is a time that has yet to happen. Choice **b**, *basic*, means simple or essential. Choice **c**, *former*, means outdated or past.

22. b. To *procure* something is to *acquire* it. Choice **a**, *discover*, means to find by chance. Choice **c**, *drop*, means to lose or fall. Choice **d**, *add*, means put in or enhance.

23. c. *Commensurate* means equal to or *proportionate*. Choice **a**, *forthcoming*, means arriving, which does not make sense in the context of the sentence. Choice **b**, *determined*, meaning decided, and choice **d**, *found*, do not make sense either.

24. b. *Converse* is contrary or *opposite*, and the word *but* in the sentence indicates a contradiction. Choice **a**, *upsetting*, means distressing or disturbing. Choice **c**, *worst*, means most horrible. Choice **d**, *extreme*, means excessive.

25. c. When something is *evocative*, it is reminiscent or *suggestive* of something else, which describes an abstract painting. Choice **a**, *difficult*, means hard or taxing. Choice **b**, *designed*, means created or patterned. Choice **d**, *pure*, means wholesome or clean.

26. d. A *harbinger* is a predecessor or a *forerunner*. Choice **a**, *follower*, means fan or one who follows. Choice **b**, *convert*, means change or alter. Choice **c**, *harbor*, means hold.

27. a. An *amulet* is a talisman or a *charm*. Choice **b**, *anklet*, is jewelry worn around the ankle. Choice **c**, *potion*, is a magical elixir. Choice **d**, *emergency*, is an urgent situation.

28. a. Someone who is a *pundit* is an authority or an *expert*. Although a pundit may be an authority on politicians, *pundit* and *politician* are not synonyms, so choice **b** is incorrect. Choice **c**, *kicker*, and choice **d**, *evil-doer*, are not synonyms of *pundit* either.

29. c. A *queue* is a row or a *line*, and people waiting to purchase movie tickets often have to wait in a queue. Although *quick* and *queue* begin with the same letters, they are not synonyms, so choice **a** is incorrect. Choice **b**, *price*, means cost. Choice **d**, *popularity*, means fame. None of these other answer choices make sense in the context of the sentence.

30. d. A *countenance* is a person's attitude, way, or *expression*. One's *goals* would not show a feeling such as being *less than pleased*, so choice **a** does not make sense. Choice **b**, *opinion*, is a belief or thought on a particular subject. Choice **c**, *abilities*, means skills.

31. a. An *aperture* is a hole or an *opening*. Choice **b**, *apparatus*, is a piece of equipment. Choice **c**, *camera*, is a device for taking pictures that has an aperture but is not a synonym for *aperture*. Choice **d**, *brightness*, may be what an aperture lets in, but it is not a synonym for *aperture*.

32. a. A *surrogate* is a substitute or a *replacement*. Choice **b**, *copy*, means replica. Choice **c**, *original*, means first. Choice **d**, *survivor*, is one who remains alive.

33. d. A *paradigm* is a pattern or an *example*. Choice **a**, *flying*, means traveling through the air. Choice **b**, *law*, means rule or principle. Choice **c**, *timely*, means on time.

34. b. A *mélange* is a combination or a *mix*. Choice **a**, *clatter*, means noise. Choice **c**, *creation*, means formation or invention. Choice **d**, *profit*, means income or earnings.

35. a. Someone who displays *bravado* shows courage or *boldness*. Choice **b**, *cowardice*, means the opposite of *bravado*. Choice **c**, *scorn*, means disgust or contempt. Choice **d**, *anti-establishment*, means against society or the establishment, which is indicated by its prefix, *anti-*, meaning against.

Part 3: Paragraph Comprehension

1. a. This is a main idea question, which is expressed in the topic sentence: *Police officers must read suspects their Miranda rights upon taking them into custody.* While choices **b** and **c** are true, they are not the main idea. Choice **d** is contradicted in the last sentence: *Therefore, officers must take care not to give suspects grounds for later claiming they believed themselves to be in custody.*

2. b. This is a facts and details question, and the answer is stated explicitly in the opening sentence: *Police officers must read suspects their Miranda rights upon taking them into custody.* That sentence contradicts choices **a**, **c**, and **d**.

3. c. This is a facts and details question, and the answer is stated explicitly in the third and fourth sentences of the passage. These sentences contradict choice **b**. Choices **a** and **d** are not stated in the passage.

4. c. This is a main idea question, and the entire tone of the passage is complimentary to Dilly's, which is intended to encourage people to eat there. The owner of Dilly's Deli (choice **a**) and the historical significance of the building (choice **d**) are not mentioned at all in the passage. Although the food service (choice **b**) is mentioned, it is a just a detail and not the main point.

5. d. This is a facts and details question, because the answer is stated explicitly in the second and third sentences of the passage. The passage mentions that the symptoms of Type II diabetes may occur gradually and thus be attributed to other causes. Left untreated, diabetes can cause damage to several major organs in the body. Choices **a**, **b**, and **c** are not addressed in this passage.

6. b. This is a facts and details question. According to the passage, only the long-term health problems are the same for these two different disorders. Choices **a**, **c**, and **d** are not mentioned anywhere in the passage.

7. a. This is a main idea question, which is expressed in the topic sentence: *New violence prevention programs in urban middle schools help reduce the crime rate by teaching both victims and perpetrators the skills of conflict resolution and how to apply reason to disputes.* Choices **b**, **c**, and **d** are not addressed in the passage at all.

8. b. This is a facts and details question, because the answer is stated explicitly in the first sentence: *Because crimes against adolescents are likely to be committed by offenders of the same age (as well as the same sex and race), preventing violence among and against adolescents is a twofold challenge.* Choice **c** may be true, but the passage does not describe it as a *twofold challenge* explicitly. Choices **a** and **d** are not mentioned in the passage at all.

9. a. This is a facts and details question, because the answer is stated explicitly in the fourth sentence of the passage: *With the shutter speed, you can freeze motion by using a fast shutter speed.* An SLR camera, not the shutter speed, allows you to hold the camera at $\frac{1}{30}$ second or faster, so choice **b** is incorrect. Choice **c** is incorrect, because the shutter itself works as a light valve, not the speed of the shutter. Choice **d** is not supported by information in the passage.

10. a. This an inference question, and the answer is suggested in the second sentence of the passage: *Opening and closing within a certain time frame, it helps determine how much light will be exposed onto the film.* Therefore, a shutter works in conjunction with time. Choices **b**, **c**, and **d** are not suggested in the passage at all.

11. d. This is an inference question, and the answer is suggested in the fifth and sixth sentences, which explain that a slow shutter speed will cause a picture to be blurry. Choices **a**, **b**, and **c** are not suggested in the passage at all.

12. a. This is an inference question, which is evident from the use of the words *suggests* and *most likely*. The answer can be deduced from the second sentence of the passage: *Another view, the deterrence theory, promotes punishment in order to discourage commission of future crimes.* Choice **b** is incorrect because the first and second sentences suggest that the retribution theory is at odds with the deterrence theory. Since all judges might not support the deterrence theory, choice **c** is incorrect. Choice **d** is incorrect because the integrity of the criminal justice system has nothing to do with the deterrence theory.

13. d. This is an inference question, which is evident from the use of the word *probably*. The last sentence notes that the deterrence theory has the effect of teaching not only criminals, but also the public, and television broadcasts of court proceedings might be effective ways of making the public aware of how convicted criminals are punished. There is no connection between non-unanimous jury verdicts and the deterrence theory, so choice **a** is incorrect. Someone who supports the deterrence theory would probably be against early prison releases, so choice **b** does not make sense. Such a person would probably also be against a broad definition of the insanity defense, so choice **c** is also wrong.

14. d. This is a facts and details question, because the answer is stated explicitly in the second sentence of the passage: *Workers are expected to use their best judgment in determining when a container weighs more than 50 pounds.* Choices **a**, **b**, and **c** may seem logical, but the passage only requires workers to make an educated guess as to the weight of the container.

15. a. This is a facts and details question, because the answer is stated explicitly in the third sentence of the passage: *If a container is too heavy, workers should attach one of the preprinted warning messages (which are carried in all trucks) to the container, informing the household that the container weighs more than 50 pounds and cannot be collected.* Choices **b**, **c**, and **d** are not mentioned in the passage at all.

Part 4: Mathematics Knowledge

1. This is an algebra problem.

    d. Subtract to get $-\frac{6}{3}$, which reduces to -2. Choice **a** is incorrect because you used $\frac{5}{3}$ in place of $-\frac{5}{3}$. Choice **b** is incorrect because you added $\frac{1}{3}$. Choice **c** is incorrect because the sign is wrong.

2. This is a geometry problem.

    c. Since volume contains three dimensions—length, width, and height—it's measured in cubic units. Choice **a** is incorrect because this is a unit of linear measure (length). Choice **b** is incorrect because this is a unit of area measure. Choice **d** is incorrect because these are the regions into which the xy-plane is divided.

3. This is a geometry problem.

    c. The area of a figure is the amount of space the object covers, in square units. Choice **a** is incorrect because this is the circumference. Choice **b** is incorrect because this is part of determining circumference. Choice **d** is incorrect because this is sometimes used to classify the type of polygon a figure is, but has nothing to do with area.

4. This is an algebra problem.

    d. Perform the operations in the parentheses first: $(12)(79) - 162 = 786$. Choice **a** is incorrect because you performed the operations as they arose from left to right; you should have simplified the parentheses first. Choice **b** is incorrect because you only multiplied 84 by 12; you should have also multiplied 5 by 12. Choice **c** is incorrect because of an arithmetic error.

5. This is a fractions problem.

    b. Fractions must be converted to the lowest common denominator, which allows you to compare the amounts: $\frac{36}{60}, \frac{32}{60}, \frac{33}{60}, \frac{33}{60}$. Choice **a** is incorrect because this is larger than $\frac{8}{15}$; in fact, this is the largest of the four fractions. Choices **c** and **d** are incorrect because they are larger than $\frac{8}{15}$.

6. This is a decimals problem.

    d. $42,549.23 \times 10^{-2} = 425.4923$ (move the decimal twice to the left because of the -2 power). Then, 425.4923 can be written as 4.254923×10^2. Choice **a** is incorrect because you moved the decimal point one too few places to the left. Choice **b** is incorrect because you moved the decimal point 3 places to the right when it should have been moved 2 places to the left. Choice **c** is incorrect because this is equal to the number before multiplying by 10^{-2}.

7. This is a geomtery problem.

    d. A football field would most likely be measured in square yards. Choices **a** and **b** are incorrect because these units of measure are too small to be a convenient way of measuring a football field. Choice **c** is incorrect because this unit of measure is too large to be a convenient way of measuring a football field.

8. This is an algebra problem.

    a. The halfway point on the number line is between 0 and $-\frac{1}{2}$, which is $-\frac{1}{4}$. Choices **b** and **c** are incorrect because these are closer to M than to N.

9. This is a geometry problem.

   b. Corresponding points on parallel lines are always the same distance apart, so the lines can never intersect. Choice **a** is incorrect because parallel lines never intersect. Choice **c** is incorrect because perpendicular lines intersect in a right angle. Choice **d** is incorrect because intersecting lines have exactly one point in common.

10. This is a geometry problem.

   b. The volume needed to add 9 more feet to the pool (it's already filled to 3 feet) is $16 \times 12 \times 9 = 1,728$ cubic feet. Choice **a** is incorrect because you didn't multiply by the depth of water needed to add to the pool. Choice **c** is incorrect because you didn't account for the water already in the pool. Choice **d** is incorrect because this would fill the pool to the very top, not the prescribed depth.

11. This is an algebra problem.

   d. This series actually has two alternating sets of numbers. The first number is doubled, giving the third number. The second number has 4 subtracted from it, giving the fourth number. Therefore, the blank space will be 12 doubled, or 24. Choice **a** is incorrect because this would be the eighth term, not the seventh term that is asked for. Choice **b** is incorrect because adding 3 to 12 doesn't follow the pattern used to form the sequence. Choice **c** is incorrect because adding the previous two terms of the sequence to get the next one doesn't follow the pattern used to form this sequence.

12. This is an algebra problem.

   c. The farther to the right the digits go, the smaller the number. Choice **a** is incorrect because 4.3 is larger than 0.43 because its whole part is larger. Choice **b** is incorrect because 0.43 is larger than 0.043 because its tenths place is larger. Choice **d** is incorrect because 0.043 is larger than 0.0043 because its hundredths place is larger.

13. This is a geometry problem.

   d. Area $= \frac{1}{2}(\text{base} \times \text{height}) = \frac{1}{2}(7 \times 3) = 10.5$ (the height must always be at a 90° angle to the base). Choice **a** is incorrect because you identified the height and base incorrectly, and forgot to multiply by $\frac{1}{2}$ when applying the area formula. Choice **b** is incorrect because you identified the height and base incorrectly. Choice **c** is incorrect because you forgot to multiply by $\frac{1}{2}$.

14. This is an algebra problem.

   d. To add the left side of the equation, find the common denominator, so that $\frac{3x}{6} + \frac{x}{6} = 4$; $\frac{4x}{6} = 4$, and $4x = 24$. Choice **a** is incorrect because you forgot to divide by 4, the coefficient of x, when solving the equation. Choice **b** is incorrect because this is the reciprocal of the correct answer. Choice **c** is incorrect because you added the tops and bottoms of the fractions on the left side of the equation rather than first getting a least common denominator.

15. This is a decimals problem.

   b. In a division problem like this, leave the whole number the same and subtract the exponents. Choice **a** is incorrect because you divided the exponents when you should be subtracting them. Choice **c** is incorrect because you added the exponents when you should be subtracting them. Choice **d** is incorrect because you multiplied the exponents when you should be subtracting them.

16. This is a decimals problem.

    d. Create a division problem without decimals by moving the decimal point three places to the right: 3,160 divided by 79 is 40. Choice **a** is incorrect because you divided in the wrong order. Choice **b** is incorrect because you divided in the wrong order and did not move the decimal point appropriately. Choice **c** is incorrect because you need to move decimal point one more place to the right.

17. This is a decimals problem.

    d. Perform long division out to the thousandths place to get 2.625. Choice **a** is incorrect because you are not interpreting the meaning of a fraction correctly; you must divide the top number by the bottom number. Choice **b** is incorrect because of an arithmetic error. Choice **c** is incorrect because you shouldn't round the answer unless instructed to do so.

18. This is a geometry problem.

    b. Find the area of two rectangles and then add the results. Use an imaginary line to block off the first rectangle at the top of the figure. This rectangle measures (5 feet)(2 feet) = 10 square feet. The second rectangle is also (5 feet)(2 feet). Add the two together for a total of 20 square feet. Choice **a** is incorrect because 16 feet is the perimeter, not the area. Choice **c** is incorrect because you counted the overlapping corner twice in the calculation. Choice **d** is incorrect because you counted the lower-left missing rectangle as part of the figure.

19. This is a percents problem.

    c. First, change the percent to a decimal: $(.072) \times (465) = 33.48$, which rounded to the nearest tenth is 33.5. Choice **a** is incorrect because you forgot to account for $\frac{1}{5}$ in $7\frac{1}{5}$%. Choice **b** is incorrect because you treated $7\frac{1}{5}$% as 0.071, which is not correct because $\frac{1}{5} = 0.2$. Choice **d** is incorrect because you (incorrectly) rounded up to the nearest ones place, not the nearest tenth.

20. This is a geometry problem.

    a. A heptagon has seven sides. Choice **b** is incorrect because this has eight sides, not seven. Choice **c** is incorrect because this has six sides, not seven. Choice **d** is incorrect because this has five sides, not seven.

21. This is an algebra problem.

    d. $3k^2 = 3 \times k \times k$ and $4k = k + k + k + k$. Choice **a** is incorrect because $3k^2$ and $4k$ are not like terms because the powers of k are different; so, you cannot add their coefficients. Choice **b** is incorrect because you added the numbers and powers of k together, and incorrectly. Choice **c** is incorrect because $4k = k + k + k + k$, not $k \times k \times k \times k$.

22. This is an algebra problem.

    a. $25 - 16 = 9$, which is the only choice that leaves you with a number less than 10. Choice **b** is incorrect because $25 - 15 = 10$ and so, is not less than 10. Choice **c** is incorrect because $25 - 14 = 11$ and so, is not less than 10. Choice **d** is incorrect because $25 - 13 = 12$ and so, is not less than 10.

23. This is a percents problem.

    a. Find 15% of $4.60: $0.15 \times 4.60 = 0.69$. Next, subtract 0.69 from 4.60 to get the decreased price. Choice **b** is incorrect because this is 15% of $4.60. You need to subtract it from $4.60. Choice **c** is incorrect because you didn't subtract 15% of $4.60; rather, you subtracted 15% of 100, which is 0.15. Choice **d** is incorrect because this is $4.60 increased by 15%.

24. This is a decimals problem.

    c. Divide 5 by 6 to convert the fraction into a decimal; $5 \div 6 = 0.833\overline{3}$. Round two decimal places to get 0.83. Choice **a** is incorrect because you are not interpreting the meaning of a fraction correctly. Choice **b** is incorrect because of an arithmetic error. Choice **d** is incorrect because this is $\frac{1}{6}$, not $\frac{5}{6}$.

25. This is a geometry problem.

    c. The volume of a cylinder equals $\pi r^2 h$, where r is the radius of the cylinder and h is the height. The radius is half the diameter, so the radius of this cylinder is 4 cm. The height of the volume is $10 - 4 = 6$ (the height of the whole cylinder minus the height of space in which the liquid has been poured out). So the volume is $\pi \times 4^2 \times 6 = \pi \times 16 \times 6 = 96\pi$ cm^3. Choices **a** and **b** are incorrect because you didn't use the correct volume formula. Choice **d** is incorrect because this is the volume of the entire cylinder, not just the volume of the liquid present.

SCORING

Write your raw score (the number you got right) for each test in the blanks below. Then, turn to Chapter 3 to find out how to convert these raw scores into the scores the armed services use.

1. Arithmetic
   Reasoning: _____ right out of 30
2. Word Knowledge: _____ right out of 35
3. Paragraph
   Comprehension: _____ right out of 15
4. Mathematics
   Knowledge: _____ right out of 25

Here are the steps you should take, depending on your AFQT score on this practice test:

- **If your AFQT is below 29,** you need more help in reading and/or math. You should spend plenty of time reviewing the lessons and practice questions found in this book.
- **If your AFQT is 29–31,** be sure to focus on your weakest subjects in the review lessons and practice questions that are found in this book.
- **If your AFQT is above 31,** review the areas that give you trouble, and then take the third practice test in Chapter 13 to make sure you are able to get a passing score again.

Using the codes below, you'll be able to log in and access additional online practice materials!

Your free online practice access code is:
FVEL267QP7H2EMC628PO

Follow these simple steps to redeem your code:

- Go to **www.learningexpresshub.com/affiliate** and have your access code handy.

If you're a new user:
- Click the **New user? Register here** button and complete the registration form to create your account and access your products.
- Be sure to enter your unique access code only once. If you have multiple access codes, you can enter them all—just use a comma to separate each code.
- The next time you visit, simply click the **Returning user? Sign in** button and enter your username and password.
- Do not re-enter previously redeemed access codes. Any products you previously accessed are saved in the **My Account** section on the site. Entering a previously redeemed access code will result in an error message.

If you're a returning user:
- Click the **Returning user? Sign in** button, enter your username and password, and click **Sign In**.
- You will automatically be brought to the **My Account** page to access your products.
- Do not re-enter previously redeemed access codes. Any products you previously accessed are saved in the **My Account** section on the site. Entering a previously redeemed access code will result in an error message.

If you're a returning user with a new access code:
- Click the **Returning user? Sign in** button, enter your username, password, and new access code, and click **Sign In**.
- If you have multiple access codes, you can enter them all—just use a comma to separate each code.
- Do not re-enter previously redeemed access codes. Any products you previously accessed are saved in the **My Account** section on the site. Entering a previously redeemed access code will result in an error message.

If you have any questions, please contact Customer Support at Support@ebsco.com. All inquiries will be responded to within a 24-hour period during our normal business hours: 9:00 A.M.–5:00 P.M. Eastern Time. Thank you!